A

MISSISSIPPI
WILDFLOWERS

JAN W. MIDGLEY

SWEET
WATER
PRESS

To my mother,
Elizabeth Douglass Windmiller,
who loves words and finds
beauty in simple things.

To my father,
Myrl Eugene Windmiller,
who taught me to believe
I can do anything I choose to do.

To both of them, for refusing
to buy a television set until
my life patterns were established.

Printed in Singapore
Published by Sweetwater Press

Library of Congress Cataloging-in-Publication Data
Midgley, Jan W.
Mississippi wildflowers / by Jan W. Midgley.
p.   cm.
Includes bibliographical references and index.
ISBN 1-58173-216-3 (trade paper)
1. Native plants for cultivation—Mississippi. 2. Wild flowers—Mississippi. 3. Wild flowers—Propagation—Mississippi. 4. Native plant gardening—Mississippi. 5 Wild flower gardening—Mississippi. 6. Plant communities—Mississippi. I. Title.
SB439.24.M7M54   1998
635.9'51762—dc21   98-32309
                                                              CIP

TABLE *of* CONTENTS

PREFACE

MY LOVE OF AND INTEREST IN WILDFLOWERS BEGAN
early in life while growing up in the middle of Missouri, where small-
town life allowed young girls to ride bikes into the countryside
unescorted. Family connections to farmland and land in general meant
weekends were spent walking along creeks, pulling rocks from fields,
making apple butter, and gathering dandelions for wine. Most of the
activities involved some kind of project, part of the ethic of constant
work passed from German and Scottish ancestors. But during the drive
to the farm or the weed pulling, someone would point out the shrike
impaling its next meal on the thorn of a locust, or a dung beetle rolling
a ball of manure in the hog yard, or a brilliant butterfly weed bright-
ening the roadside. Few knew the scientific names of the flowers or
birds, but they knew the habits of these critters, such as which ones ate
what, and that certain birds returned when certain flowers bloomed.
They knew where to look for morel mushrooms in the spring. They
understood the interconnection of the elements and the cycles in
nature. As Aldo Leopold said in A Sand County Almanac, "there is
value in any experience that reminds us of our dependence on the soil-
plant-animal-man-food chain, and of the fundamental organization of
the biota." Our fate is inextricably tied to the fate of plants.

Plants provide food, medicine, beauty, erosion control, and filtra-
tion, to mention just a few benefits to mankind. Plants are the base of
the food chain. Whether we eat plants or meat that has developed from
plants, we are dependent on plants. From time immemorial, plants
have been the pharmacopoeia of humans. Many products that originally came from plants are now synthesized, but the chemical recipe
originally came from the plant. Each day, unknown numbers of species
of plants become extinct. We will never know if the cure for some disease also died with that plant.

When we destroy plants and their entire habitats with development
and pollution, my heart aches. We destroy pieces of the world that are
essential for our physical and emotional well-being. I am not a
Luddite, a hater of technological development, but I fear the loss of the
experience of nature for the general population. When we pave the
world, we can no longer experience nature and realize how we are
interconnected with it. We lose our sense of home—of who we are and
what role we play in the interaction of all the creatures, plants, soil,
water, and air.

I believe each of us can preserve a piece of our heritage by beginning
to recognize native plants and the insects, birds, and animals interact-
ing with those plants. If we plant a few natives in our yards, we can
delight in the butterfly on the phlox and show a child a caterpillar on
the milkweed leaf. In this book, I try to help gardeners of all stripes—
beginners and veterans—incorporate more native plants into their
landscapes. Add a variety of native plants and the wildlife will come.

Humans respond to richness of variety, whether in numbers of
species or textures of leaves. Patterns and repetition weave the various
elements into a meaningful whole. We also have a need to learn, an
inquisitiveness that gives us a feeling of delight when we discover something new. Nature offers unending mystery and surprise, whether it be

the fawn around the bend of the path or the four-leaf clover among the typical three-leafers. In nature, there are no rules and variation is common. Change is inevitable and healthy.

Nature has a resilience that offers the hope of rebirth to any who will observe. Spring fire ravages a woodland, and within weeks bracken fern and bird foot violets and merrybells rise above the charred earth. Fire is a natural element. Bulldozers are another matter. Once the top 6–12 inches of soil are removed, natural succession will replace the community if it remains undisturbed, but the process will take many generations. It can be restored, but it will never be quite the same.

If restoration is our best hope, then we must know how to propagate the plant material. For twenty-five years, I have grown native plants from seeds, cuttings, and division. I have read every book I can find on the topic and I have kept records on each species I grow I will know more tomorrow and may find that something new works a bit better, but this book represents the current state of my knowledge at this time. Native plants frequently become robust in cultivation. Given better sunlight than the woodland offers, a wild geranium blooms heavily. Likewise, seeds grown in cultivation germinate in much higher percentages than in nature. Collect seeds, clean them, and sow them. Delight when they germinate, nurture the seedlings, and plant them when they are strong. You have now become a part of the intricate web of nature and can no longer pass by with blinders on, unaware of the miracle occurring daily before your very eyes.

THIS BOOK IS THE RESULT OF THIRTY YEARS OF gardening and growing. Along the way, many people have molded my thinking and helped me.

My children, Frank and Elizabeth Midgley, have more than tolerated my passion. They potted, made picture signs, created computer programs, and collected money. They even caught the ecology bug.

The Cullowhee Native Plant Conference gave me the gift of community with large numbers of people of every stripe who share my desire to give back as much as I take from the earth.

The librarians at the Harrison Regional Library in Columbiana, Alabama, especially Naomi Absher, cheerfully located materials from libraries near and far.

Many friends shared their vast knowledge. Hugs to Charles Allen, Linda Askey, C. Colston Burrell, Ed Clebsch, Caroline Dean, Beth Erwin, Bill Fontenot, Jennifer Greer, Jessie Harris, Kim Hawks, Sally Kurtz, Anne Lindsey, Peter Loos, Bob McCartney, Gretchen Minners, Ken Moore, Carole Otteson, Elaine Nash, Mary Painter, and Al Schotz. Special thanks to Weesie Smith for allowing me to photograph in her garden and to Larry Mellichamp, UNCC, for sharing his diagram of wetland habitats. I extend heartfelt gratitude to Dan Pittillo, WCU, for reviewing the manuscript.

My final thanks go to my partner, Dean Clark, who enthusiastically assumed day-to-day operation of our nursery, Wildflower, while I wrote. His confidence sustained me in moments of self-doubt.

Fall Line

PHYSIOGRAPHIC PROVINCES OF THE SOUTHEAST

- INTERIOR LOW PLATEAU
- CUMBERLAND PLATEAU
- RIDGE AND VALLEY
- BLUE RIDGE
- PIEDMONT
- COASTAL PLAIN

INTRODUCTION

MISSISSIPPI IS IN A PART OF THE COUNTRY CALLED THE Coastal Plain. At one time, the Appalachian Mountain chain extended all the way to Mexico, but it eroded over time and the ocean moved in and out over the land. The present topography of the state is rolling hills. The length of the state is 300 miles, with a latitude difference of 5 degrees. In addition, the elevation or height above sea level varies from 800 feet at the northeastern corner to sea level along the coast. The northeastern corner of the state is home to plants typical of more northern areas. Likewise, the southern third of the state has some Coastal Plain species not found in northern regions.

Many factors influence the variety of plants in a given area: temperature, moisture, light, elevation, slope, soil, other plants, insects, animals, and man, to list a few. Most of the herbaceous plants in Mississippi are mesophytes. They thrive where the air and soil are moist but not continuously saturated. Specialized plants occupy sites which are wet for most of the year or are extremely dry.

In general, the climate of Mississippi is mild with some variations due to altitude, latitude, and the seasons. In addition, the coastal area temperature is moderated slightly by the Gulf of Mexico. The annual average temperature ranges from 63 degrees to 68 degrees. Rainfall averages 51 to 62 inches, with more along the coast.

Soil characteristics are probably the most important factor in the development of particular types of plant communities. The nutrient content, pH, and porosity of soils strongly determine what plants occur in any given area.

PHYSIOGRAPHIC
PROVINCES
OF MISSISSIPPI

Fall Line

- Fall Line Hills
- Black Belt Prairie
- Pontotoc Ridge
- Flatwoods
- North Central Plateau or Plains
- Jackson Prairie Belt
- Loess or Bluff Region
- Mississippi Delta (Alluvial Plain)
- Pine Hills
- Coastal Strip

FALL LINE HILLS

At one time, this narrow band was a plateau, sloping from the Appalachian fold to the south. Over time, the plateau eroded into ridges and valleys. Gravel deposits from the Cretaceous Period cap the upper 50–75′ of the ridges. Limestone, shale, and chert comprise the steep slopes and cliffs along the valley of the Tennessee River and its tributaries. Continue south to find Carboniferous rocks rising here and there through beds of cretaceous sand over gravel. In this region, upland soils are light, sandy and infertile. In stream bottoms, the soil is more fertile. Most of the trees on the hills are second and third growth. Some common trees include yellow and loblolly pine, and mountain and chinquapin oak. Blueberries, hazelnut, mountain laurel, witch hazel, and sweet shrub form the woody understory. The ground layer includes bird's foot violet, prairie phlox, fire pink, and bluets. Lovelies like alumroot, *iris cristata*, and *sedum ternatum* cling to limestone ledges. Among the wildflowers on lower slopes are wild geranium, liverleaf, wild ginger, Allegheny spurge, rue anemone, and large flowered white trillium. Many of these species are common in more northern areas but are uncommon in the Coastal Plain of Mississippi.

Tishomingo State Park has 8 miles of hiking trails in the Fall Line Hills region. For information: Box 880, Tishomingo, MS 38873; 601/438-6914.

➤ *See pages 16–25 for lists of plants of the Mixed Mesophytic Forest, the Western Mesophytic Forest, and the Oak-Pine Forest.*

BLACK BELT PRAIRIE

Seventy-five to 100 million years ago, ocean covered all of the Coastal Plain. The shells of sea-dwelling creatures can still be found in the heavy, calcareous, loamy clay. The dark soil gives this prairie area the name Black Belt Prairie. Originally, the prairie was probably a big bluestem prairie with a few blackjack oak and post oak. The soil was difficult to work but it was rich, so it was farmed intensively from settlement up until World War I. Farming eventually ceased because the soil was depleted and the boll weevil struck the cotton. The region now has many old fields in various stages of succession, but where the soil conditions are conducive and fire has not been overly controlled, remnant bits of prairie exist. The dark soil now supports few trees other than red cedar and hackberry. In part of the region, lighter, yellowish brown loamy soils support post, blackjack, and Spanish oak. Showy wildflowers of the open prairies include coreopsis, rosinweed, butterflyweeds, black-eyed Susan, and blazing stars. In the heavier, richer soils of stream bottoms reside wild blue phlox and jack-in-the-pulpit.

Mixed into the prairies are some red, sandy hills, which have plants characteristic of the North Central Plateau region.

Along the 15-mile length of the Witch Dance Trail in the Tombigbee National Forest, one can see outcrops containing marine fossils from the Upper Cretaceous Period the birthplace of prairie soils.

For information: Tombigbee National Forest, Route 1, Box 98A, Ackerman, MS 39735; 601/285-3264.

➤ *See page 42 for a list of prairie plants.*

PONTOTOC RIDGE

This ridge of hills and valleys is the headwater for streams flowing southeast and southwest. The soils are red, sandy loams formed from layers of rock and sediment deposited about 70 million years ago when oceans covered the land. Except for the lean, sandy soil of the northern part of the ridge, the soils are richer than prairie soil. Various pines, oaks, sweet gum, hickory, tulip poplar, and bigleaf magnolia form the tree layer. Hydrangeas, strawberry bush, spice bush, bladder nut, and hazel nut are common shrubs. The wildflower species might include wild ginger, bloodroot, wild geranium, spring beauty, toothwort, and trillium.

▪ Trace State Park is in the Pontotoc Hills. It has 25 miles of hiking trails. For information: Route 1, Box 254, Belden, MS 38826; 601/489-2958.

➤ *See pages 16–21 for a list of plants of the Mixed Mesophytic Forest and pages 22–25 for plants of the Oak-Pine Forest.*

FLATWOODS

A thin ribbon, 3 to 15 miles wide, of acidic gray subsoil clay arches from the north to the central eastern border of Mississippi. This heavy soil is deficient in lime and other nutrients. It can be abnormally wet or dry. Pines and hardwoods mix with herbaceous plants such as jack-in-the-pulpit, ladies' tresses, butterwort, and swamp sunflower.

▪ Legion State Park has 440 acres of forest maintained by managed fires. For information: 635 Legion State Park Road, Louisville, MS 39339; 601/773-8323.

➤ *See page 31 for a list of plants in flatwoods.*

NORTH CENTRAL PLATEAU

The plateau region covers about one-fourth of the state. It varies from 400 to 600 feet above sea level. Many mature streams thread throughout the plateau. Over time, erosion cut deep stream valleys with wide bottomlands. The wide valleys can be 200 feet lower than the general plateau. The soil varies from east to west. The more easterly soil is somewhat like the clay of the flatwoods, but sandier. The western section is much sandier. This area is blessed with a farmable, tawny, silt loam, moist but well drained.

The Oak-Pine Forest has several variants in this region of Mississippi. In the drier eastern section, the plant community is mixed oak-pine with elm, plum, sassafras, dogwood, blueberry, and persimmon. The second layer of poison ivy, grape, sumacs, and low blueberry is indicative of the dryness of the area. Within these woods, one might see lyre-leaved sage, Carolina anemone, butterfly weed, and coreopsis.

The woody species in the western section with better soils are similar to the ones in the eastern portion, but hardwoods may outnumber pines. Hardwood forests allow a richer herbaceous layer, because light reaches the forest floor in winter and spring. In addition to the wildflowers seen in the eastern section, one might also see pussytoes, wild

False Solomon's Seal

petunia, bird's foot violet, May apple, false Solomon's seal, partridge-berry, alumroot, fairy wand, spiderwort, and Indian pink.

Soils in the stream bottoms support wild blue phlox, jack-in-the-pulpit, green dragons, merrybells, and trillium in the shade; and asters, boneset, hibiscus, ragwort, and meadow beauty in areas with more light.

■ Holly Springs National Forest boasts two areas of old-growth forests representative of the vegetation of the plateau province. For information contact the Holly Springs National Forest, 1000 Front Street, Oxford, MS 38655; 601/236-6550.

➤ *See page 23 for a list of plants of the Oak-Pine Forest.*

JACKSON PRAIRIE BELT

The topography of this midstate prairie belt is gently rolling countryside. The prairie patches mix with soils and plants more characteristic of adjacent southeastern and western regions. The prairie soils are heavy, gray clays, high in calcium carbonate. They intergrade with brown loam from the west and sandier soils from the longleaf pine belt to the southeast. Typical woody plants in the region are pines, oaks, hickory, persimmon, cedar, and sumac. The typical prairie flora includes a matrix of grasses (especially little bluestem and Indian grass), delphinium, penstemon, baptisia, prairie clovers, rosinweed, black-eyed Susan, purple coneflower, sneezeweed, butterfly weeds, and false aloe. Most of the Jackson Prairie was plowed by 1860 and agricultural activities continue to threaten the remnants.

■ As many as sixty-eight prairie pieces exist in the Bienville National Forest. The largest piece, Harrell Prairie Hill Botanical Area, demonstrates what a southern prairie might have looked like 400 years ago. For information: 3473 Highway 35 South, Forest, MS 39074; 601/469-3811.

➤ *See page 42 for a list of prairie plants.*

LOESS OR BLUFF REGION

The Loess or Bluff region is a north-south strip, 15 to 20 miles wide, that runs along the edge of the alluvial soils of the delta area. Loess is wind-deposited silt. Ages ago, glaciers in more northern areas ground rocks into bits. The fine silt traveled south in water and in the air. This rock dust soil can be 30 to 90 feet deep. The topography is broken because the loess erodes easily. The calcareous loess has a high lime content, which encourages a wide variety of plant growth. Because the strip of loess extends the entire length of the state, some plants will be found at the northern end that will not be found at the southern end, and vice versa. The woody plant palette is extensive but consists of mainly hardwoods. Pines and cedars invade as second growth and in old fields. The three dominant trees in the original forests in the southern part of this region were beech, southern magnolia, and American holly. Some unexpected plants with more northern, eastern, and western affinities are wild hydrangea, Allegheny spurge, doll's eyes, ginseng, and northern maidenhair fern.

■ The Homochitto National Forest lies within the rugged Loess Hills. The forest service can direct you to old-growth timber stands. For more information, contact one or both ranger districts: Bude Ranger District, USDA Forest Service, Route 1, Box 1, Meadville, MS 39653, 601/384-5876 or Homochitto Ranger District, USDA Forest Service, 950 Highway 24 East, Box 398, Gloster, MS 39638; 601/225-4281.

■ Clark Creek Natural Area in the southernmost part of the Loess Hills offers rugged topography, waterfalls, and great diversity of plant and animal life. For more information, contact the Mississippi Department of Wildlife, Fisheries, and Parks, Box 451, Jackson, MS 39205; 601/362-9212 or 800/GO-PARKS.

➤ *See pages 16–21 for a list of plants of the Mixed Mesophytic Forest, and pages 25–34 for plants of the Southern Mixed Hardwood Forest.*

MISSISSIPPI DELTA (ALLUVIAL PLAIN)

The flat Alluvial Plain is about 60 by 200 miles in area. The tail tapers to the south. The soil of this area is either clay or sands deposited by the Mississippi River and its tributaries. Alluvial means "water deposited." The soil tends to be swampy, and the plants reflect the high moisture level of the soil. The hardwoods include gum, oak, bald cypress, maple, elm, pecan, and cottonwood. Here one can see thickets of cane and palmettos and masses of Spanish moss. The darkness of the forest and the wetness of the soil limit the wildflower variety, but higher ground supports cardinal flower, lizard's tail, asters, and sunflowers, as well as many common aggressive wetland plants not profiled in this book.

■ The Delta National Forest, the only bottomland forest in the national forest system, lies in the Mississippi alluvial plain. Contact Delta

National Forest, Sharkey-Ag. Building, 402 Highway 61 North, Rolling Fork, MS 39159; 601/873-6256.

➤ *See page 35 for a list of plants in flood plains and swamps.*

PINE HILLS

This large area across the southern third of the state is flat to hilly. The soil is a reddish-brown, acidic, sandy loam that is low in nutrients. Most of the original longleaf pine forest has been replaced by a mixed hardwood climax forest. Pines appear in areas where the canopy is open.

In upland areas, the soil may drain adequately to support beech, oak, southern magnolia, pine, Florida anise, jack-in-the-pulpit, partridge-berry, trillium, broad beech fern, ebony spleenwort, and Christmas fern. Patches of this Southern Mixed Hardwood Forest can be seen in the DeSoto National Forest.

Flatwoods occupy lower areas with poor drainage. Very little acreage of longleaf pine-wire grass savanna remains, but examples still exist in the DeSoto National Forest.

▪ Examples of a longleaf pine woodland can be seen in the southern portion of the Bienville National Forest and the Homochitto National Forest.

▪ Chickasawhay Ranger District of the DeSoto Nation Forest lies within the Pine Hills. Two long, looped hiking trails lead one through many different plant communities. For more information, contact the Chickasawhay Ranger District, 481 S. Magnolia Street, Box 426, Laurel, MS 39441; 601/428-0594.

➤ *See pages 25–34 for a list of plants in the Southern Mixed Hardwood Forest and flatwoods.*

COASTAL STRIP

This low (less than 20 to 30 feet above sea level) Coastal Strip consists of savannas, marshes, dunes, and beaches, and includes the barrier islands. Groundwater is near or at the surface in marshes and swamps. In higher areas the soil is gray sand. In lower areas, it is dark, peaty, and acidic. Pines grow throughout, but the canopy is open, allowing for a rich herbaceous layer common only in this section of the state.

The savannas (open areas with a few trees) are flatwoods with poorly draining sandy soils. They contain pitcher plants, sundews, Stoke's aster, sunbonnets, meadow beauties, and other plants that like a high water table. Marshes support sabatias, sedges, seaside goldenrod, and sea ox-eye. The dunes and beaches have unique, sometimes protected, vegetation. Many of the plants of the coastal area are so site-specific that they are beyond the scope of this book. For the same reason, they are not likely candidates for the average garden.

▪ An excellent example of a savanna can be seen in Jackson County at the Sandhill Crane National Wildlife Refuge, 7200 Crane Lane, Gautier, MS 39553; 601/497-6322.

▪ Examples of marsh, swamp, flatwood, dune, and maritime plant communities can be seen in the Gulf Islands National Seashore, 3500 Park Road, Ocean Springs, MS 39564; 228/875-0821.

The Crosby Arboretum has an entry fee to support its mission to preserve, restore, and study native plants. It has self-guided trails, special programs, plant sales, and opportunities for volunteers to contribute and learn. For information: Box 190, Picayune, MS 39466; 601/799-2311.

➤ *See page 31 for a list of plants in savannas, and pages 39–41 for plants in marshes.*

Sarracenia flava

IN ADDITION

To join other wildflower enthusiasts for lectures and field trips, contact the Mississippi Native Plant Society and ask about a group in your area.

Mississippi Native Plant Society c/o Mississippi Museum of Natural Sciences, 111 North Jefferson Street, Jackson, MS 39202

You can find an abundance of wildflowers in Mississippi's parks and wildlife areas. The national forests are managed as one unit with ten different ranger districts. For a free guide to the national forests,

Mississippi National Forests Recreation Guide, contact the forest supervisor's office:

■ National Forests in Mississippi, 100 W. Capitol Street, Suite 1141, Jackson, MS 39269; 601/965-4391.

Mississippi has three national parks. Two are particularly rich in wildflowers. Gulf Islands National Seashore which extends into Florida preserves plant communities of the Lower Coastal Plain.

■ Contact: 3500 Park Road, Ocean Spring, MS 39564, 228/875-9057.

Natchez Trace Parkway has twelve interpretive trails with signs naming plants.

■ Contact: Route 1, NT-143, Tupelo, MS 38801; 601/680-4025.

The twenty-eight state parks in Mississippi offer many opportunities for outdoor recreation.

■ For more information, contact the Public Information Office, Division of State Parks, Department of Wildlife, Fisheries, and Parks, Box 23093, Jackson, MS 39225, 601/304-2140 or 800/GO-PARKS.

For general information about all the parks, call 800/467-2757 (GO-PARKS).

For detailed information on outdoor recreation in Mississippi's natural areas, refer to the book, *Hiking in Mississippi* (Helen McGinnis, 1994).

NATIVE PLANTS

WHAT IS A NATIVE PLANT? THE DEFINITION IS NOT straightforward; it is even controversial. I use a simple formula: Any plant that was on this continent when the colonists came about 400 years ago is a native plant. But what about the ginkgo tree that we know was here millions of years ago because we have fossil records? It was extirpated from this continent 150 million years ago and was later re-introduced from China. And what about plants from California? Can we really say the orange California poppy planted in roadside wildflower beds is native to the Southeast? In this book I do not attempt to address these native vs. exotic plant debates. If the plant was here when the first colonists came, I consider it to be native.

Many flowering plants that we call wildflowers are not native plants, but are naturalized plants. Some came with the colonists for medicinal use, and some hitched a ride in packing material or in ballast on ships. Naturalized plants thrive and reproduce with no assistance from man. Some are neighborly and some are pushy bullies.

The plants profiled in this book are found in seven southeastern states: Alabama, Georgia, Louisiana, Mississippi, North Carolina, South Carolina, and Tennessee. Some of the plants are found in northern Florida, but the more temperate subtropical plants of mid- to lower Florida are not typical of most of the flora of the Southeast.

NOMENCLATURE

All plants, whether native or non-native, are organized into families, genera, and species. Each one has a botanical name that is the same in any language in the world.

Botanical names are often called "Latin names," but the names come from Latin or are Latinized from Greek and many other languages. Plants in the same genus are related. Families are groups of related genera. Plants with the same specific epithet, such as *Manfreda virginica* and *Claytonia virginica*, are not related. Virginica means of Virginia, so these plants were named for the same geographic region. The specific epithet may describe the appearance of the plant, the habitat, or even honor an individual. Species names often include the surname of someone who found the plant or who contributed to the study of plants. The primary nomenclatural reference for this book is the National Plants Database, accessed through a website (http://plants.usda.gov/plant proj/plants/index.html). This database is based on the work of John Kartesz, *A Synonymized Checklist of the Vascular Flora of the United States, Canada, and Greenland* (second edition, Timber Press, 1994).

DEFINITIONS

Most of the plants profiled here are perennials, plants that die down to the rootstock in the winter but survive for many years. A few of the plants are annuals that self-seed readily and return year after year. One or two vines are also included because they are so common throughout the Southeast.

Other terms used frequently in this book may need clarification. An herbaceous plant is one that is not woody—in other words, it dies down in cold weather. A forb is an herbaceous plant that is not a grass. The natural habitat of a plant is the area in which it is usually found and where the conditions are conducive to its growth. Plant species have a geographical range in which they can be found, because the conditions favor their perpetuation. Some may have a limited range, while others may have a wide range, even spreading over the continent and beyond.

Provenance means the origin of something, such as where a seed was collected. Over long periods of time, plants adapt to the soils and climates of a region. Some species have very wide geographic ranges, and provenance determines their heartiness. Plants grown in the Southeast from Indian grass seeds collected in Minnesota will not thrive as well as plants grown from seeds collected in the Southeast. If you plan to grow native plants, try to obtain seeds from your own state or an adjoining state.

CONSERVATION

Through local groups you can also learn what plants are considered rare or endangered in your state. Most states have lists that are often available through the various state Natural Heritage programs. It is important to know whether a plant is protected in your state before you collect seeds. Some states impose fines for collecting any type of plant material, not just rare plants, without written permission of the landowner.

In 1973, the United States enacted the Federal Endangered Species Act, which covers plants and animals. A landowner has the right to protect plants on his property, but he cannot sell one in public commerce if it is nationally listed as endangered or threatened. Because of this law, cooperative efforts between federal and state agencies identify endangered plants, establish their distribution, monitor their status, and provide penalties for disturbance of the species. Sometimes this law seems to tie the hands of nursery workers who wish to sell an easily propagated but rare plant across state lines. On the plus side, funding of the basic identification and monitoring procedures set the stage for agencies such as the Nature Conservancy to buy and protect particularly valuable habitats.

The activities of man are the biggest threat to our native species. As cities sprawl into the surrounding countryside, we build and widen roads to service the new houses, schools, and malls. Just recently I rescued plants from a roadside. Butter and Egg Road wove through a pineland that sheltered trillium, bird's foot violet, pussytoes, dwarf iris, hairy phlox, asters, false aloe, and merrybells—all plants uncommon in the commercial trade. Within two weeks, that road was scheduled to be widened. A few days later, I photographed golden club at a friend's house, where the creek has not eroded and the water flows clear year-round. I decided to drive the scenic route home in order to look for photo opportunities on another gravel road. I photographed a breath-taking woodland filled with blooming blue phlox, golden Alexander, rare trillium, toothworts, geranium, blue star, lilies, ferns, May apple, and much more. Feeling radiant from the beauty of all these spring flowers among dark tree trunks, I came face to face with a wide-load tractor-trailer unloading a bulldozer. Since the road was blocked and the crew confirmed my suspicion of imminent widening and paving, I grabbed a shovel and saved a few trillium and lilies, then dug up a few for a small group of birders who happened on the scene. When that road is paved, the water will rush off the pavement, carrying silt and pollutants into the stream at a rapid pace. The sides of the stream will begin to crumble with the increased flow of water. In a balanced environment, the water and pollutants slowly perk through the soil, slowing the flow and cleansing the water through the plant and soil filter.

The widened and paved road is only one negative result of development. Initially, plants are removed in the clearing process, eliminating the genetic pool. Secondly, the natural filtering of the native flora and soils is lost or altered. Thirdly, water sheets off compacted soils and pavement and erodes the sides of creeks and rivers, uprooting plant material downstream. Lastly, the native flora is usually replaced with non-native grasses that require frequent doses of chemical to achieve the desired green monoculture. Chemicals and fertilizers spread on the lawns travel at a rapid pace into streams and rivers, polluting our waterways.

The imbalance and downward spiral in the association of plants, soil, and water are only part of the detriment of the loss of native plants. The visual connection to the environment of the area is lost. Over the past 25 years, bluets, lupines, butterfly weed, and dozens of other plants have disappeared from roadside banks. Widening roads and increasing use of herbicides to maintain roadsides have been a death knell for roadside flowering plants. The view from the car window is now an endless green expanse of mowed exotic grasses. Occasional relief in the form of an exotic canna or poppy gives us no sense of place or connection to the complexity of a natural habitat. Even so-called wildflower plantings along our state highways are usually full of annual plants from Europe or California that will not reproduce because they are not in their natural soils and climates.

Clear-cutting for housing, roads, and agriculture chops the forest into bits that are less resilient to catastrophic events. Fire started by lightning and by man was once common in the eastern deciduous forest and actually was essential to plants such as the carnivorous pitcher plants. Fire kept undergrowth in check and maintained the longleaf pine system. Regular fires kept the amount of fuel low enough that the fire did not burn too hot and damage trees beyond recovery. If an occasional tree died, it was quickly replaced from nearby seed sources such as the wind or a bird.

Fragmenting the forest also hampers the movement of wildlife, whether on semiannual migrations or on daily rounds. Even box turtles have well-established territories and regularly traveled routes. When we disturb plants, we disturb organisms in the soil, insects, and animals. We need to maintain corridors of green that allow the animals to travel, and also to allow enough of a seed bank so that we do not lose plant species needlessly.

One of the most heavily damaged ecosystems in the Southeast is wetlands. From 1985 to 1995, we lost 500,000 acres of wetlands. Half of the wetlands that colonists found when they came to the Southeast are now gone. Wetlands are the great filters and purifiers of our waters.

We cut the trees, bulldoze the shrub and herb layer, leave forests in patches, and drain wetlands. In addition, we introduce exotic plants that have no natural predators in this country. They grow out of control and crowd out or shade out native plants. Examples of invasive exotics are Japanese honeysuckle, privet, and kudzu. Kudzu is a well-known example of an aggressive plant that we planted with the best of intentions. It was introduced to control erosion and to serve as fodder. It certainly can stabilize a bank—it can grow a foot a day. For fodder, it is a problem because it is not easy to bale like hay. When it is not grazed, it grows like the plant that ate Manhattan and develops a tuber the size of a wheelbarrow. The flower is beautiful and fragrant. So what is the big deal? The big deal is that when you have kudzu, it defeats other plants. A few plants may survive under the blanket of kudzu, but the diversity of the community is reduced. Many other exotic plants spread on their own in the wild and may or may not be as aggressive as kudzu.

The plant is just one part of the large natural web. It makes food out of sunlight, soil, and carbon dioxide. It provides food for insects, birds, and other creatures. Bats, birds, and dragonflies feed on the insects. At the end of the growing season, the herbaceous litter decays and becomes rich compost with the help of fungi, worms, insects, bacteria, and water. Plants are just part of a self-regenerating system that functions smoothly and efficiently until its cycle is disturbed.

What can we do as individuals to encourage native plants? If I plant a few and you plant a few and your neighbor plants a few, a butterfly can pause here and there and at the elementary school and so on during its cycle of nectar sipping, egg laying, and larvae feeding. If we purchase native plants responsibly and increase their numbers by propagating them, planting more, or sharing them with friends, we increase the chances of survival of all the insects, birds, and other life that depend on them.

RESOURCES

Gardeners can purchase some native plants in local garden centers, and mail-order sources for seeds and plants are listed on page 293, but I would recommend everyone join a local wildflower society and ask the members about plant and seed sources. In fact, local groups often sponsor sales of propagated native plants. Contact your state wildflower society for information on joining a local chapter. Addresses of state societies are listed on page 292.

Bear in mind two important points when buying plants: The plants should be nursery propagated, and the provenance should be as close to home as possible.

Nursery propagated means someone grew the plants from seed, cuttings, division, or in tissue culture. The term "nursery grown" is not good enough. Wild collected plants can be purchased and put in holding beds for a few months and be called nursery grown. Feel free to ask about the source of plants you know to be uncommon and difficult to propagate. Bonus plants growing in the pot might suggest the plant is wild collected. Propagated plants usually have no freebie wildflowers growing in the pot with the labeled plant. Another way to identify wild collected material is by the price. Some species, such as trillium, take seven years to grow from seed to flowering plant. Taking care of a plant for seven years would require the grower to put a price of about $15 to $25 on a flowering plant. Younger, non-flowering plants are frequently sold via mail order for a reasonable price. Only one species of native orchid is readily available commercially, *Spiranthes odorata*. It is increased by division. Other species of orchid are grown in tissue culture but are not readily available. The mycorrhizal fungi essential for nutrient processing by the orchid proliferate more readily on tissue culture media than the plant tissue itself. Do not purchase native terrestrial orchids unless you know they have been grown legally. Buying wild-collected material encourages diggers to continue depleting our natural treasures.

FOREST TYPES &
PLANT COMMUNITIES

There are four main forest types in the Southeast; they are outlined on the map on page 16. My map is derived from the work of E. Lucy Brown (1950) and A. W. Kuchler (1964) (see the Bibliography, page 288). There are few sharp lines in the distribution of plants. Transitions between communities are gradual, and a species typical of one forest type can be found in another. For example, beech trees are dominant trees in the Mixed Mesophytic Forest, but can be found in especially moist areas of the Oak-Pine Forest.

The Southeast is divided into physiographic provinces (see map, page vi) based mainly on topographical differences. Starting in the northwest and proceeding southeast, the provinces are the Interior Low Plateau, the Cumberland Plateau, the Ridge and Valley, the Blue Ridge, the Piedmont, and the Coastal Plain. Only the Coastal Plain Province crosses all states in the Southeast. It also covers the most acreage. Forest types correlate closely with physiographic provinces. Notice the similarity between the forest regions on the map on page 16 and the physiographic provinces on the map on page vi.

Designation of a forest type to a plat of land can be difficult. Is one talking about the tree that one can see at this point in time or is one talking about the community of plants that might exist if the site were undisturbed for sixty years? In general we are talking about the latter, the climax community. Natural succession in an open field starts with annual weeds, perennial herbs, and later, shrubby invaders like sumac and brambles. After a few years, pine trees sprout and grow rapidly. Once the pines offer a bit of shelter, hardwood seeds germinate. Once the hardwoods create a shady canopy over the pines, the pines gradually die. The more competitive hardwoods lead to a climax community.

Light is not the only factor determining the climax species. In the Midwest, low rainfall can favor a prairie community over a woodland. In the East we have more rain, which encourages forests, but the activities of man have drastically altered the forest types of the Southeast. As many as 10,000 years ago, Native Americans started fires to create open woodlands and encourage game. In the Piedmont, this burning favored pines over hardwoods. When the European settlers took over the region, they cleared trees, especially hardwoods, for row crop agriculture. Fires started by man or lightning continued to influence the landscape until about 1940, when we began to control fires (with both positive and negative effects).

Specific combinations of climate, soil, exposure, and fire create specialized habitats. Cutting through the forest regions are rock outcrops, waterways, streams, and rivers, which have specific plant communities associated with them. Different combinations of water and light levels result in several types of wetland habitats. Special factors in the soil (edaphic conditions) may favor prairie plants. Highly exposed limestone outcrops favor cedar glade communities. High altitudes and the associated climate produce Spruce-Fir Communities. These special habitats are discussed in the section following the forest types.

Certain species characterize any given community; they are called the dominant species in that community. They usually comprise the upper layer, which is why trees often define a community that also has a shrub layer and a herbaceous layer. To remain dominant, the trees have to be able to reproduce, and tree seedlings or stump sprouts must be able to compete with the plants in the lower layers. A plant that is dominant in one community may also exist in other communities.

Indicator plants prefer a certain community. They may be found occasionally in another community but are very likely to be found exclusively in a single community. When you see an indicator plant, you can identify the forest type with some confidence.

The following is a sampling of plants that occur in certain communities; the list will help you locate the plants you see.

The division into four main forest types in the Southeast helps organize the many plant communities in the Southeast. For more definitive information about plant communities see Bibliography, page 288 (Schafale and Weakley, 1990; Wharton, 1989; and Grossman, D.H. et al., 1998).

MAIN FOREST TYPES OF THE SOUTHEAST

■ Mixed Mesophytic Forest
■ Western Mesophytic Forest
■ Oak-Pine Forest (oak-hickory-pine)
■ Southern Mixed Hardwood Forest

FOREST TYPES
MIXED MESOPHYTIC FOREST

The Mixed Mesophytic Forest occupies rich, acidic, moist, well-drained sites in any of the physiographic provinces. This is the most diverse plant community in the Southeast. Bits of this community occur on north-facing bluffs, seepage slopes, and in cool ravines in the Piedmont and Coastal Plain, but it is more characteristic of the Cumberland (Appalachian) Plateau Region. In the higher Appalachians, it is often called a type of cove forest. The soil is dark with humus, which is well incorporated into the soil, whether the soil is crumbly or compact. The dominant trees are beech and oak. In the Deep South, plant species unique to the Coastal Plain mix in with the Mixed Mesophytic vegetation, giving the patches of beech-oak forest of that region a unique flavor. Some of the shrubs and herbaceous plants are limited to areas of higher elevation but many have wide ranges and occur in all of the forest regions.

DOMINANT TREES:

Beech ~ *Fagus grandiflora*
Northern red oak ~ *Quercus rubra*
White oak ~ *Quercus alba*

OTHER TREES:

American ash ~ *Fraxinus americana*
Basswoods ~ *Tilia* spp.
Bitternut hickory ~ *Carya cordiformis*
Black gum ~ *Nyssa sylvatica*
Chestnut oak ~ *Quercus montana*
Deciduous magnolias ~ *Magnolia acuminata, fraseri, tripetala*
Red maple ~ *Acer rubrum*
Tulip poplar ~ *Liriodendron tulipifera*
Wild cherry ~ *Prunus serotina*

INDICATORS IN MOUNTAINS:

White basswood ~ *Tilia americana* var. *heterophylla*
Yellow buckeye ~ *Aesculus flava (A. octandra)*

OTHER MOUNTAINOUS SPECIES:

American chestnut ~ *Castanea dentata*
Eastern hemlock ~ *Tsuga canadensis*
Sugar maple ~ *Acer saccharum*

NORTHERN SPECIES:

(may occur at upper ends of coves)
Mountain maple ~ *Acer spicatum*
Striped maple ~ *Acer pensylvanicum*
Yellow birch ~ *Betula alleghaniensis*

SMALL TREES AND SHRUBS:

Alternate-leaved dogwood ~ *Cornus alternifolia*
Blueberries ~ *Vaccinium corymbosum, stamineum*
Cinnamon clethra ~ *Clethra acuminata*
Devil's walking stick ~ *Aralia spinosa*

Flowering raspberry, beebalm, and Carolina phlox in the mountains of western North Carolina

Elderberry ～ *Sambucus canadensis*
Flowering raspberry ～ *Rubus odoratus*
Hearts a bustin' ～ *Euonymous americana*
Ironwood ～ *Carpinus caroliniana*
Maple leaf viburnum ～ *Viburnum acerifolium*
Mountain camellia ～ *Stewartia ovata*
Mountain laurel ～ *Kalmia latifolia*
Paw paw ～ *Asimina triloba*
Rosebay rhododendron ～ *Rhododendron maximum*
Spice bush ～ *Lindera benzoin*
Wild hydrangea ～ *Hydrangea arborescens*
Witch hazel ～ *Hamamelis virginiana*

VINES:

Big-leaf Dutchman's pipe ～ *Aristolochia macrophylla*
Bittersweet ～ *Celastrus scandens*

HERBACEOUS:

Alumroots ～ *Heuchera* spp.
American bellflower ～ *Campanulastrum
americanum*
Asters ～ *Aster curtisii, cordifolius,
divaricatus*
Beebalm ～ *Monarda didyma*
Black cohosh ～ *Cimicifuga racemosa*
Bloodroot ～ *Sanguinaria canadensis*
Blue cohosh ～ *Caulophyllum thalictroides*
Blue phlox ～ *Phlox divaricata*
Blue-stemmed
goldenrod ～ *Solidago caesia*
Bluets ～ *Houstonia caerulea,
serpentifolia*
Carolina phlox ～ *Phlox carolina*
Doll's eyes ～ *Actaea pachypoda*
Dwarf larkspur ～ *Delphinium tricorne*
Evergreen gingers ～ *Hexastylis* spp.
Fairy wand ～ *Chamaelirium luteum*
False lily of the valley ～ *Mainthemum canadense*
False Solomon's seal ～ *Mainthemum racemosa*
Fire pink ～ *Silene virginica*
Fly poison ～ *Amianthemum muscatoxicum*
Foamflower ～ *Tiarella cordifolia*
Galax ～ *Galax urceolata (G. aphylla)*
Giant chickweed ～ *Stellaria pubescens*
Golden seal ～ *Hydrastis canadensis*
Jack-in-the-pulpit ～ *Arisaema triphyllum*
Jewel weeds ～ *Impatiens capensis, pallida*
Joe Pye weed ～ *Eupatorium maculatum,
purpureum*
Liverleaf ～ *Hepatica nobilis*

*Delphinium
tricorne*

May apple ‑ *Podophyllum peltatum*
Monkshood ‑ *Aconitum uncinatum*
Partridgeberry ‑ *Mitchella repens*
Pink turtlehead ‑ *Chelone lyonii*
Rue anemone ‑ *Thalictrum thalictroides*
Skullcaps ‑ *Scutellaria incana, serrata*
Spring beauties ‑ *Claytonia* spp.
Squirrel corn,
Dutchman's breeches ‑ *Dicentra canadensis, cucularia*
Toothworts ‑ *Cardamine* spp.
Trout lilies ‑ *Erythronium* spp.
Umbrella leaf ‑ *Diphylleia cymosa*
Violets ‑ *Viola* spp.
Virginia snakeroot ‑ *Aristolochia serpentaria*
Wake robins ‑ *Trillium* spp.
Waterleaf ‑ *Hydrophyllum* spp.
Waterleaves ‑ *Hydophyllum* spp.
White snakeroot ‑ *Ageratina altissima*
Wild ginger ‑ *Asarum canadense*
Wind anemone ‑ *Anemone quinquefolia*
Wood nettle ‑ *Laportea canadensis*
Wood poppy ‑ *Stylophorum diphyllum*
Yellow ladies' slippers ‑ *Cypripedium parviflorum, pubescens*

Hepatica nobilis

FERNS:

Broad beach fern ‑ *Phegopteris hexagonoptera*
Christmas fern ‑ *Polystichum acrostichoides*
Cinnamon fern ‑ *Osmunda cinnamomea*
Fancy wood fern ‑ *Dryopteris intermedia*
Goldie's fern ‑ *Dryopteris goldiana*
Interrupted fern ‑ *Osmunda claytoniana*
Marginal wood fern ‑ *Dryopteris marginalis*
Northern maidenhair fern ‑ *Adiantum pedatum*

SPECIAL COMMUNITIES WITHIN MIXED MESOPHYTIC FOREST REGION

BALDS

Grass or shrub balds occur at elevations of 4,700 to 6,200 feet. These acidic slopes usually occur on the south and west sides of domes and ridges. They are either grass covered with patches of shrubs or densely shrub-covered. The shrubs are mainly ericaceous plants; in other words, they are heaths. Trees are slowly invading balds. Management by manual removal or periodic fire may be necessary to preserve the community.

Catawba rhododendron and grass bald on Roan Mountain, North Carolina

SOME SPECIES ON A SHRUB BALD:

Black chokeberry — *Aronia melanocarpa*
Blueberries — *Vaccinium corymbosum, erythrocarpum*
Mountain laurel — *Kalmia latifolia*
Rhododendrons — *Rhododendron catawbiense, maximum*

ON THE GROUND LAYER:

Galax — *Galax urceolata (G. aphylla)*
Mosses — *Bryophytes*
Reindeer lichen — *Cladonia cushions*
Sand myrtle — *Leiophyllum buxifolium*
Trailing arbutus — *Epigea repens*
Wintergreen — *Gaultheria procumbens*

SOUTHEASTERN SPRUCE–FIR COMMUNITY

Spruce-fir forests of the southern Appalachian Mountains are forests of high-elevation areas, usually above 4,455 feet. In the Southeast, these high-elevation communities occur in Tennessee and North Carolina. The strong wood of spruce trees made them desirable for industrial use. From the early 1800s to about 1930, steam power and railroads changed the environment. Spruce was logged heavily. Environmental concern led to the formation of the Great Smoky Mountain National Park in 1934. In spite of these measures, Fraser fir trees are dying from damage by the balsam woolly adelgid, and some mature red spruce is failing to thrive. Air pollution and acid rain are suspect and under study.

Herbaceous plants of the Spruce-Fir Forest tolerate dark, acidic, and moist conditions. Mosses and ferns thrive in these sites.

DOMINANT TREES:

Fraser fir — *Abies fraseri*
Red spruce — *Picea rubens*

Spruce-Fir Forest along the Blue Ridge Parkway

OTHER WOODY PLANTS:

American beech ∼ *Fagus grandifolia*
Blackberry ∼ *Rubus canadensis*
Canadian hemlock ∼ *Tsuga canadensis*
Catawba rhododendron ∼ *Rhododendron catawbiense*
Mountain ash ∼ *Sorbus americana*
Mountain maple ∼ *Acer spicatum*
Northern red oak ∼ *Quercus rubra*
Yellow birch ∼ *Betula alleghaniensis (B. lutea)*

HERBACEOUS:

Bead lily ∼ *Clintonia borealis*
Mountain, white wood aster ∼ *Aster acuminatus, divaricatus*
Mountain wood fern ∼ *Dryopteris x campylopter*
Pennsylvania sedge ∼ *Carex pensylvanica*
Pink turtlehead ∼ *Chelone lyonii*
Wood sorrel ∼ *Oxalis acetosella*

WESTERN MESOPHYTIC FOREST

The Western Mesophytic Oak-Hickory Forest is a transition area from communities of eastern and southern Mixed Mesophytic Forest to oak-hickory communities to pure oak, becoming less luxuriant as you go west. It is a forest of tall, broad-leaved deciduous trees. This change in forest type occurs because annual rainfall is lower in this area. It occurs in the Interior Low Plateau in Alabama and Tennessee, and in the Coastal Plain of Tennessee, Mississippi, and Louisiana.

The soils are generally fertile, being derived from limestone, sandstone, and shale. Loess soils are wind-deposited. Alluvial soils are water-deposited. No glacial action occurred this far south in the Western Mesophytic Forest.

As is true of all forests of the Southeast, the Oak-Hickory Forest has been altered by man. Where fields were abandoned, red cedar (*Juniperus virginiana*) is the primary successional tree among the herbaceous plants on the limestone soils. Over time, oak forests whether moist or dry, will develop on about 70 percent of the land. The other areas will regrow bottomland forests or moist slope communities.

Pockets of different forest types and habitats create a patchwork. Within the beech-oak, oak-hickory, or plain oak forest, barrens occur in open areas. Dry barrens support cedar trees (see cedar glades, page 45). Wet alluvial areas support swamp forest communities (see page 35). The soils are gray-brown podzolic, lateritic, and melanized soils, plus intrazonal types.

The vegetation changes in the forest from one area to another. As one goes from east to west within the area, hickories give way to pure oak forests. As one goes south, Oak-Hickory Forests become more diverse with many additional species. Pines also become more common as one proceeds south.

DOMINANT TREES:

Bitternut hickory ∼ *Carya cordiformis*
Black oak ∼ *Quercus velutina*

Northern red oak ∽ *Quercus rubra*
Shagbark hickory ∽ *Carya ovata*
White oak ∽ *Quercus alba*

OTHER TREES:

American basswood ∽ *Tilia americana*
American elm ∽ *Ulmus americana*
Black cherry ∽ *Prunus serotina*
Black walnut ∽ *Juglans nigra*
Chinquapin oak ∽ *Quercus muehlenbergii*
Persimmon ∽ *Diospyros virginiana*
Pignut hickory ∽ *Carya glabra*
Tulip poplar ∽ *Liriodendron tulilpifera*
White ash ∽ *Fraxinus americana*

SMALL TREES AND SHRUBS:

American hazelnut ∽ *Corylus americana*
Coralberry ∽ *Symphoricarpos orbiculatus*
Devil's walking stick ∽ *Aralia spinosa*
Dogwood ∽ *Cornus florida*
Mulberry ∽ *Morus rubra*
Sassafras ∽ *Sassafras albidum*
Upland privet ∽ *Forestiera ligustrina*

HERBACEOUS INDICATORS:

Allegheny spurge ∽ *Pachysandra procumbens*
Prairie trillium ∽ *Trillium recurvatum*

Pachysandra procumbens

OAK-PINE FOREST

(OR OAK-HICKORY-PINE)

The dominant trees are oak, hickory, and pine, but I use the short title, Oak-Pine Forest, to distinguish this association from the oak-hickory of the Midwest. Little virgin forest exists today, and secondary forests are dominated by pine, especially loblolly and yellow pine. Sandstone is the dominant surface rock. The thin soil layer is composed of red clays and yellow or gray-to-brown sandy loams. Oak-Pine Forests are drier than Southern Beech Forests, but patches of vegetation typical of the Mixed Mesophytic Forest (see page 16) appear on moist slopes.

This forest type covers part of the Ridge and Valley Province, the Piedmont Province, and the Coastal Plain, north of the Savannah River.

It also extends into the Coastal Plain in Alabama and Mississippi. The wetland areas within the boundaries of the Oak-Pine Forest have their own characteristic soils and plant species (see wetlands, page 34).

A line across the middle of Georgia divides the Oak-Pine Forest region into two sections: the streams of the Atlantic Slope drain into the Atlantic Ocean. The streams of the Gulf Slope drain into the Gulf of Mexico.

DOMINANT TREES:

Hickories – *Carya* spp.
Loblolly pine – *Pinus taeda*
Northern red oak – *Quercus rubra*
Post oak – *Quercus stellata*
Southern red oak – *Quercus falcata*
White Oak – *Quercus alba*

OTHER TREES:

Black gum – *Nyssa sylvatica*
Persimmon – *Diospyros virginiana*
Red cedar – *Juniperis virginiana*
Shortleaf pine – *Pinus echinata*
Sweet gum – *Liquidamber styraciflua*

SMALL TREES AND SHRUBS:

American crabapple – *Malus angustifolia*
Beautyberry – *Callicarpa americana*
Big-leaf snowbell – *Styrax grandiflora*
Blueberries – *Vaccinium arboreum, pallidum*
Carolina rose – *Rosa caroliniana*
Common or smooth sumac – *Rhus glabra*
Dogwood – *Cornus florida*
Fringe tree – *Chionanthus virginicus*
Hawthorns – *Craetegus spathulata, C.* spp.
Horse sugar – *Symplocus tinctoria*
Indigo bush – *Amorpha fruticosa*
New Jersey tea – *Ceanothus americanus*
Possumhaw – *Ilex decidua*
Red buckeye – *Aesculus pavia*
Redbud – *Cercis canadensis*
Shadbush – *Amelanchier canadensis*
Sourwood – *Oxydendrum arboreum*
Southern pinxter azalea – *Rhododendron canescens*
Sweetshrub – *Calycanthus floridus*
Viburnums – *Viburnum acerfolium, rufidulum, prunifolium*
Winged elm – *Ulmus alata*

VINES:

Catbriers – *Smilax* spp.
Coral honeysuckle – *Lonicera sempervirens*
Grapes – *Vitis* spp.
Passion vine – *Passiflora incarnata*

GRASSES:

Bamboo, giant cane – *Arundinaria gigantea*
Bent awn plumegrass – *Saccharum contortus*
Big bluestem or Turkeyfoot – *Andropogon gerardii*
Bottle brush grass – *Hystrix patula*
Broomsedge – *Andropogon virginicus*
Bushy beardtongue – *Andropogon glomeratus*
Indian grass – *Sorghastrum nutans*
Little bluestem – *Schizachyrium scoparius*
Poverty oat grass – *Danthonia sericea*
Purple top – *Tridens flavus*
River oats – *Chasmantheum latifolium*
Silver plumegrass – *Saccharum aloepecuroides*
Spike grass – *Chasmantheum sessifolium*
Split beard bluestem – *Andropogon ternarius*
Sugarcane plumegrass – *Saccharum giganteum*
Switchgrass – *Panicum virgatum*

SEDGES:

Sedges – *Carex* spp.

FLOWERING PLANTS:

American ipecac – *Porteranthus stipulatus*
Asters – *Aster concolor, patens*
Beardtongues – *Penstemon australis,
digitalis, pallidus*
Bellwort – *Uvularia perfoliata*
Bird's foot violet – *Viola pedata*
Blue-eyed grass – *Sisyrinchium angustifolium*
Blue star – *Amsonia tabernaemontana*
Bluets – *Houstonia caerulea,
purpurea, tenuifolia*
Carolina lily – *Lilium michauxii*
Crane fly orchid – *Tipularia discolor*
Cream wild indigo – *Baptisia bracteata*
Dwarf iris – *Iris verna*
Evergreen wild ginger – *Hexastylis arifolia*
Fleabanes – *Erigeron pulchellus,
philadelphicus*
Flowering spurge – *Euphorbia corollata*
Goat's rue – *Tephrosia virginiana*

*Baptisia
bracteata*

Iris verna

Golden aster ⁓ *Chrysopsis mariana*
Goldenrods ⁓ *Solidago caesia, nemoralis, odora, rugosa*
Grass-leaved blazing star ⁓ *Liatris graminifolia*
Green and gold ⁓ *Chrysoganum virginianum*
Hairy phlox, blue phlox ⁓ *Phlox amoena, divaricata*
Indian pink ⁓ *Spigelia marilandica*
Ironweed ⁓ *Vernonia angustifolia, gigantea*
Milkweeds ⁓ *Asclepias tuberosa, variegata*
Partridgeberry ⁓ *Mitchella repens*
Prickly pear cactus ⁓ *Opuntia humifusa*
Pussytoes ⁓ *Antennaria plantaginifolia*
Rosinweeds ⁓ *Silphium astericus, compositum, laciniatum*
Rue anemone ⁓ *Thalictrum thalictroides*
Silk grass ⁓ *Pityopsis graminifolia*
Skullcaps ⁓ *Scutellaria* spp.
Solomon's seal ⁓ *Polygonatum biflorum*
Southern ragwort ⁓ *Senecio anonymous*
Spiderwort ⁓ *Tradescantia hirsuticaulis, virginiana*
Spotted wintergreen ⁓ *Chimaphila maculata*
St. Andrews cross ⁓ *Hypericum hypericoides*
Swamp sunflower,
ashy sunflower ⁓ *Helianthus angustifolius, mollis*
Thoroughworts ⁓ *Eupatorium* spp.
Veined hawkweed ⁓ *Hieracium venosum*
Wake robin ⁓ *Trillium cuneatum*
White-topped aster ⁓ *Seriocarpus asteroides*
Whorled coreopsis ⁓ *Coreopsis major*
Wild bergamot ⁓ *Monarda fistulosa*
Wild geranium ⁓ *Geranium maculataum*
Wild petunia ⁓ *Ruellia caroliniensis*
Wild quinine ⁓ *Parthenium integrifolium*
Yellow star grass ⁓ *Hypoxis hirsutis*

FERNS:

Bracken fern ⁓ *Pteridium aquilinum*
Christmas fern ⁓ *Polystichum acrostichoides*
Cinnamon fern ⁓ *Osmunda cinnamomea*
Ebony spleenwort ⁓ *Asplenium platyneuron*
Southern lady fern ⁓ *Athyrium felix femina*

SOUTHERN MIXED HARDWOOD FOREST

(Quarterman and Keever; 1962; Quarterman, 1981)

This area has also been called the Southeastern Evergreen Forest (Braun, 1950) because of the large number of broad-leaved evergreens and pines. Pines (especially longleaf pine), magnolias (especially *M. grandiflora*), and live oak with Spanish moss were the predominant

signature plants. At the time of settlement, longleaf pine was the dominant tree in 40 percent of the region (62 percent in upland regions).
By 1990, less than 1 percent of the area was dominated by longleaf
pine. Unsuppressed fires strongly influence the components of a plant
community. Since man began tapping (for naval stores) and cutting
(for timber) the longleaf pines and controlling fires (since the 1930s
and 1940s), the forest has changed. Slash pine, loblolly, and shortleaf
pine have been associates of longleaf all along; they become more predominant when burning is controlled. Deciduous trees form a sub-
dominant layer in pine communities, and the hardwoods can become
dominant after clear-cutting or other interference. None of the pines
can thrive in woodlands that have a dense canopy and little light. The
main upland vegetation is now pine or a pine-hardwood mix.

Broad-leaved evergreens are more abundant in the Coastal Plain
because of the mild climate and long growing season associated with the
low altitude. This area forms the transition between the deciduous forest regions and the subtropical evergreen forest of southern Florida. The
Southern Mixed Hardwood Forest occurs only in the Coastal Plain.

There are several different plant communities within this region.
The factors that cause the diversity are: geologic age, soil deposits, fire
frequency, and historical land use.

The underlying rock of the Coastal Plain is young compared to areas
inland. Tertiary rock is the common substrate for the whole area, but
bands of rock of varying ages form terraces. The inner band of
Cretaceous origin is the oldest rock. The youngest band toward the
coast is Pleistocene in origin. On the Atlantic Slope, the older terraces
are dissected, and the younger terraces are relatively smooth. On the
Gulf Slope, there is little evidence of older rock strata, and instead one
sees stream terraces. Many terraces of the Pleistocene Age create topographical relief.

Soils differ in texture and ability to hold water. Soils deposited during the Tertiary Age are sandy and peaty. These are the main soils of the
Atlantic Slope. The Gulf Slope has those and several other bands. The
red hills have red soils that come from calcareous deposits and are fertile, supporting hardwood trees. The cretaceous soils of the Black Belt
are dark clay with calcium carbonate, which originally supported
prairie grasses, forbs, and an open deciduous forest.

Fire sustains some communities and damages others. Some need fire
every two to three years, and at least every ten years, to prevent woody
plants from moving in. Some trees, such as longleaf pine, are fire-adapted
and can survive a quick, cool-burning fire. Even the animals in fire communities are adapted to regular fire. They are critters like the gopher tor-
toise, who live underground. A few trees, such as *Magnolia virginiana,*
can resprout into shrub-like plants after fire. When fire does not occur
for many decades, the fuel on the ground builds. Then if a fire were to
occur, it would be very hot and would destroy everything in its path.

Land use probably has changed the southeastern forest more than any
of these other factors. Land use includes all the activities of man: collection of sap for naval stores (tar, pitch, rosin, and turpentine), farming,
timbering, and development. Even the Native Americans shaped the forest with their use of fire to open forests for hunting and to clear fields.

Just as the geology of the Coastal Plain is relatively young, the
vegetation of the area is fairly new. Water came in and out over the
land many times, submerging existing vegetation in water and in soil

deposits. Plant species from the Appalachians overlap with southern species more on the Gulf Slope than on the Atlantic Slope. The plants are a mix of temperate deciduous, typically Coastal Plain, and partly warm temperate-subtropical. Bottomland forests are fairly similar throughout the 1,200 miles of the region.

SPECIAL COMMUNITIES WITHIN SOUTHERN MIXED HARDWOOD FOREST

LONGLEAF PINE FORESTS

Open, park-like pine forests of longleaf pine and wire grass dominated most of the uplands of the southeastern Coastal Plain from 5,000 years ago to settlement. Upland Longleaf Pine Forest is found on fine, sandy, acidic loam, with a clay substrate. The acreage covered by longleaf pine is down to 1 percent of its original range (Martin, et. al., *Biodiversity*, Lowland vol., Ch. 10, 1993), for many reasons. It is dependent on the occurrence of low-intensity fires at least every ten years. Fire control, farming, timbering, and grazing by feral hogs have all contributed to the demise of the Longleaf Pine Forest. Longleaf pine is a subclimax community, and oak moves in if fire does not remove the hardwoods. Where remnant patches of the longleaf-wiregrass ecosystem remain, species diversity is high. The undisturbed soils are fertile, and areas of varying moisture support a wide variety of plants. The moister areas are called flatwoods (see below).

TREES

Longleaf pine ~ *Pinus palustris*

SHRUBS:

Gallberry ~ *Ilex glabra*
Runner oak ~ *Quercus pumila*

HERBACEOUS:

Black-eyed Susan ~ *Rudbeckia hirta*
Blazing stars ~ *Liatris* spp.
Golden asters ~ *Heterotheca* spp.
Gopher apple ~ *Geobalanus oblongifolius*
Legumes ~ *Lespedeza* spp.
Marsh fleabane ~ *Pluchea rosea*
Thoroughwort ~ *Eupatorium rotundifolium*
Wild indigo ~ *Baptisia lanceolata*
Wire grass ~ *Aristida stricta*

Longleaf pine-wiregrass savanna in the Croatan National Forest, North Carolina

DAN PITTILLO

HARDWOOD FORESTS:
COASTAL PLAIN UPLAND
MIXED HARDWOOD FOREST

The forests of the Coastal Plain are highly variable in species content because almost all the areas are regrowth, following disturbance. In addition, some sites are mesic (average moisture) and some are xeric (dry). The species of oak and hickory vary with the amount of available moisture.

The evergreen southern magnolia and American beech distinguish this forest from the Oak-Pine Forest of the Piedmont. North of the range of the southern magnolia, the beech becomes the most important signature tree. The middle layer of shrubs and vines, both deciduous and evergreen, is limited, since the tree canopy mutes light. Legumes and grasses dominate drier sites. Showy wildflowers occur in some areas. In the most southern areas, tropical elements appear including American olive, red bay, and cherry laurel. These evergreens add shade, decreasing the herbaceous layer.

*Main trees of the potential climax forest of the former longleaf pine region (Quarterman and Keever, l962).

TREES:

American beech	*Fagus grandiflora**
Basswood	*Tilia americana*
Black gum	*Nyssa sylvatica*
Magnolias	*Magnolia grandiflora**, virginiana*
Pignut, mockernut hickory	*Carya glabra*, tomentosa**
Southern sugar maple	*Acer barbatum*
Spruce pine, longleaf pine, loblolly pine	*Pinus glabra, palustris, taeda*
Sweet gum	*Liquidamber styraciflua**
White, Southern red, laurel, and water oaks	*Quercus alba*, falcata*, laurifolia*, nigra**

SMALL TREES:

American and yaupon holly	*Ilex opaca*, vomitoria*
American olive	*Osmanthus americanus*
Crabapple	*Malus angustifolia*
Dogwood	*Cornus florida**
Fringetree	*Chionanthus virginicus*
Hop hornbeam	*Ostrya virginica**
Horse sugar	*Symplocos tinctoria*
Large-leaf storax	*Styrax grandifolia*
Red bay	*Persea borbonia*
Red mulberry	*Morus rubra*
Redbud	*Cercis canadensis*
Sassafras	*Sassafras albidum*
Silverbell	*Halesia diptera*
Sourwood	*Oxydendrum arboreum*
Sparkleberry	*Vaccinium arboreum**

SHRUBS:

Beautyberry — *Callicarpa americana*
Cherry laurel — *Prunus caroliniana*
Dwarf palmetto — *Sabal minor*
Mountain laurel — *Kalmia latifolia*
Southern wax myrtle — *Myrica cerifera*
Virginia sweetspire — *Itea virginica*

*Callicarpa
americana*

VINES:

Scarlet honeysuckle — *Lonicera
sempervirens*

HERBACEOUS:

Beggar's lice — *Desmodium* spp.
Blazing star — *Liatris elegans*
Butterfly pea — *Clitoria mariana*
Coral bean — *Erythrina herbaceae*
Dwarf iris — *Iris verna*
False foxglove — *Aureolaria flava*
Goldenrods — *Solidago* spp.
Horse mint — *Monarda punctata*
Indian pink — *Spigelia marilandica*
Lespedezas — *Lespedeza* spp.
Lousewort — *Pedicularis canadensis*
Lyre-leaf sage — *Salvia lyrata*
Milkweeds — *Asclepias* spp.
Partridge pea — *Cassia fasciculata*
Passion flower — *Passiflora incarnata*
Prickly pear cactus — *Opuntia humifusa*
Pussytoes — *Antennaria* spp.
Rose verbena — *Verbena canadensis*
Silk grass — *Pityopsis graminifolia*
Thin-leaved bluestars — *Amsonia* spp.
White wild indigoes — *Baptisia* spp.
Wild petunia — *Ruellia caroliniensis*
Wild pink — *Silene caroliniana*

HARDWOOD FORESTS:

COASTAL PLAIN UPLAND
BEECH-MAGNOLIA FOREST

**(also LOESS BLUFF FOREST, MESIC HAMMOCK,
or BEECH RAVINES IN THE CAROLINAS)**

A Beech-Magnolia Forest that resembles the Mixed Mesophytic Forest occurs on hammocks, on river bluffs and ravines, and in the red lands of the Coastal Plain. The soil is moist but well-drained, and the well-shaded slopes are cool. It is a microclimate agreeable to diverse species more common in the Piedmont and the Cumberland Plateau. In some sites, the soil is slightly calcareous. On the Gulf Slope this community can be found on acidic, sandy soils.

DOMINANT TREES:

American beech – *Fagus grandiflora*
Southern magnolia – *Magnolia grandiflora*

SOME OTHER TREES:

American holly – *Ilex opaca*
Bigleaf magnolia – *Magnolia macrophylla*
Loblolly pine – *Pinus taeda (some sites)*
Northern red oak – *Quercus rubra*
Red buckeye – *Aesculus pavia*
Spruce pine – *Pinus glabra (some sites)*
Tulip poplar – *Liriodendron tulipifera*
White oak – *Quercus alba*

SMALL TREES AND SHRUBS:

Dogwood – *Cornus florida*
Highbush blueberry – *Vaccinium corymbosum*
Hop hornbeam – *Ostrya virginica*
Ironwood – *Carpinus caroliniana*
Pinxter azalea – *Rhododendron canescens*
Redbud – *Cercis canadensis*
Silky camellia – *Stewartia malecodendron*
Silverbell – *Halesia diptera*
Sourwood – *Oxydendrum arboreum*

Podophyllum peltatum

HERBACEOUS:

Bloodroot – *Sanguinaria canadensis*
Carolina lily – *Lilium michauxii*
Cranefly orchid – *Tipularia discolor*
Dwarf coreopsis – *Coreopsis auriculata*
Evergreen wild ginger – *Hexastylis arifolia*
False Solomon's seal – *Maianthemum racemosum*
Green and gold – *Chrysogonum virginianum*
Jack-in-the-pulpit – *Arisaema triphyllum*
May apple – *Podophyllum peltatum*
Merrybells – *Uvularia perfoliata*
Partridgeberry – *Mitchella repens*
Solomon's seal – *Polygonatum biflorum*
Spotted wintergreen – *Chimaphila maculata*
Summer phlox – *Phlox paniculata*
Wake robin – *Trillium cuneatum*
Wild ginger – *Asarum canadense*

FERNS:

Broad beech fern – *Phegopteris hexagonoptera*
Christmas fern – *Polystichum acrostichoides*
Rattlesnake fern – *Botrychium virginianum*

FLATWOODS :
(all have poor drainage)
LONGLEAF PINE SAVANNAS

Poor drainage due to a hardpan layer created savannas of grasses with few trees. The dominant grass is toothache grass (*Ctenium aromaticum*), dotted with a few longleaf pines (*Pinus palustris*) and slash pines (*Pinus elliottii).* Among the grasses and sedges are many showy flowers, including many orchids and carnivorous plants. Many of these species are dependent on regular, low-intensity fire to survive.

Once dominated by the longleaf pine and some oak and black gum, few savannas have endured changes in drainage and fire control, which encouraged invasion by other species, such as sweet gum and loblolly pine. The roots of sweet bay magnolia are fire tolerant, and what appears to be a small tree or shrub may in fact be quite old. Acreage of Longleaf Pine Savannas is dwindling rapidly due to development, drainage of the high water table, and control of fires.

HERBACEOUS:

Asters ⁓ *Aster dumosus, farinosa, paludosus*
Barbara's buttons ⁓ *Marshallia graminifolia*
Blue-eyed grasses ⁓ *Sisyrinchium* spp.
Bog milkweed ⁓ *Asclepias lanceolata*
Butterworts ⁓ *Pinguicula* spp.
Candy flowers, milkworts ⁓ *Polygala* spp.
Clasping coneflower ⁓ *Dracopis amplexicaulis*
False dragonheads ⁓ *Physostegia* spp.
Fleabane ⁓ *Erigeron vernus*
Fly poison ⁓ *Amianthium muscaetoxicum*
Fringed orchids ⁓ *Platanthera ciliaris,*
    cristata, nivea
Gayfeathers ⁓ *Liatris pycnostacia,*
    spicata
Gentians ⁓ *Gentiana* spp.
Goldenrod ⁓ *Solidago patula*
Grass pinks ⁓ *Calopogon* spp.
Meadow beauties ⁓ *Rhexia* spp.
Narrow-leaved skullcap ⁓ *Scutellaria integrifolia*
Pine lily ⁓ *Lilium catesbaei*
Pineland hibiscus ⁓ *Hibiscus aculeatus*
Pitcher plants ⁓ *Sarracenia* spp.
Primrose-leaved violet ⁓ *Viola primulifolia*
Rattlesnake masters ⁓ *Eryngium aquaticum, integrifolium*
Rose pinks ⁓ *Sabatia* spp.
Rose pogonia ⁓ *Pogonia ophioglossoides*
Slender seedbox ⁓ *Ludwigia virgata*
Sunbonnets ⁓ *Chaptalia tomentosa*
Sundews ⁓ *Drosera* spp.
Swamp sunflower ⁓ *Helianthus angustifolius*
White star grass ⁓ *Aletris farinosa*
White thoroughworts ⁓ *Eupatorium* spp.

*Platanthera
ciliaris*

FLATWOODS :
LONGLEAF PINE FLATWOODS

Flatwoods are similar to savannas, but are wetter and and endure fewer fires. Pines and shrubs predominate, and the ground layer is limited. The herbaceous plants that exist are much less showy than those in the savannas. There is no toothache grass, and there are no pitcher plants. The pine flatwoods may have started as pine savannas, but when they did not burn, woodies shaded out the herbaceous layer. Loblolly pine moves in when fire is suppressed for a long time.

TREES:

Longleaf pine ⁓ *Pinus palustris*
Oaks ⁓ *Quercus* spp.
Slash pine ⁓ *Pinus elliottii*
Swamp black gum ⁓ *Nyssa sylvatica var. biflora*
Sweet bay ⁓ *Magnolia virginiana*

SHRUBS:

Aronia arbutifolia

Black titi or
buckwheat tree ⁓ *Cliftonia monophylla*
Blueberries ⁓ *Vaccinium* spp.
Fetterbush ⁓ *Lyonia lucida*
Huckleberries ⁓ *Gaylussacia* spp.
Inkberry ⁓ *Ilex glabra*
Large-leaved
gallberry ⁓ *Ilex coriacea*
Red bay ⁓ *Persea borbonia*
Red chokeberry ⁓ *Aronia arbutifolia*
Saw palmetto ⁓ *Serenoa repens*
Southern wax myrtle ⁓ *Myrica cerrifera*
Sweet pepperbush ⁓ *Clethra alnifolia*
Titi, swamp cyrilla ⁓ *Cyrilla racemiflora*

FERNS:

Bracken fern ⁓ *Pteridium aquilinum*

SLASH PINE FLATWOODS

This community occurs on wetter sites than the Longleaf Pine Flatwoods.

DOMINANT TREES:

Pond pine ⁓ *Pinus serotina*
Slash pine ⁓ *Pinus elliottii*

OTHER TREES:

Oaks ⁓ *Quercus* spp. *(sparse)*

DOMINANT SHRUBS:

Gallberry ⁓ *Ilex coriaceae*
Saw palmetto ⁓ *Serenoa repens*

OTHER SHRUBS:

Evergreen blueberry ∼ *Vaccinium myrsinites*
Hairy wicky ∼ *Kalmia hirsuta*
Highbush blueberry ∼ *Vaccinium corymbosum*
Honeycup ∼ *Zenobia puberulenta*
Red bay ∼ *Persea borbonia*
Stagger bushes ∼ *Lyonia ferruginea, lucida*
Sweet bay ∼ *Magnolia virginiana*
Sweet pepperbush ∼ *Clethra alnifolia*

XERIC SAND HILLS

A belt of sand hills extends from southern North Carolina across South Carolina and Georgia into Alabama. Water drains quickly from these sandy soils, carrying minerals with it. The main plants are longleaf pine (if it has not been cut) and turkey oak, with some wire grass. Intense light and low amounts of water and nutrients determine the vegetation. The plants often have small, thick, waxy, or hairy leaves, and thick roots. Areas of nutrient-poor, dry, sandy soils can occur in any area of the Southeast and would support a similar community of plants.

Plants found in sand hills include:

Deerberry ∼ *Vaccinium stamineum*
Ironweed ∼ *Vernonia angustifolia*
Longleaf pine ∼ *Pinus palustris*
Prickly pear cactus ∼ *Opuntia humifusa*
Silk grass ∼ *Pityopsis graminifolia*
Turkey oak ∼ *Quercus laevis*
Winged sumac ∼ *Rhus copallina*
Wire grass ∼ *Aristida stricta*
Yucca ∼ *Yucca filamentosa*

Opuntia humifusa

COASTAL EVERGREEN OAK FORESTS (MARITIME FORESTS)

These communities occur right on the edge of the coast and on barrier islands. They are found on coastal ridges and on dunes of coastal islands. The signature species is live oak. It occurs in a narrow belt along the south Atlantic and Gulf Coasts. Slash pine forests are in the same belt. Proceed inland, and other trees join the live oak. Few herbaceous plants survive in the shade of the trees. In somewhat open areas, trailing bluets and prickly pear cactus survive. Sea oats, a dune plant, survives at the very edge of dunes, because it tolerates salt spray better than live oak does.

Most of the Evergreen Oak Forests are successional. Live oak was harvested for shipbuilding early in our history. The biggest threat to the community now is land clearing for development.

Coastal plant communities are highly specialized. For an excellent reference, refer to Porcher's, *Wildflowers of the Carolina Lowcountry and Lower Pee Dee*.

DOMINANT TREES:

Live oak ⁀ *Quercus virginiana*
Slash pine ⁀ *Pinus elliottii*

OTHER WOODY PLANTS:

American olive ⁀ *Osmanthus americanus*
Laurel and myrtle oak ⁀ *Quercus laurifolia, myrtifolia*
Red bay ⁀ *Persea borbonia*
Saw palmetto ⁀ *Serenoa repens*
Southern magnolia ⁀ *Magnolia grandiflora*
Wax myrtle ⁀ *Myrica cerifera*
Yaupon holly ⁀ *Ilex vomitoria*

Serenoa repens

SPECIAL PLANT COMMUNITIES

Some special plant communities can occur in more than one forest type and in more than one physiographic province. Rivers flow through all the regions, and the land alongside them supports wetland vegetation that is similar throughout the Southeast.

The vegetation of wetlands varies with the amount of moisture and light. Two other special communities occur in more than one region. They are prairies and rock outcrops. All these communities are described below.

WETLANDS

The Southeast is home to almost half the wetlands in the lower forty-eight states. These areas are important for many reasons besides beauty, wildlife habitat, and plant diversity. By filtering water, they help control its quality. They are reservoirs for stormwater runoff, which helps control flooding. They offer food and shelter for diverse animal life, and they are living classrooms. Amphibians, migratory waterfowl, turtles, aquatic insects, and freshwater mollusks are heavily dependent on wetlands. Unfortunately, wetlands are lost yearly due to development, ditching, draining for agriculture, canal-building, peat and phosphate mining, and gas and oil extraction.

There are three kinds of wetlands that can occur in more than one physiographic province or forest type: swamps, peatlands, and marshes. Swamps have trees and are inundated three or more months per year. Grass- or shrub-dominated peatlands are areas of pure organic matter which are seasonally flooded. Marshes support herbaceous plants and are submerged year-round.

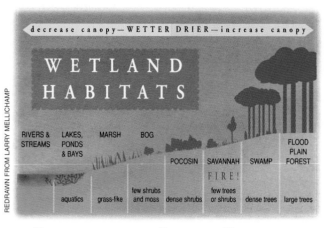

decrease canopy—WETTER DRIER—increase canopy

WETLAND HABITATS

REDRAWN FROM LARRY MELLICHAMP

RIVERS & STREAMS	LAKES, PONDS & BAYS	MARSH	BOG		POCOSIN	SAVANNAH FIRE!	SWAMP	FLOOD PLAIN FOREST
	aquatics	grass-like	few shrubs and moss	dense shrubs		few trees or shrubs	dense trees	large trees

BOTTOMLAND SWAMP FORESTS

Bottomland forests occur on flat, alluvial flood plains. Alluvial means the topsoil has been deposited by water. These areas are far enough away from the ocean that they are not influenced by the tide. The water level fluctuates throughout the year. In the wettest areas, the bald cypress and tupelo gum dominate the landscape. A limited number of herbaceous plants live in this shady water world. Standing water limits the oxygen-holding capacity of the soil, a strong factor in the ability of plants to survive. Moving to slightly higher ground, hardwoods begin to dominate the alluvial flood plain or swamp. As the depth of the water decreases, or the amount of time the plants are submerged decreases, the variety of woody and herbaceous plants increases.

The acreage covered by alluvial swamps in the Coastal Plain is very large compared to that covered by river bottom swamps in the other physiographic regions of the Southeast. The Mississippi River forms a huge alluvial plain that cuts through the Oak-Pine and Southern Mixed Hardwood Forest regions, going from Mississippi to Louisiana. Many other southern rivers have large flood plains. Some drain into the Gulf, and some drain into the Atlantic. Tributaries and streams also have flood plains. In addition, the streams crossing the Coastal Plain flow slowly and drop large amounts of silt. Natural bars and levees block the flow of water, and large areas of land remain wet all year.

The following lists review these plant communities, from the wettest to the driest.

* Dominant species (see *Biodiversity*, Lowland vol., Chap. 8, Martin, et al, 1993).

RIVER SWAMP

The River Swamp is the wettest of the four communities.

TREES:

Bald cypress ⁓ *Taxodium distichum* *
Black willow ⁓ *Salix nigra*
Pond pine ⁓ *Pinus serotina*
Pond pine ⁓ *Taxodium ascendens*
River birch ⁓ *Betula nigra*
Swamp black gum ⁓ *Nyssa sylvatica var. biflora*

Sweet bay ⁓ *Magnolia virginiana*
Sweet gum ⁓ *Liquidamber styraciflua*
Tupelo gum ⁓ *Nyssa aquatica**
Water elm ⁓ *Planera aquatica*

SHRUBS:

Buttonbush ⁓ *Cephalanthus occidentalis*
Swamp privet ⁓ *Forestiera acuminata*
Virginia sweetspire ⁓ *Itea virginica*

HERBACEOUS:

Blue flag ⁓ *Iris virginica*
Golden club ⁓ *Orontium aquaticum*
Spanish needles ⁓ *Bidens* spp.
Swamp lily ⁓ *Crinum americanum*

Cephalanthus occidentalis

LOWER HARDWOOD SWAMP FOREST

This forest contains communities in low, poorly drained areas where water stands into the growing season. The forest has many of the plants of the river swamp community, plus more, including:

TREES:

Box elder ⁓ *Acer negundo*
Cottonwood ⁓ *Populus deltoides*
Green ash ⁓ *Fraxinus pennsylvanica*
Hackberry ⁓ *Celtis occidentalis*
Nuttall's oak ⁓ *Quercus nuttallii*
Overcup oak ⁓ *Quercus lyrata**
Red maple ⁓ *Acer rubum*
Storax ⁓ *Styrax americana*
Swamp dogwood ⁓ *Cornus stricta*
Water hickory ⁓ *Carya aquatica**
Water locust ⁓ *Gleditsia aquatica*

VINES:

Laurel leaf greenbrier ⁓ *Smilax laurifolia*

HERBACEOUS:

Butterweed ⁓ *Senecio glabellus*
False nettle ⁓ *Boehmeria cylindrica*

Jewel weed ~ *Impatiens capensis*
Lizard's tail ~ *Saururus cernuus*

FERNS:

Net-vein chain fern ~ *Woodwardia areolata*
Royal fern ~ *Osmunda regalis*
Sensitive fern ~ *Onoclea sensibilis*

Osmunda regalis

BACKWATER SWAMPS

Communities on backwaters and flats are seasonally flooded. They may have some of the plants from the wetter communities.

TREES:

American elm ~ *Ulmus americana**
Box elder ~ *Acer negundo*
Laurel oak ~ *Quercus laurifolia**
Pecan ~ *Carya illinoensis* (*Gulf Coast drainage only*)
Sweet gum ~ *Liquidambar styraciflua**
Sycamore ~ *Platanus occidentalis**
Water oak ~ *Quercus nigra**
Willow oak ~ *Quercus phellos**

SMALL TREES AND SHRUBS:

Black haw ~ *Viburnum obovatum*
Cabbage palm ~ *Sabal palmetto*
Dwarf palmetto ~ *Sabal minor*
Ironwood ~ *Carpinus caroliniana*
Possumhaw ~ *Ilex decidua*
Sugarberry ~ *Celtis laevigata*

VINES:

Climbing hydrangea ~ *Decumaria barbara*
Poison ivy ~ *Toxidendron radicans*
Rattan vine ~ *Berchemia scandens*
Trumpet creeper ~ *Campsis radicans*

SEDGES AND GRASSES:

Panic grasses ~ *Panicum* spp.
Swamp grasses ~ *Leersia* spp.

HERBACEOUS:

Green-headed coneflower ~ *Rudbeckia laciniata*
Justicia ~ *Justicia ovata*
Swamp rose mallow ~ *Hibiscus moscheutos*

TRANSITIONAL WETLANDS OR
SECOND BOTTOM HARDWOOD FOREST

Communities in higher areas, with short periods of flooding that are transitional to the uplands (levees, ridges, dunes):

TREES:

American holly	*Ilex opaca*
Hickories	*Carya* spp.
Oaks	*Quercus alba, michauxii, pagodaeifolia**
Paw paw	*Asimina triloba*
Pines	*Pinus glabra, taeda*
Winged elm	*Ulmus alata*

SHRUBS:

Arrowwood	*Viburnum dentatum*
Elderberry	*Sambucus canadensis*
Spice bush	*Lindera benzoin*

VINES:

Carolina jasmine	*Gelsemium sempervirens*
Cross vine	*Bignonia capreolata*
Muscadine	*Vitis rotundifolia*

CANE OR BAMBOO:

Switchcane	*Arundinaria gigantea*

FERNS:

Christmas fern	*Polystichum acrostichoides*
Cinnamon fern	*Osmunda cinnamomea*

HERBACEOUS:

Zephranthes atamasco

Atamasco lily	*Zephranthes atamasco*
Cut-leaf toothwort	*Cardamine concatenata*
Golden alexander	*Zizea aurea*
Green dragon	*Arisaema dracontium*
Ladies' tresses	*Spiranthes cernua*
May apple	*Podophyllum peltatum*
Obedient plant	*Physostegia virginiana*
Spider lily	*Hymenocallis caroliniana*
Spiderwort	*Tradescantia virginiana*
Spring beauty	*Claytonia virginica*
Tall meadow rue	*Thalictrum pubescens*
Violets	*Viola* spp.
Wild ageratum	*Eupatorium coelestinum*

PEATLANDS

Pocosins, bays, and shrub bogs are peat-filled depressions that are seasonally flooded with fresh water and are nutrient poor. What little nutrients the plants get comes in with rain water. Lower peatlands can be permanently flooded. The vegetation is part of the Subtropical Evergreen Forest. It is a dense tangle of evergreen shrubs, vines, and small trees. There may be a few pines. Bits of shrub bogs occur along shallow edges of swamps. Herbaceous plants are present only when a site has burned recently.

SHRUBS:

Black titi	*Cliftonia monophylla*
Dog hobbles	*Leucothoe axillaris, racemosa*
Fetterbush	*Lyonia lucida*
Highbush blueberry	*Vaccinium corymbosum*
Hollies	*Ilex cassine, coriacea, glabra*
Honeycup	*Zenobia pulverulenta*
Huckleberries	*Gaylussacia* spp.
Leatherleaf	*Chamaedaphne calyculata*
Myrtles	*Myrica cerifera, heterophylla, inodora*
Red chokeberry	*Aronia arbutifolia*
Sheep kill	*Kalmia carolina*
Sweet pepperbush	*Clethra alnifolia*
Titi	*Cyrilla racemiflora*

Zenobia pulverulenta

VINES:

Carolina jasmine	*Gelsemium sempervirens*
Cranberry	*Vaccinium macrocarpon*
Greenbriers	*Smilax glauca, laurifolia, walteri*

SOME TREES:

Atlantic white cedar	*Chamaecyparis thyoides*
Loblolly bay	*Gordonia lasianthus*
Pond pine	*Pinus serotina*
Red bay	*Persea borbonia, palustris*
Red maple	*Acer rubrum*
Sweet bay	*Magnolia virginiana*

GRASSES:

Bamboo or cane	*Arundinaria gigantea*
Bushy beard grass	*Andropogon glomeratus*

FERNS AND MOSSES:

Cinnamon fern	*Osmunda cinnamomea*
Sphagnum mosses	*Sphagnum* spp.
Virginia chain fern	*Woodwardia virginica*

FRESH, BRACKISH, AND SALTWATER MARSHES

The dominant plants in marshes are herbaceous. Their roots are in soil, and their leaves are partially immersed in water. Grasses, rushes, and sedges dominate, with some flowering plants. Smooth cordgrass (*Spartina alterniflora*) dominates saltwater marshes. Species from freshwater marshes and saltwater marshes intermingle in the brackish marsh. Needle rush (*Juncus roemerianus*) is common in brackish water. Freshwater marshes can be inland beside ponds and lakes or beside tidal rivers. Grasses still dominate, but showy flowering plants are more common in freshwater marshes than in the saltier ones.

FRESHWATER MARSH SPECIES:

DOMINANTS (IN ORDER):

Southern wild rice	~ *Zizaniopsis miliacea*
Wild rice	~ *Zizania aquatica*
Pickeral weed	~ *Pontederia cordata*
Arrow arum	~ *Peltandra virginica*

GRASSES, SEDGES, AND RUSHES:

Big cordgrass	~ *Spartina cynosuroides*
Bulrushes	~ *Scirpus americanus, cyperinus, validus*
Narrow and common cattails	~ *Typha angustifolia, latifolia*
Saw grass	~ *Cladium mariscus* var. *jamaicense*
Soft rush	~ *Juncus effusus*
Sugarcane plumegrass	~ *Saccharum giganteum*
Tussock sedge	~ *Carex alata, stricta*

POSSIBLE SHRUBS:

Buttonbush	~ *Cephalanthus occidentalis*
Groundsel	~ *Baccharis halimifolia*
Indigo bush	~ *Amorpha fruticosa*
Swamp rose	~ *Rosa palustris*
Water willow	~ *Decodon verticillatus*

VINES:

Climbing hempweed	~ *Mikania scandens*
Ground nut	~ *Apios americana*
Native wisteria	~ *Wisteria frutescens*
Passion flower	~ *Passiflora incarnata*

HERBACEOUS:

Alligator weed	~ *Alternanthera philoxeroides* (exotic)
Aquatic milkweed	~ *Asclepias perennis*
Arrow arums	~ *Sagittaria* spp.
Blue flag	~ *Iris prismatica, virginica*
Bur-marigold	~ *Bidens laevis*
Butterweed	~ *Senecio glabellus*
Cardinal flower	~ *Lobelia cardinalis*
Climbing aster	~ *Aster carolinianus*
Crinum	~ *Crinum americanum*
Eryngo	~ *Eryngium aquaticum*
Fragrant ladies' tresses	~ *Spiranthes odorata*
Fringed orchids	~ *Platanthera* spp.

Golden club ~ *Orontium aquaticum*
Jewel weed ~ *Impatiens capensis*
Lizard's tail ~ *Saururus cernuus*
Mad dog skullcap ~ *Scutellaria lateriflora*
Marsh aster ~ *Aster tenuifolius*
Marsh daisy ~ *Boltonia asteroides*
Obedient plants ~ *Physostegia leptophylla,
denticulata*
Salt marsh, large marsh pink ~ *Sabatia calycina, dodecondra*
Seashore mallow ~ *Kosteletskya virginica*
Seedboxes ~ *Ludwigia* spp.
Spider lily ~ *Hymenocallis crassifolia*
Swamp milkweed ~ *Asclepias incarnata*
Swamp rose mallow ~ *Hibiscus moscheutos*
Water hemlock ~ *Cicuta maculata*
Water parsnip ~ *Sium suave*
Water willow ~ *Justicia ovata*

*Asclepias
incarnata*

FERNS:

Marsh fern ~ *Thelypteris palustris*
Royal fern ~ *Omunda regalis*
Virginia chain fern ~ *Woodwardia virginica*

PRAIRIES

The main prairie region of the southeastern United States is a 25-mile-wide crescent starting in the Western Mesophytic Forest region in southern Tennessee, crossing the northeastern corner of Mississippi, and extending across central Alabama. Much of this region is now covered with trees, especially sweet gum, post oak, and red cedar. Other prairie patches exist in southern Mississippi in the Jackson Prairie, in southern Louisiana in pleistocene terraces south of the Longleaf Pine region, and in Clay County, North Carolina.

Prairies have characteristic soils, topography, and vegetation. The heavy black or reddish brown soils are derived from soft, gray limestone of cretaceous age. Although these soils are high in calcium, the plants they support are not necessarily calcium or lime-dependent. Limestone dissolves quickly and releases the plant foods combined in it, providing a wide variety of readily available nutrients.

The Black Belt Prairie has few small streams, but rivers have cut bluffs into the chalk, giving some relief to the rolling topography.

The majority of the herbaceous and woody plant species of the prairie come from the interior of the country, not the east. The herbaceous layer dominates, with a high percentage of grasses such as bluestems and Indian grass. Mixed in with the grasses is a glorious display of flowering plants. One sees occasional groves of trees on higher ridges.

The proliferation of trees is limited by the impervious subsoil layer and by fire. Under the black loam formed by years of grass decomposition, the tight clay layer prevents drainage or upward capillary movement of water. When the prairie loses its grass layer, it rapidly loses the organic component in the top layer of soil that allows water to percolate slowly to lower levels. Regular fire also keeps woody growth in check, but does not harm the crowns of the herbaceous plants if it is a quick, cool fire. When an area does not burn for many years (more than ten), the available fuel increases, and a fire in that situation is hotter and can damage normally fire-resistant species.

Farming, grazing, timbering, fire suppression, and other activities of man compromise the ecological interactions necessary to sustain a prairie system. The remaining prairie vegetation of the Southeast is found in patches, not in the wide expanses of yesteryear.

The following lists contain some of the plants that might occur in a southeastern prairie, starting with the dominant species.

GRASSES:

Little bluestem	*Schizachyrium scoparius*
Indian grass	*Sorghastrum nutans*
Panic grasses	*Panicum and Dicanthelium* spp.
Plumegrasses	*Saccharum alopecuroides, contorum, giganteum*
Wild rye	*Elymus* spp.
Brownseed paspalum	*Paspalum plicatulum*
Eastern gamagrass	*Tripsacum dactyloides*
Bushy beardgrass	*Andropogon glomeratus*
Broomsedge	*Andropogon virginicus*
Side oats grama	*Bouteloua curtipendula*
Lovegrasses	*Eragrostis* spp.
Dropseeds	*Sporobolis* spp.
Longspike tridens	*Tridens strictus*
Slim spike three awn	*Aristida longispica*
Big bluestem	*Andropogon gerardii*

RUSHES:

Rushes	*Juncus filipendulus, torreyi*
Wool grass	*Scirpus cyperinus*

SEDGES:

Sedges	*Carex cherokeensis, crawei, crinita, gigantea, glaucescens, lupulina*
Spikerushes	*Eleocharis* spp.
Three-way sedge	*Dulichium arundinaceus*

HERBACEOUS:

Alumroot	*Heuchera americana*
American ipecac	*Porteranthus stipulatus*
Angelica	*Angelica venosa*
Asters	*Aster concolor, dumosus, laevis, linarifolius, lucidulus, novae angliae, paludosus, patens, paternus, pilosus, praealtus, sericeus, solidagineus, surculosus, tortifolius, undulatus*
Barbara's buttons	*Marshallia* spp.

Beardtongues ~ *Penstemon australis, digitalis*
Black-eyed Susans ~ *Rudbeckia fulgida,*
heliopsidis, hirta
Blazing stars ~ *Liatris aspera,*
graminifolia,
microcephala, spicata,
squarrosa, squarrulosa
Blue sages ~ *Salvia azurea, lyrata,*
urticifolia
Blue wild indigo ~ *Baptisia australis*
Blue-eyed grass ~ *Sisyrinchium angustifolium*
Bluets ~ *Houstonia caerulea,*
purpurea, pusilla, tenuifolia

Liatris
squarrosa

Boltonia, doll's daisy ~ *Boltonia asteroides, caroliniana*
Bush clovers ~ *Lespedeza* spp.
Butterfly weed ~ *Asclepias tuberosa*
Butterweeds, ragworts ~ *Senecio* spp.
Carolina anemone ~ *Anemone caroliniana*
Cherokee bean ~ *Erythrina herbaceae*
Coreopsis ~ *Coreopsis auriculata,*
lanceolata, major,
pubescens,
tinctoria, tripteris
Culver's root ~ *Veronicastrum*
virginicum
False aloe ~ *Manfreda virginica*
Fleabanes ~ *Erigeron* spp.
Gaura ~ *Gaura filipes*
Giant ironweed ~ *Vernonia gigantea*
Goldenrods ~ *Solidago arguta, erecta, nemoralis,*
odora, ptarmicoides,
rigida, rugosa, speciosa

Anemone
caroliniana

Grey-headed coneflower ~ *Ratibida pinnata*
Indian blanket ~ *Gaillardia aestivalis*
Lizard's tail ~ *Saururus cernuus*
Marsh mallow ~ *Hibiscus moscheutos*
Milkworts ~ *Polygala* spp.
Mints ~ *Monarda citriodora,*
fistulosa
Mountain mints ~ *Pycnanthemum*
incanum, tenuifolium,
virginianum
Obedient plant ~ *Physostegia virginiana*
Ohio horse mint ~ *Blephilia ciliata*
Pale meadow beauty ~ *Rhexia mariana*
Partridge peas ~ *Chamaecrista*
fasciculata, nictitans
Passion vines ~ *Passiflora incarnata, lutea*
Phlox ~ *Phlox amoena, glaberrima,*
maculata, pilosa

Ratibida
pinnata

*Sabatia
capitata*

Pinks ~ *Sabatia angularis, capitata*
Prairie larkspur ~ *Delphinium carolinianum*
Purple coneflowers ~ *Echinacea pallida, purpurea*
Purple prairie clover ~ *Dalea purpurea*
Rattlesnake master ~ *Eryngium yuccifolium*
Rosinweeds ~ *Silphium astericus, compositum, terebinthinaceum, trifoliatum*
Rue anemone ~ *Thalictrum thalictroides*
Shooting star ~ *Dodecatheon media*
Silk grass ~ *Pityopsis graminifolia*
Skullcaps ~ *Scutellaria elliptica, integrefolia*
Sneezeweed ~ *Helenium autumnale*
Soapwort gentian ~ *Gentiana saponaria*
Southern ladies' tresses ~ *Spiranthes lacera, magnicamporum*
Spanish needles ~ *Bidens aristosa, bipinnata*
Spider milkweed ~ *Asclepias viridis*
Spiked lobelia ~ *Lobelia spicata*
Spurges ~ *Euphorbia* spp.
St. John's worts ~ *Hypericum* spp.
Sundrops ~ *Oenothera fruticosa*
Sunflowers ~ *Helianthus angustifolius, atrorubens, divaricatus, hirsutus, microcephalus, mollis, occidentalis, strumosus, verticillatus*
Tall meadow rues ~ *Thalictrum dasycarpum, pubescens*
Thimbleweed ~ *Anemone virginiana*
Thoroughworts ~ *Eupatorium altissiumum, capillifolium, fistulosum, hyssopifolium, perfoliatum, rotundifolium, serotinum*
Verbenas ~ *Verbena* spp.
Vernal iris ~ *Iris verna*
Violets ~ *Viola pedata, walteri*
White sweet clover ~ *Meliotus alba*
White wild indigo ~ *Baptisia alba*
Whorled milkweed ~ *Asclepias verticillata*
Wild geranium ~ *Geranium maculatum*
Wild hyacinth ~ *Camassia scilloides*
Wild petunias ~ *Ruellia caroliniensis, humilis, strepens*
Yellow star grass ~ *Hypoxis hirsuta*
Yucca or bear grass ~ *Yucca filamentosa*

VINES:

Summer grape ~ *Vitis aestivalis*

TREES:

Blackjack oak ～ *Quercus marilandica*
Chinquapin ～ *Q. muehlenbergii*
Elms ～ *Ulmus* spp.
Hickories ～ *Carya* spp.
Nuttall's oak ～ *Q. nuttalli*
Post oak ～ *Q. stellata*
Red cedar ～ *Juniperus virginiana*
Sweet gum ～ *Liquidamber styraciflua*

SMALL TREES AND SHRUBS:

Blue haw ～ *Viburnum rufidulum*
Blueberries ～ *Vaccinium arborea, corymbosa*
Bottlebrush buckeye ～ *Aesculus parviflora*
Carolina rose, prairie rose ～ *Rosa carolina, R. setigera*
Carolina buckthorn ～ *Rhamnus caroliniana*
Crabapple ～ *Malus angustifolia*
Dwarf paw paw ～ *Asimina parviflora*
False buckthorn ～ *Bumelia lanuginosa*
False indigo bush ～ *Amorpha fruticosa*
Fragrant sumac ～ *Rhus aromatica*
Hawthorns ～ *Crataegus* spp.
New Jersey tea ～ *Ceanothus americana*
Plums ～ *Prunus* spp.
Possumhaw ～ *Ilex decidua*
Redbud ～ *Cercis canadensis*
Swamp dogwood ～ *Cornus amomum*
Wafer ash ～ *Ptelia trifoliata*

Rosa carolina

*Hypericum buckleyi at Devil's Courthouse
on the Blue Ridge Parkway in North Carolina*

ROCK OUTCROP COMMUNITIES

Rock Outcrop Communities can occur on limestone, sandstone, or granite. They all tend to have dry eroded soil and are dominated by herbaceous plants. Trees and shrubs exist only where a crack or hole in the rock admits the roots. The paucity of trees means light is readily available.

CEDAR GLADES

Cedar glades occur in central Tennessee (Nashville Basin), northern Alabama (a pocket between the Highland Rim and Appalachian Plateau), and in the Ridge and Valley Province of Georgia (Chicka-mauga Valley). They consist of shallow soil over limestone and are dry in summer. They are open grasslands, low to medium in height, with scattered needle-leaf evergreen shrubs and groves of low- to medium-tall broadleaf deciduous trees. Cedar glades are wet in winter and spring and dry in summer and fall. Plant communities in glades are fascinating because they have disjunct species (not contiguous with the plant's range). For example, a Texas species might appear in the middle of Tennessee. Periodic droughts control woody species.

HERBACEOUS:

(many annuals)
Beardtongue – *Penstemon tenuiflorus*
Biennial evening primrose – *Oenothera triloba*
Black-eyed Susan (biennial) – *Rudbeckia hirta*
False aloe – *Manfreda virginca*
Fleabane – *Erigeron strigosus*
Prairie clover – *Dalea gattingeri*
Prickly pear – *Opuntia humifusa*
Sand phlox – *Phlox bifida*
Sandwort (annual) – *Minuartia patula*
Scurf pea – *Psoralea subacaulis*
Texas stonecrop – *Sedum pulchellum*
Wild petunia – *Ruellia humilis*
Winter annuals – *Leavenworthia* spp.
Yucca – *Yucca filamentosa*

FERNS:

Hairy lip fern – *Cheilanthes lanuosa*

GRASSES:

Broomsedge – *Andropogon virginicus*
Common witchgrass – *Panicum capillare, flexile*
Little bluestem – *Schizachyrium scoparium*
Poverty grass – *Sporobolus vaginiflorus*
Side oats gama – *Bouteloua curtipendula*
Slim spike three awn – *Aristida longispica*

SHRUBS ADJACENT TO GLADES:

(also occur in other communities)
Aromatic sumac – *Rhus aromatica*
Blue haw – *Viburnum rufidulum*
Coralberry – *Symphoricarpos orbiculatus*
Glade privet – *Forestiera ligustrina*
St. John's worts – *Hypericum frondosum, sphaerocarpum*

TREES THAT SPROUT
IN SHRUB BORDERS:

Blue ash ◝ *Fraxinus quadrangulata*
Post oak ◝ *Q. stellata (a few)*
Red cedar ◝ *Juniperus virginiana*
  (dominant)
Redbud ◝ *Cercis canadensis*
Sugarberry ◝ *Celtis laevigata*
Winged elm ◝ *Ulmus alata*

SANDSTONE GLADES (OUTCROPS)

Sandstone outcrops are more acidic than the limy cedar glades. They occur throughout the Southeast, but the dominant plants are different at each site in each state. Once again, grasses and herbaceous plants predominate, especially little bluestem, coreopsis, hypericums, and liatris. Nonvascular plants are common and vulnerable to the traffic of picnickers who find the views from these rock ledges irresistible.

GRANITE ROCK OUTCROPS

The composition of the rock in these outcrops varies throughout the Southeast, but granite outcrop is the accepted name. Soils are shallow, and water runs off quickly. Some water may collect in small depressions. Intense light exposure and extremes in temperature and moisture create an almost desert-like habitat. The state of Georgia has a large concentration of granite outcrops in the central Piedmont. Most granite outcrops are in the Oak-Pine Forest area. Low lichens and mosses carpet these flatrocks. In winter, a red cast over most of the flatrock is the annual, *Diamorpha smallii*. Annuals flower all spring. Where thin soil exists, grasses, sedges, and a few perennial flowering plants grow. As the soil gets deeper at the edges of the outcrop, the diversity of herbaceous plants increases, and a few stunted woody plants appear.

Diamorpha cymosa on Forty-acre Rock in South Carolina

WILDFLOWER BASICS

BASIC BOTANICAL TERMS

Achene: a small, dry, one-seeded fruit that does not open to release its seed; for example, sunflower seed.

Apex: usually refers to the end of the leaf, bud, or petal away from the attachment point.

Aril: an appendage or outer covering of a seed.

Awn: a slender, bristle-like appendage (an additional plant part), often on a fruit or seed.

Basal: literally, at the base of the plant or defined structure, usually referring to leaves.

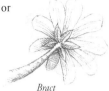

Bract

Bract: a modified leaf, e.g., those beneath a flower or inflorescence.

Bulb: a round structure in which fleshy, scale leaves enfold a bit of stem and its growing point. The layers of scales attach to a disc of tissue at the bottom called the basal plate; the point at which the scales join the disc is the site of cells capable of division, making propagation of the plant possible from scales (see page 49).

Calyx: all of the sepals, separate or joined in a cup.

Capsule: a dry seed case that splits along three or more lines when mature to release multiple seeds (from two or more carpels).

Carpel: a simple pistil or one member of a compound pistil of a flower. It bears the ovules.

Cauline: on the stem.

Corm: a bulb look-alike but without scales and composed mainly of stem tissue; a round underground stem; leaves emerge from the top, roots from the bottom.

Corolla: a collective term for the petals, which may be arranged in regular or irregular fashion.

Dioecious: having male and female flowers on separate plants, normally requiring pollen from the male plant to fertilize the female flowers.

Disc Flower: the small flowers amassed in the middle of the flat head of the inflorescence of Asteraceae (see drawing on page 54).

Discoid: an Asteraceae flower head composed of only disc flowers.

Ellipsoid: shaped like an American football.

Flower: the part of the plant that produces the seed. The stalk of a single flower, fruit, or leaf is a pedicel.

Follicle: a dry, one-celled fruit that splits along one seam, only when mature (from one carpel).

Fruit: the structure that contains the seed; a mature ovary or ovaries.

Glandular: having secretory glands or hair-like structures.

Glaucous: covered with a whitish, waxy substance.

Inflorescence: a cluster of flowers on a stem. The stalk of an inflorescence is a peduncle (see the drawings on page 54).

Involucre: a whorl of bracts (modified leaves) beneath a cluster of flowers (see the bract illustration on page 54).

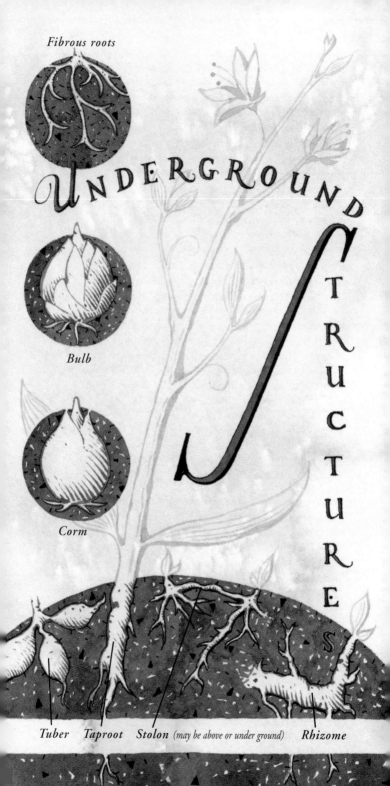

Fibrous roots

UNDERGROUND Structures

Bulb

Corm

Tuber Taproot Stolon (may be above or under ground) Rhizome

Irregular Flowers: either totally asymmetrical or, if cut along only one axis, will reveal bilateral symmetry (mirror images, like those of a human face when vertically bisected).

Leaf Node: the place where the leaf joins the stem; the site of cells capable of division, and thus, growth into new shoots or roots.

Leaves: food-producing organs of plants.

Pedicel: stalk of a single flower of an inflorescence.

Peduncle: stalk of an inflorescence or of a solitary flower on a species having single flowers.

Perfect: flower having both female and male parts.

Petals: the parts of a flower that are usually colored. They may be separate or united. Together they form the corolla.

Pistil: the female reproductive part of a flower, including the stigma, style, and ovary (see the illustration on page 51).

Pubescent: covered with soft hairs.

Radiate: a flower head with both disc and ray flowers.

Ray Flower: the outer ring of flowers on the inflorescence or head of Asteraceae; looks like a petal (see diagram on page 54).

Receptacle: the expanded end of the flower stalk that bears the flower organs, or in the Asteraceae, the flowers.

Regular Flowers: all the same parts of a flower alike in size and shape; may be cut along more than one line to obtain mirror images.

Rhizome: an elongated, underground stem with vestigial leaves and leaf nodes; the presence of cells that divide quickly at these leaf nodes make propagation easy (see page 49); a creeping, root-like structure used for the storage of food and water.

Roots: the smooth, uniform part of the plant that grows downward, anchors the plant, and transports water and nutrients from the ground into the upper parts of the plant.

Rosette: a circle or cluster of leaves, usually at ground level.

Salverform: a corolla tube that is long and thin (see the drawing on page 53).

Sepals: the outer whorl of the flower; may be green and leaf-like or colored and petal-like.

Simple: used in two situations, one in reference to the stem, and the other in reference to a leaf. In the first case, it is an unbranched stem. In the second, it is a leaf that has only one main blade (no compound leaflets) (see the drawing on page 51).

Stamen: the male reproductive part of the flower including the anther and filament (see the drawing on page 51).

Stipules: small, leaf-like appendages at the base of a leaf stalk (see the drawing of a simple leaf on page 51).

Stolon: a slender, horizontal stem running above or just below ground level. It tends to form roots and new plants at the tip (see the drawing on page 49).

Tuber: a swollen, underground stem that stores food (see drawing on page 49).

PARTS OF A FLOWER

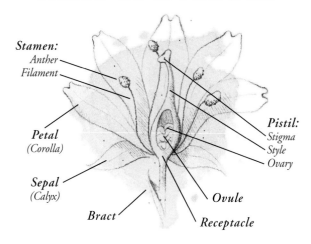

Stamen:
Anther
Filament

Pistil:
Stigma
Style
Ovary

Petal
(Corolla)

Sepal
(Calyx)

Bract

Ovule

Receptacle

PARTS OF A LEAF

All leaves are made up of the same parts whether they are simple or compound.

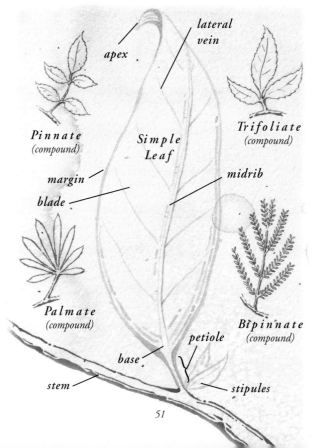

apex

lateral vein

Pinnate
(compound)

Simple Leaf

Trifoliate
(compound)

margin

midrib

blade

Palmate
(compound)

Bipinnate
(compound)

petiole

base

stem

stipules

COROLLA SHAPES

Rotate

Regular

Irregular

Urn Shaped

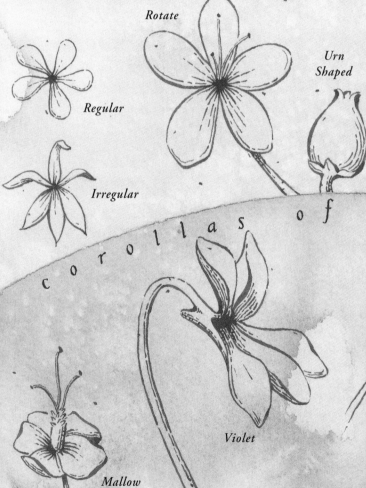

corollas of

Mallow

Violet

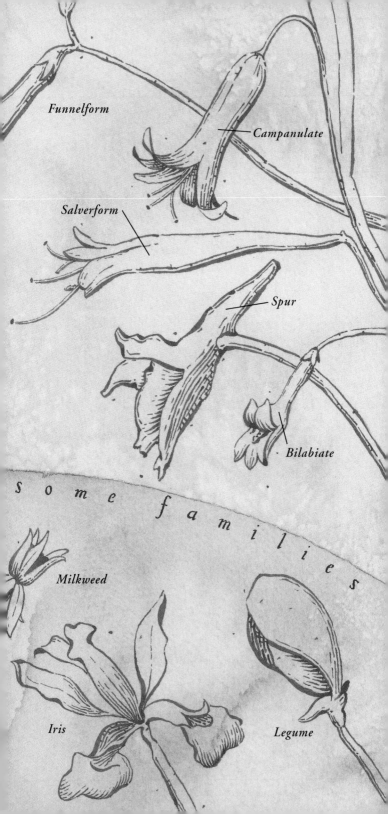

Funnelform

Campanulate

Salverform

Spur

Bilabiate

some families

Milkweed

Iris

Legume

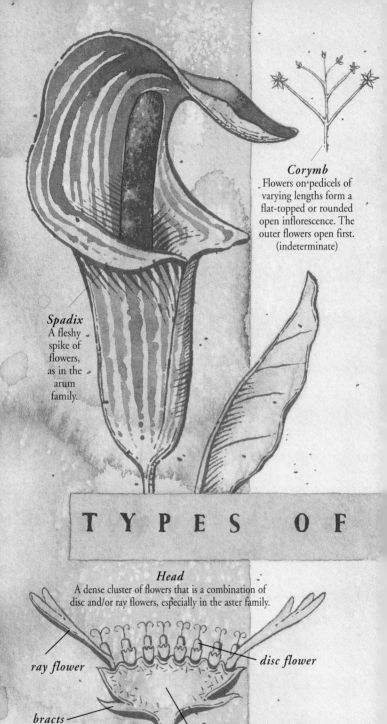

Corymb
Flowers on pedicels of varying lengths form a flat-topped or rounded open inflorescence. The outer flowers open first. (indeterminate)

Spadix
A fleshy spike of flowers, as in the arum family.

TYPES OF

Head
A dense cluster of flowers that is a combination of disc and/or ray flowers, especially in the aster family.

ray flower

disc flower

bracts

peduncle

receptacle

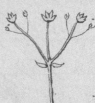

Cyme
In this broad flower cluster, there is a central flower at the top of the main stalk and in the middle of each flower side branch. These central flowers open first. (determinate)

Panicle
A loose, diversely branching flower cluster; branches numerous times.

Umbel
Many small flowers on pedicels of varied length form a flat or rounded inflorescence. The pedicels arise from a central point.

Simple Umbel

Compound Umbel

INFLORESCENCE

Spike
Stalkless flowers on an elongated stalk; flowering begins at the bottom.

Raceme
An elongated flower cluster of stalked flowers along a main peduncle; flowering begins at the bottom.

FLOWER ARRANGEMENTS

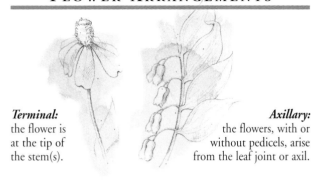

Terminal:
the flower is
at the tip of
the stem(s).

Axillary:
the flowers, with or
without pedicels, arise
from the leaf joint or axil.

LEAF VEINATION:

Parallel   *Pinnate*   *Palmate*   *Netted*

LEAF ARRANGEMENTS:

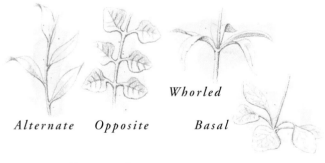

Whorled

Alternate   *Opposite*   *Basal*

LEAF ATTACHMENTS:

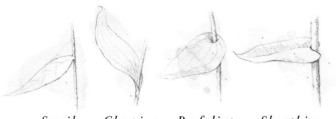

Sessile   *Clasping*   *Perfoliate*   *Sheathing*

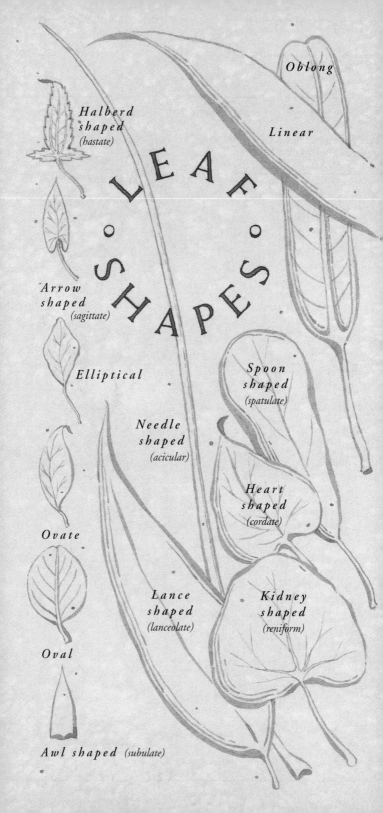

Oblong

Linear

Halberd
shaped
(hastate)

Arrow
shaped
(sagittate)

Elliptical

Needle
shaped
(acicular)

Spoon
shaped
(spatulate)

Heart
shaped
(cordate)

Ovate

Lance
shaped
(lanceolate)

Kidney
shaped
(reniform)

Oval

Awl shaped *(subulate)*

LEAF MARGINS

Crenate

Incised
(cut or dissected)

Serrate
(finely toothed)

Entire
(even, unbroken)

Ciliate

Lobed

Dentate
*(coarsely or
roundly toothed)*

Wavy

CHARACTERISTICS OF PLANT FAMILIES

Plants are organized into groups called families on the basis of similar plant parts and arrangements. Within each family is one or more genera, and within each genus is one or more species. Differences abound and make the identification of plants a challenge, but similarities usually outweigh the differences and help both amateurs and professionals identify plants new to them. In order to discover the name of a plant, one must learn to look carefully at a plant. Most people begin with an examination of the flower. Color is less important than the number of petals, the symmetry, and the arrangement of the flowers on the stem. Next in importance is the leaf and its attachment to the stem. If a plant is not in bloom, you can often ascertain the genus by the leaves, with or without the seed stalk. The roots can be the deciding factor, but I do not recommend digging up plants just to look at the roots, unless they are in your own back yard. I often collect seed and grow a plant from the seed in order to identify it later. The process may take two to three years, but the fun is in the search as much as the solution.

Families are in one of two categories: monocotyledons and dicotyledons. A cotyledon is the embryonic leaf in the seed of a plant. It is the first leaf to emerge when the seed germinates. When the seed first germinates, monocotyledons have one seed leaf and dicotyledons have two. Monocots usually have parallel-veined leaves and flowers with parts in threes or multiples of three or 3-merous.

The majority of plants in this book are dicots. They may have regular or irregular flowers and arrangements of flower and leaf in enough diversity to entertain you for a lifetime.

MONOCOTYLEDONS

(PARALLEL-VEINED LEAVES, FLOWER PARTS IN THREES)

Agavaceae (century plant family): fragrant, regular, perfect flowers on a tall, erect stalk; mostly basal narrow leaves; fruit a capsule.

Araceae (arum family): inflorescence a spadix, sheltered beneath a hood-like sheath; long petioled leaves simple or compound in parts of 3, 5, 7, or 9; fruit a berry.

Commelinaceae (spiderwort family): 3 petals, 3 sepals, 6 stamens with colorful, hairy filaments; flower clusters look triangular; flower color blue to purple; narrow leaves form sheath around stem, which is swollen at the leaf axil; fruit a capsule.

Iridaceae (iris family): flowers regular, 3-merous in all genera except iris, which has erect petals, the "standards," and recurved sepals, the "falls"; leaves long and narrow; fruit a capsule.

Liliaceae (includes Amaryllidaceae, lily family): 3 petals, 3 sepals (petals and sepals usually similar and may be united), 6 stamens; leaves mostly narrow, but wide in trillium; fruit a capsule or berry.

Orchidaceae (orchid family): 3 petals, 3 sepals (2 may be fused), 1 or 2 stamens may be combined with the style and stigma; irregular flowers; shiny leaves that are broad elliptical or lanceolate; fruit a capsule; seeds miniscule.

DICOTYLEDONS

Acanthaceae (acanthus family): flowers irregular or regular, 2–4 stamens; leaves opposite; fruit a capsule.

Apiaceae or Umbelliferaceae (carrot family): 5 petals, sepals, and stamens, tiny flowers in an umbel or compact head; leaves compound or simple, may be deeply cut; mass of seeds.

Apocynaceae (dogbane family): corolla funnel-shaped; leaves alternate or opposite; plants have white sap; fruit a follicle.

Aristolochiaceae (birthwort family): no petals, 3 sepals united at the base; flowers at leaf axils; leaves alternate; fruit a capsule.

Asclepiadaceae (milkweed family): intricate flowers with parts in fives; leaves opposite, whorled, or alternate and entire; fruit a follicle.

Asteraceae (aster or sunflower family): many small flowers on a flat to rounded receptacle, surrounded by the involucre (ring of bracts); 2 types of flowers: ray and disc; can be ray only, disc only, or ray and disc flowers; leaves highly variable; fruit an achene.

Balsaminaceae (touch-me-not family): plants succulent annuals or perennials; flowers irregular; 5 petals, orange or yellow, 3 sepals with the lower one forming a spurred sac, 5 stamens; simple, alternate leaves; mature capsule bursts open when touched.

Berberidaceae (barberry family): solitary flower at leaf axil; petals and sepals similar, twice as many stamens as petals; opposite leaves; rhizomatous; fruit a berry.

Brassicaceae (mustard family): 4 petals form a cross; sepals green; racemes have flowers and seed pods simultaneously; leaves alternate, pinnately lobed; long, thin, 2-celled fruit separates on both sides, from the bottom up.

Buxaceae (box family): no petals or sepals; flowers imperfect; male flowers at top of spike, female flowers at the bottom; 4 stamens; leaves alternate, turn ruddy and spotted through winter; sprawling; fruit a 6-seeded capsule.

Cactaceae (cactus family): sepals and petals similar; many stamens; succulent, spiny stems; leaves absent or fall early; fruit a berry.

Campanulaceae (bellflower family): corolla regular or irregular; 5 sepals, 5 stamens; leaves alternate; fruit a capsule.

Caprifoliaceae (honeysuckle family): regular or irregular flower; calyx and corolla 5-lobed, 5 stamens; leaves opposite, simple or compound; fruit has a soft pulp.

Caryophyllaceae (pink family): 5 petals, frequently notched; 5 sepals may be united into a long calyx, 5–10 stamens; leaves entire, opposite, narrow; leaf nodes swollen; fruit usually a capsule.

Euphorbiaceae (spurge family): petals, 0–5 petal-like appendages often present; leaves opposite, alternate, or whorled, simple or compound; fruit a capsule or a bladder-like container with a thin seed coat.

Fabaceae (bean family): 5 petals (lower 2 often joined), 5 sepals; united at base; many stamens, may be fused in groups; leaves alternate, compound; fruit a pod (legume) with many seeds that cling to one side of the pod when it splits open.

Gentianaceae (gentian family): 4–13 petals and sepals, both united at the base; stamens same number as petals; simple leaves basal, alternate, opposite, or whorled; fruit a capsule.

Geraniaceae (geranium family): 5 petals and sepals, 10 stamens; leaves alternate or opposite, simple, palmately, or pinnately divided or compound; fruit a beaked capsule.

Lamiaceae (mint family): flowers in spikes or clusters at the leaf axils; flower has 2 lips, the lower 3-lobed, the upper 2-lobed; 5 fused sepals; 2–4 stamens; leaves simple, opposite, smell minty because the foliage is covered with tiny glands that secrete a fragrant oil; stem usually square; 4 nutlets inside a dry calyx that makes the fruit.

Loganiaceae (logania family): corolla and calyx 4–5 lobed; 4–5 stamens; leaves opposite or alternate; fruit a capsule.

Malvaceae (mallow family): showy flowers; 5 petals, 5 united sepals, many stamens; leaves alternate, usually palmately veined and lobed; fruit a capsule.

Melastomataceae (melastome family): 4 petals and sepals, 8 stamens, usually spurred; leaves simple, opposite; fruit a capsule containing many seeds.

Onagraceae (evening primrose family): 0–9 petals, usually 4, if present, partially united; stamens twice the number of petals; ovary 4-lobed, cross-shaped; simple leaves opposite or alternate; fruit is a capsule or nutlet, usually 4-celled.

Papaveraceae (poppy family): 4–12 petals; 2–3 sepals; numerous stamens; simple or compound leaves, alternate, may appear basal; fruit a capsule.

Passifloraceae (passion flower family): vines; flower has 5 petals, 5 sepals, 5 stamens; leaves simple but lobed; fruit a berry with many seeds.

Polemoniaceae (phlox family): perfect flowers; 5-merous; petals flare from a tube that may be slim or bell-shaped; leaves simple or compound, entire, alternate or opposite; fruit is a capsule.

Portulacaceae (purslane family): 4–6 petals, 2 sepals, 5 or more stamens; leaves alternate or opposite, simple, succulent; fruit a capsule.

Primulaceae (primrose family): 5 petals fused at base in tube; 5 sepals united; 5 stamens; simple leaves in a basal rosette; fruit a capsule.

Ranunculaceae (crowfoot family): flowers mostly regular, some hooded or spurred; many petals or none; many stamens and carpels; compound leaves alternate, opposite, or whorled, usually basal; fruit an aggregate of achenes, follicles, or berries.

Rubiaceae (madder family): small flowers; 4-lobed corolla tube; 4-lobed united sepals; 4 stamens; leaves opposite or whorled, entire; fruit usually a capsule or berry.

Saururaceae (lizard's tail family): no sepals or petals, 3–7 stamens; flowering stalk opposite a leaf; simple leaves alternate; fruit a capsule.

Saxifragaceae (saxifrage family): 4–5 petals; calyx 4–5 lobed; leaves alternate or opposite; fruit a capsule; seed without endosperm (stored food).

Scrophulariaceae (figwort or snapdragon family): corolla irregular to nearly regular, 2-lipped, usually has a distinct tube and 5 lobes; 2–5 stamens; simple leaves opposite, alternate, or whorled; fruit a capsule.

Verbenaceae (vervain family): corolla and calyx 4–5 lobed; toothed leaves opposite; often has angled stem and irregular flowers but lacks mint smell of Lamiaceae (mints); fruit dry, 1 nutlet in each of 4 compartments.

Violaceae (violet family): solitary flowers irregular; 5 petals and sepals; simple leaves alternate, usually basal; fruit a capsule that splits into 3 sections.

CULTIVATION

SOIL AND pH

Bits of rock, decaying plant material, fungi, critters, and water interact to create soil. The underlying rock and weathering determine the pH level. When limestone breaks down, it creates a fairly neutral, fertile soil. Sandstone and shale break down to yield more acidic, less fertile soils. Limestone and shale typically occur in valleys and on plains, while sandstone occupies ridges.

The measure of the acidity or alkalinity of a solution is expressed as pH. The pH scale ranges from 0–14, with pH 7 being neutral. Below 7 is acidic, while above 7 is alkaline or sweet. Soil pH ranges between pH 3 and pH 10. The pH is important in cell metabolism of plants. At certain levels, plants may not be able to absorb the nutrients they need to thrive.

Following are some pH ranges and plants that thrive in those conditions.

Superacid, pH 3–4: Some peat bogs are superacid. Very few plants tolerate this range.

Very acid, pH 4–5: Extremely acidic conditions occur in peat bogs and in varying degrees in oak woodlands, especially when rhododendrons are present. Very acidic microhabitats can exist in a less acidic area, such as under conifers or in rotting bark.

Acid, pH 5–6: The majority of soils in the South—woodlands, meadows, marshes—fall into this range. Any of the wildflowers described in this book would grow well in this range.

Circumneutral, pH 6–8: Many cultivated plants and vegetables grow well at a neutral pH. Some wildflowers tolerate this range.

The homeowner can deal with pH in one of three ways. First, the homeowner can observe the existing plants. The trees and shrubs tell a story. Evergreen conifers, oak, hickory, beech, and blueberries all suggest an acidic soil, which will be suitable for most wildflowers. In this first situation, you will not have to do a thing. If you live in a development with few trees and soil that has been rearranged by bulldozers, you can test the soil yourself or get professional help. You can test the soil with a kit purchased at a garden shop, but this test will not tell you anything about the structure of the soil. To garner information on pH and the makeup of the sample, call the county extension service for instructions. They provide testing services.

To raise the pH, add ground limestone, crushed oyster shell, or calcium nitrate fertilizer. To lower the pH, add powdered sulfur. Some organic materials slowly lower the pH as they decay. These include cottonseed meal, pine needles, and oak leaves.

SOIL STRUCTURE AND AMENDMENTS

Humus: Over time, organic material decomposes into a dark brown component of soil. Moisture, worms, bacteria, and fungi all play a role in the transformation of coarse vegetable matter (leaves, stems, pine needles, straw) into humus. Humus holds moisture and slowly releases water as well as nutrients.

Clay: Many miniscule particles compose clay, so it has smaller air spaces but retains a great deal of water. Clay needs structural amendment to increase aeration and to enhance drainage. For a permanent change in the soil, add pea gravel or crushed granite (available as chicken starter grit at feed-supply stores). Ask for grade 2 granite, not oyster shell. Builders sand or sharp sand can be used with care, but the sand must have large particles. In addition, add composted material, such as leaves, pine bark, or just about any material that will add humus. Compost is preferable to peat moss. The latter is difficult to get wet when it is thoroughly dry and is low in nutrients. Use composted material first and peat moss as a last resort.

Sand: Sandy soil drains rapidly and benefits from the addition of humus of any kind. The nutrient level may be low in a sandy soil. Humus will increase available nutrients as well as slow their loss.

MOISTURE

All of the Southeast is blessed with sufficient rainfall to produce forests, so it certainly can support herbaceous plants. Many authors say the pattern of rainfall is evenly distributed over the year. If you have gardened at all, you will raise your eyebrows at that comment. We have all experienced long periods without rain when we may wish to water special plant treasures or newly planted material.

Most plants need supplemental moisture the first year they are planted. If you use species that are appropriate for the forest type (see page 16) in which you live, you should not have to water the plants after that first year. If you covet all sorts of plants as I do, you will have to give the out-of-habitat species additional water during periods of drought. Limiting oneself to one plant palette takes great self-control —more than I have—so I do a bit of watering during droughts.

Too much water can be just as deadly as too little. Poorly regulated irrigation systems are the death knell for more plants than they save. If one sites plants in appropriate microhabitats, irrigation systems are not necessary.

AERATION AND MULCHING

Aeration: Healthy soils have lots of air spaces. Heavy equipment or foot traffic compacts soils, reducing the amount of air space. Try to keep machinery off of garden areas. If the damage is already done, add plenty of humus to the soil either by turning it in or by mulching. As it decomposes, it will help restore the soil aeration. Clay soils compact easily and may need amendment with coarse materials, both inorganic and organic, to increase the amount of air spaces.

Mulch: Mulch is any material applied to the surface of the soil to suppress the germination and growth of weeds and to conserve moisture. Mulch can be organic, inorganic (rock), or manmade material. Organic or vegetable matter is preferable because it adds structure and nutrients to the soil as it decomposes. Good mulch materials include shredded bark (pine or hardwood), pine needles, straw, shredded leaves, peanut hulls, and cocoa hulls. Grass clippings, whole leaves, and manure are best added to the compost pile because their decomposition as mulch reduces soil nitrogen. Apply mulch no more than 3 inches in thickness and do not cover the crowns of plants.

In nature, leaves do fall on top of plants. But too much of a good thing occurs when homeowners rake or blow all the leaves from the lawn into the wildflower garden. Herbaceous plants can rot under a wet, heavy pile of leaves.

LIGHT

Light is essential for plant growth. Even so-called shade plants need filtered light to bloom well. A wild geranium in a heavy-shade woodland is straggly and only has a few blooms. Under more light, it grows stocky and blooms prolifically.

During the summer, identify the trees and shrubs in your woodland and decide if the trees should be thinned. Tie a colorful tape on the tree you wish to remove, and the work can be done in the winter when some of the leaves will be off of the trees and less damage will occur during the removal process. At the very least, remove some of the lower limbs on the trees to let more light into the forest floor. When a woodland is selectively thinned, blooming plants and ferns often appear. You may even have a native azalea you did not know you had because it could not set bloom buds until it received adequate light.

FERTILIZERS

One can apply chemical fertilizers in the form of slow-release pellets or liquid solution, but generally they are not necessary. A healthy soil provides most of the nutrients required by plants. Addition of organic material provides fodder for worms, bacteria, and fungi. As these organisms digest the vegetable matter, they release inorganic nutrients. Organic material can be incorporated into the soil at the time of planting, or spread on top as mulch. Ideally, organic materials and animal waste should be composted thoroughly. Bacteria and fungi use nitrogen and other elements as they digest leaves and other matter. When using freshly chipped wood and/or bark, add a high nitrogen, rapid-release fertilizer. Always keep granular fertilizer off of the leaves and crowns of plants, because it causes chemical burn on the leaves.

The prominent numbers on plant fertilizer bags tell the buyer the amount of nitrogen, phosphorus, and potassium (N-P-K) in the fertilizer. The first number is the amount of nitrogen. It encourages leaf growth, but in high amounts discourages flowering. The first number can be equal to or slightly higher than the second number. The second number tells the proportion of phosphorus (P), which is important for all stages of growth. The third number represents the amount of potassium (K), or potash, which is essential for many processes and aids in root growth. It is especially important in the development of fruit. If you wish to apply fertilizer, use 12-6-6 once a year in late winter or early spring before new growth emerges.

Nitrogen, phosphorus, and potassium are the main ingredients we think of when we think of fertilizer because they are the nutrients plants need in the largest amounts. They are called macronutrients. Other macronutrients are calcium, magnesium, and sulfur. Plants need micronutrients in smaller quantities. These are iron, manganese, copper, zinc, boron, molybdenum, chlorine, and cobalt.

Needs for macronutrients and micronutrients are relative. Each one of the nutrients has a pH range at which it is most available to the plant. Acid-loving plants need more of the microelements available in the soil than alkaline-loving plants do, because the micronutrients are less available in the low pH of an acidic soil.

Inorganic compounds release elements quickly, and organic materials release them more slowly. Sandy soils are inorganic and may need nitrogen applied more often than humus-rich soils. Red clay soils and cool wet soils release phosphorus poorly. The quick release forms of phosphorus are bonemeal, superphosphate, and fish emulsion. Bulbs need plenty of phosphorus. Clay soils bind potassium, and it can build up in those soils, so don't apply more than once a year there. Banana peels and grapefruit rinds are good sources of potassium, as are wood ashes (not charcoal ashes). But ashes also raise the pH, so be careful around acid-loving plants.

PLANTS OR SEEDS

With a few exceptions, most of the native plants that one can purchase for gardens are perennials, meaning they come up year after year. Most of them can be grown from seeds, but you may have more trouble locating a source for seeds than a source for rooted plants. If you buy a plant, you can then collect seeds from your own yard, which is the easiest place to monitor the progress of ripening seeds. Some of the mail-order nurseries listed on page 293 sell seeds as well as plants.

WHEN TO PLANT

Fall is the best time to plant in the South. We do not have the March soil heaving problems of the Northeast and mid-Atlantic. Fall planting works so well because the plant is not trying to produce new leaf growth or flowers and can concentrate on putting down deep roots to sustain shoot growth the following spring and summer.

Lobelia siphilitica, Water Ways Nursery, Lovettesville, Virginia

PROPAGATION

PLANTS CAN BE REPRODUCED BY SEVERAL METHODS, including seeds, cuttings (stem, leaf, or root), division, and tissue culture. In this book, I will refer to the first three methods. Tissue culture requires more controlled techniques that are beyond the means of most commercial growers, much less homeowners. Increasingly, labs are working to propagate natives such as orchids, trillium, and pachysandra. Commercial growers are already offering plants started from bits of cloned tissue.

The cloning of mammals is a hot topic in the news these days, but people have been cloning plants for years. A clone is a replication of the parent plant, and the genetic material is identical. A plant produced by division or from a cutting is a clone.

Growing plants from seeds provides considerable genetic diversity. Seeds are produced from a set of parents, male and female. The resulting offspring are a mix of the genes of the parents. The male and female parts may both be on one flower or on separate plants of the same species. About 75 percent of flowering plants are self-incompatible. In other words, they cannot fertilize themselves even when they have both male and female flower parts. Plants that have both male and female parts on different parts of the plant are termed monoecious. Species with male flowers on one plant and female flowers on other plants of the same species are called dioecious plants. Whatever the sexual arrangement of the flowers of a plant, the reproduction is aided by insects, animals, wind, and water. Pollen is carried from flower to flower by bats, bees, butterflies, and beetles. Some pollen is released into the air and carried to another flower on the breeze. Pollen from the male part on one flower arrives at the female part of that or another flower. The pollen tube grows down the stigma and style into the ovule, and fertilization occurs.

Genetic diversity is healthy, because the plants with the strongest resistance to disease and the vagaries of soil and climate survive. Weak plants die and do not contribute to the gene pool. When too many cloned or identical plants occupy an area, all become susceptible to decimation by blight or insects.

PROPAGATION BY SEED

SEED TYPES

There are two types of wildflower seeds—wet and dry. Wet seeds are not really wet but have a moist, fleshy white appendage called an aril or elaiosome. The seeds are usually shiny, brown or black, and fairly sizeable. Wet seeds are a bit slippery. Dry seeds really are dry, like the annual vegetable and flower seeds you buy in paper packets.

SEED CULTIVARS

A cultivar is a named selection of a particular species. Cultivars have a name in single quotes after the species name, for example, *Phlox paniculata* 'David'. It may or may not be a clone, which causes many a disagreement among botanists and amateurs alike. Some believe that a plant should not be assigned a cultivar designation unless every plant is a clone. Currently, some plants that are grown from seeds have cultivar names. They are called seed cultivars and usually bear recessive characteristics. By selecting the special forms to produce seeds, they can be propagated from seeds and expected to reproduce the characteristics of the parent plants. Examples of seed cultivars are *Echinacea* 'White Swan', *Physostegia* 'Summer Snow', and *Salvia* 'Coral Nymph'. All of these cultivars were selected for an unusual bloom color. Among a bunch of seedlings, someone found a different colored bloom, saved that plant, collected seeds, started new plants, and found that the progeny retained the new color. Cultivars are selected for many traits in addition to color, such as leaf color, mildew resistance, and whim.

Seed cultivars need to be planted a great distance from plants of the same species or they may cross. The desired trait may be lost among new seedlings. The parent plants will not change, but their seeds will have mixed genetics with other nearby flowers of the same species.

TIME OF SEED COLLECTION

Seeds can ripen any time from three weeks after flowering to months later. Experience is going to be the best teacher in learning to judge ripeness. Wet seeds are often contained in explosive capsules that eject the seeds with force when they split. Bloodroot is a good example of a plant with wet seeds. When the bloodroot capsule begins to fatten and change from green to yellow, squeeze one. If the seams split easily and the seeds are shiny brownish black, you can harvest the seeds.

Dry seeds are easier to collect, because the seed container will remain intact for a long period after the seeds are ripe. When the capsule begins to split or the seeds can be plucked from their fruit, they are ready for collection. A few dry seed species have explosive capsules. Geranium, ruellia, and spigelia capsules will pop open in the paper collection bag on the shelf in the pantry. It sounds as if one has a sack of Mexican jumping beans on the shelf.

SEED COLLECTION

In the home garden, you can check plants daily for ripeness. In the wild, plants should be flagged at the time of bloom. ("In the wild" is a loose phrase; all land has an owner. Always obtain written permission from the owner to collect plant material.) Never collect more than 10 percent of the seeds from a stand of plants. Even perennials need to replenish themselves. A very small amount of seeds is enough to start a few plants for further propagation.

In general, rare plants are rare because they have very specific habitat and nutritional requirements. To take seeds from those plants when one cannot provide the identical conditions is unconscionable. Absolutely never collect orchid seeds of any kind. They have no endosperm and require undefined mycorrhizal fungi for seed germination and for plant nutrition. Starter plants of

Sanguinaria canadensis seed pod

uncommon species such as trillium are available from reputable growers, and after a few years, the ambitious gardener can collect seeds from his own plants. (See the Plant Source List, on page 293.)

I prefer to collect my own seeds rather than buy commercial seeds for two reasons. First, local seeds are adapted to the conditions of my garden. Some purists specify seeds from within a 50-mile radius of the planting location. I gladly accept gifts of seeds from friends in Georgia and Mississippi or anywhere else in the Southeast. But I avoid using seeds that are adapted to conditions 500 miles away if the same species grows closer to home. Second, purchased seeds often don't germinate well. They may have been stored poorly or may be older than stated. Purchase seeds as a last resort and attempt to verify the provenance.

Wet seeds need to stay damp to prevent the aril from drying. If it does dry, the seeds may never germinate or may not germinate for years. You can sow them immediately or collect them in a zip-top plastic bag containing moist sphagnum moss. Be sure to squeeze excess moisture from the moss when preparing the container. The bag of moss and seeds can be stored in a refrigerator at 40 degrees for several weeks to months before sowing.

Collect dry seeds into brown paper bags. Either shake the seeds into a bag or cut off the whole seed head and invert it into the bag. Let the bag sit for a few days before attempting to clean the seeds.

Birds eat the seeds of the aster and sunflower family before the seeds are completely ripe. Usually there are enough seeds for everyone, but you can protect a few seed heads if necessary. If the bloom head is small, cover it with a cap of stocking material or a brown paper bag until the seeds are ripe. Alternatively, collect the seeds when still slightly green. Many seeds continue to mature if collected a few days before they are completely brown. Cut the entire flowering head and invert it into a large brown paper bag. Keep the open bag in a room with good air circulation, preferably air-conditioned, for the drying action. After a week or so, give the stem a shake and listen for seeds to fall from their receptacles.

FUMIGATION

I have never seen any larvae or insects (other than ants) among wet seeds but see them often in dry seeds. Not all the insects are harmful to the seeds. Many small spiders lurk among seeds but don't eat them. Most damage to certain species is caused by the larvae of insects. Among the susceptible are gentians, hibiscus, and iris. To destroy harmful insects, you can place a snippet of pest strip in the paper bag with the cleaned seeds for two weeks. I find the odor objectionable and place the fumigant and the bag inside a metal tin (like the ones popcorn comes in). Cookie tins accommodate small bags.

If you wish to avoid all chemicals, clean the seeds, making sure they are totally dry, and put them in the freezer for a day or two.

SEED CLEANING

WET SEEDS

Wet seeds have a pheromone in the aril that attracts ants. They carry the seeds to their nests, eat the aril, and dump the seeds in a side chamber or outside on the ground. Potassium is high in the soil around ant hills, perhaps enhancing germination or seedling growth. Unfortunately, this system stymies the efforts of man to get the seeds to germinate in an outdoor bed. To foil the ants, store the seeds in moist sphagnum in a zip-top plastic bag in the refrigerator for a few weeks. I have tried to remove the aril from wet seeds. Even with a good set of fingernails, this is an impossible chore—you just can't get a grip on the slippery seeds.

DRY SEEDS

Let dry seeds sit in the collection bag for a day or two before cleaning, but try to get to the job before months pass.

Dry seed–cleaning is a matter of getting rid of spent petals, sepals, capsules, stems, and leaves. Work over a clean white sheet of paper on a tray. You may have to crush hard capsules with a rolling pin. The heads of the aster group may be broken apart by hand to release the nutlets. Various grades of sieves can be used to separate chaff and seeds (see the source list, page 293, for a commercial source for sieves). A small to moderate amount of debris does not interfere with seeds that are hand sown.

Penstemon seed cap

Once again, experience teaches you what individual species' seeds look like. When you first begin, a 10X botanical hand lens or magnifying glass is helpful in identifying the seeds among the chaff. Some composites, such as coneflowers and asters, have a lot of infertile seeds. The keepers are larger and fatter.

Some dry seeds, such as those of jack-in-the-pulpit, have a pulpy outer seed coat that contains a germination inhibitor. It needs to be removed. In nature, the flesh would be removed by passing

Arisaema triphyllum seeds

through the intestinal system of a bird or other animal. If the material is not removed, the seeds will eventually germinate, but may take another year to do so. Soak the seed head in water for a day and then rub the mass in a sieve or strainer. The seeds can be spread on paper, dried, and then stored or sown immediately. I prefer the latter method.

SEED STORAGE

Wet seeds can be refrigerated up to two months. I do not like to hold them any longer than that because the medium may begin to grow mold.

Store dry seeds in brown manila coin envelopes available at office-supply stores. Write the name of the plant, the date, and provenance on the top of the envelope. Place the envelopes in an airtight container—glass, plastic, or tin. I use plastic shoe storage boxes for large numbers of envelopes. Place the seed collection in a dark place where the temperature is around 40 to 70 degrees. Storage temperature is a controversial issue; at one time, all seeds were stored at 40 degrees.

Recent research reports that a 40-degree storage temperature may be deadly for some composites. How this can be true when seeds over-winter outside eludes me. Most seeds last longer when stored as close to 40 degrees as possible. Ongoing studies on germination and seed storage continue to provide useful information about the special requirements of seeds (Deno, 1993).

I keep seeds for five or more years and find most of them quite viable for at least three years. Never give away all of last year's seeds! Some species fail to set seeds every year, or the collector might miss the time or just plain forget. You always need old seeds as a backup. For seeds needing after-ripening, you may choose to use year-old seeds.

AFTER-RIPENING OR VERNALIZATION

Vernalization literally means to render vernal or spring-like. Some seeds are mature upon collection. Others may continue to mature for varying periods of time after collection. It may take one to six months before the embryo is ready to respond to moisture and begin growing. Such seeds must be stored—or vernalized—until they are mature or ripe enough to germinate. After-ripening is a type of dormancy that cannot be broken. You just have to wait. Other types of dormancy can be overcome.

DORMANCY

Nature has methods to prevent seeds from germinating too early. If all seeds sprouted in the summer or fall, most small seedlings would be frozen to death by winter temperatures. Some seeds require a certain time period of cold temperature or a combination of cold and a moist environment. Some even require alternation between warm/cold/warm temperatures in order to germinate. Others have a thick, hard seed coat that must be worn away or broken by freezing or cracking. Some seeds have fleshy coverings that contain a germination inhibitor. Whatever the special factor, the seed must undergo a period of rest and come up against various natural factors (or human intervention) before germination will commence. If you have no information about a seed, try to reproduce the conditions it would experience in nature.

SEED TREATMENTS

STRATIFICATION

All stratification involves moisture and temperature changes. At lower temperatures, more oxygen is soluble in water, so the oxygen needs of an embryo are more easily satisfied. Sow the seeds over a moist (but not soaking wet) medium and place the container outside with a screen cover. Cold, moist stratification should be done in the South from mid-November through January or February, depending on the number of weeks or months of cold required. A cold, moist treatment can also be accomplished in a refrigerator. Place the seeds in a zip-top plastic bag with a few tablespoons of builder's sand. (This is coarser than play sand.) Store the bag in a section of the refrigerator that does not freeze. I prefer outdoor stratification, because natural fluctuations in temperature enhance germination rates in some species, especially the flag irises.

The disadvantage of outdoor chilling is the danger of losing seeds to washing by heavy rain or to rodents. The ideal location is a cold green-house or an open shed or carport. Get creative to deflect heavy rainfall that might disturb the seeds. Watch for signs of rodent damage, such as holes dug in the medium of the seedling tray. Set a mousetrap if necessary.

For seeds that require a warm, moist stratification followed by a cold, moist stratification, start the seeds in July or August outside. In colder months, warm stratification can be done in a plastic bag or a film canister. Label the bag or can. Add a small amount of sand, the seed, and about five drops of water. Place the container on your desk or any place in the house where the temperature will remain around 70 degrees. Check the contents occasionally to see if it seems too dry and just for the fun of seeing what is happening.

Whatever the type of stratification, keep a record of the starting date and label the container! Write a reminder to yourself in your daybook on the day the stratification will finish, so you will remember to advance the seed to its next stage.

SCARIFICATION

Some seeds have a thick, hard seed coat. Water cannot get through this outer layer to the embryo, and you must clip or file the seed coat to crack it without harming the embryo. Most seeds requiring scarification are quite large. Professional labs use acid to etch or soften the seed coat. The home gardener can use a hand file or can hold the seed against an emery wheel to make an opening in the seed coat. Scarification is most often required on the seeds of trees.

I've heard of a man who fed a problematic, hard-coated tree seed to his turkeys. Passing through the birds' alimentary canals, they encountered acid and the mechanical action of grit in the gizzard. The method of seed collection following evacuation was not elucidated, but the seed germinated.

TEPID-WATER SOAK

Place the seeds in a small bowl and cover with about ¹/₂ cup of tepid water. Let seeds soak twelve to twenty-four hours before sowing them.

BOILING-WATER SOAK

Some seeds with tough seed coats may require a boiling-water treatment to get oxygen to the embryo. Place the seeds in a small, heat-proof bowl. Bring a pan of water to a boil. Take it off the heat. When the bubbling stops, pour the water over the seeds and let them soak twelve to twenty-four hours before sowing.

LIGHT

Some seeds require light to germinate. Conversely, some need dark. When a seed needs light, either surface sow the seed or cover lightly with seed-starting medium or chicken grit. I use a light covering of something because I find the seed desiccates when surface-sown. If you have only small numbers of seed trays to monitor, you can cover them with a sheet of glass or improvise a plastic tent to keep the humidity high around the seed and still admit light. The disadvantage to this enclosure method is the development of fungal growths on the media. Homeowners can provide light and keep the moisture level high by sowing the seeds in clear plastic containers that once held strawberries or blueberries. Once the seeds germinate, remove any cover promptly.

SEED-STARTING MEDIA

Commercial seed-starting mixes contain mixtures of peat, perlite, vermiculite, and fine bark or charcoal. Any well-drained mix such as equal parts of peat moss, vermiculite, and sand is acceptable. The advantage of purchased mixes is that they are free of pathogens and weed seed.

Seed frame in moist woodland

CONTAINERS

Any shape container is fine as long as it has plenty of drainage holes. Usually a container with a depth of 2 to 3 inches allows the medium to drain adequately between watering.

OUTDOOR SEED BEDS

Improve the soil in an outdoor seed bed with coarse sand and plenty of organic matter. A cold-frame type structure is ideal, because the lid can be fitted with hardware cloth instead of plastic and will deter squirrels and other digging rodents. The bed should be in a naturally moist site or it will need regular irrigation.

SEED SOWING

Spread the media in the container. Tamp it down lightly and water it well. For larger seeds, place two seeds in a plug hole or space them in rows. For seeds in the aster family, sow heavily. For other small seeds, sow lightly over the top of the medium. Cover very small seeds or seeds that need light to germinate with a dusting of the medium, or chicken grit. Cover larger seeds with soil to a depth equal to the diameter of the seed. Gently water again and label the tray with the name of the plant and the date. If possible, place the flat on a wire or lathe bench. If you must place the flat on the ground, squirt three lines of slug bait under the flat, or else slugs, pill bugs, and snails will feast on the seedlings as fast as they germinate.

The temperature during the day should be 70 to 75 degrees, but the nighttime temperature can drop to 55 degrees. A few seeds need a lower temperature, and some need a higher temperature. Any special requirements are outlined in the section on individual species (see plant profile section, page 93).

DISEASES THAT IMPEDE GERMINATION

The main threat to young seedlings is fungal growth on the growing medium. Several practices help prevent this problem.

Use clean, even sterile, equipment. Use sterile, soil-free media. The term "sterile" is used very loosely in reference to commercial seed-starting mixes purchased in garden shops. You can bake soil or compost as you would a baked potato and kill pathogens, but the smell can drive you from your home for the next twenty-four hours. I did it once.

Keep the temperature as close to the specified germination temperature as possible. If the temperature is too low, the time for the seeds to germinate is prolonged, and fungal spores can settle from the air onto the medium.

Apply only as much moisture as necessary. Too much water and a heavy soil encourage growth of fungi, mosses, and liverworts. A vented plastic lid keeps the ambient moisture high around the seeds and prevents the surface of the medium from drying. Frequently, the surface appears dry but if you lift the flat or container, you will feel that it is still heavy with water.

Good air circulation is another method of maintaining health in seedlings and mature plants. In a greenhouse, ceiling fans are crucial pieces of equipment. Keep them running at all times. Most homes in the South have ceiling fans, too. If you are starting seeds in the house, a ceiling fan or small house fan will help keep the air moving. Don't direct a strong breeze at the tray; just keep the air in the vicinity stirring. The disadvantage of the vented plastic lids is the decreased air flow. Check all covered containers each day and uncover them immediately at the first sign of any green or cottony growth.

TROUBLESOME INSECTS

During the period of seed germination, you may begin to see small black gnats flying around the seed trays near the soil surface. These are fungus gnats. Their larvae are detrimental to the young plants. Large commercial growers use chemical drenches to kill these beasts. I try not to over-water, which helps prevent their increase. When the plants are placed outside, the problem disappears.

Around the middle of March, black, green, and/or orange aphids may begin to appear on hot-house–grown plants. The best cure is to move the plants outside. Within a few weeks, the aphids will be gone. Better plant health, better light, beneficial insects, whatever the factors —nature solves the aphid problem, usually. As a last resort, use insecticidal soap or neem oil. The soap is widely available commercially. The neem oil is made from the seeds of a tree from India. Look at the list of ingredients on the back of bottles of insecticides for roses or other ornamentals. You can find a product that is about 90 percent neem oil. Mix according to package directions. Spray well, especially the undersides of the leaves. In four days, spray again. On mature plants, a good blast of water from a nozzle on a hose is a good aphid treatment. Avoid using chemical sprays as much as possible. You may kill the good guys as well as the bad.

FERTILIZING SEEDLINGS

When the seedlings develop true leaves, fertilize once a week with one-third-strength liquid fertilizer that has N-P-K in the proportions 20-20-20.

TRANSPLANTING SEEDLINGS

Seedlings can be transplanted to a pot containing soil, microelements, and slow-release fertilizer when they have two sets of true leaves. A plastic picnic fork is a good tool for lifting seedlings out of a row of plants. A clam knife (a dull knife with an inch-wide blade available in most grocery stores) lifts plugs with the greatest of ease. If the plant has been sitting in the germination tray for a long time, the roots may be in a tight knot. Tease them apart and let them hang to the bottom of the new pot, filling the soil in around them. If the roots are longer than the depth of the pot, prune them. They will wind around on the bottom of the pot soon enough on their own. Keep the young plant at the same level in the new soil as it was in the germination tray. Gently press the soil around the plant but do not pack it tightly.

PLANTING SEEDLINGS

By fall, the new plants should have a well-developed set of roots. Luckily, fall is the best time of year to put plants in the ground. Choose the site according to the natural habitat of that species and amend the soil (see Cultural Information, page 62). Knock the plant out of the pot and loosen the roots, cutting the plaque off the bottom if the roots have formed a solid mass. If you prune the roots, prune a bit of the foliage, too. Position the plant at the same level in the ground as in the pot. Firm the soil gently around the plant and water it well to settle air spaces. Mulch lightly around the plant but not over the top.

PLANTS EASILY PROPAGATED BY SEED

Alumroot ⁓ *Heuchera americana*
American bellflower ⁓ *Campanulastrum americanum*
Anemones ⁓ *Anemone* spp.
Asters ⁓ *Aster* spp.
Beardtongues ⁓ *Penstemon* spp.
Beggar ticks ⁓ *Bidens* spp.
Black-eyed Susans ⁓ *Rudbeckia* spp.
Blazing stars ⁓ *Liatris* spp.
Blue stars ⁓ *Amsonia* spp.
Bluets ⁓ *Houstonia* spp.
Coreopsis ⁓ *Coreopsis* spp.
Culver's root ⁓ *Veronicastrum virginicum*
Fairy wand ⁓ *Chamaelirium luteum*
False aloe ⁓ *Manfreda virginica*
Fire pink ⁓ *Silene virginica*
Fleabanes ⁓ *Erigeron* spp.
Gentians ⁓ *Gentiana* spp.
Golden alexander ⁓ *Zizea aurea*
Golden club ⁓ *Orontium aquaticum*
Goldenrods ⁓ *Solidago* spp.
Green dragon, jack-in-the-pulpits ⁓ *Arisaema* spp.
Helmetflowers ⁓ *Scutellaria* spp.
Hibiscus ⁓ *Hibiscus* spp.
Iris ⁓ *Iris* spp.
Ironweed ⁓ *Vernonia* spp.

Lobelias ⇀ *Lobilia* spp.
Meadow beauties ⇀ *Rhexia* spp.
Meadow rues ⇀ *Thalictrum* spp.
Milkweeds ⇀ *Asclepias* spp.
Mountain mints ⇀ *Pycnanthemum* spp.
Passionflower ⇀ *Passiflora incarnata*
Prairie larkspur ⇀ *Delphinium carolinianum*
Purple coneflower ⇀ *Echinacea purpurea*
Rattlesnake master ⇀ *Eryngium yuccifolium*
Rosinweeds ⇀ *Silphium* spp.
Shooting star ⇀ *Dodecatheon media*
Silk grass ⇀ *Pityopsis graminifolia*
Sneezeweed ⇀ *Helenium autumnale*
Spider lily ⇀ *Hymenocallis caroliniana*
Sunflowers ⇀ *Helianthus* spp.
Thoroughworts ⇀ *Eupatorium* spp.
Trillium ⇀ *Trillium* spp.
Violets ⇀ *Viola* spp.
White snakeroot ⇀ *Ageratina altissima*
Wild ageratum ⇀ *Eupatorium coelestinum*
Wild hyacinth ⇀ *Camassia scilloides*
Wild indigoes ⇀ *Baptisia* spp.
Wild petunias ⇀ *Ruellia* spp.
Yuccas ⇀ *Yucca* spp.

PROPAGATION BY CUTTING
STEM CUTTINGS

Why grow plants from cuttings instead of seeds? There are three good reasons: genetic duplication, ease of handling, and bloom in one year. First, genetic duplication is necessary to produce cloned selections of species. With seedlings, the genetic structure is always a mixture. Second, rooted cuttings are easier to handle than delicate seedlings. Trying to pick tiny plants out of a tray full of seedlings requires a steady, light touch. Third, plants grown from cuttings usually bloom the first year. Seedlings can take as long as seven years to bloom.

To propagate herbaceous perennials by cuttings means to remove a section of a plant and to induce roots to emerge. The plant part is usually a piece of stem or root. On herbaceous plants, the best time to take a stem cutting is when the new growth has become slightly firm. When bent, the stem will snap like a fresh green bean. If the stem piece is floppy, like a piece of cooked spaghetti, it is not ready to be cut.

Many herbaceous plants will form roots on cuttings without any outside hormone inducement, but most growers use auxins to encourage the formation of roots. Auxins are hormones, both natural and synthetic, that speed the formation of new roots and the number and quality of the roots. At the retail level, IBA (indole 3-butyric acid) is available in both powder and liquid form. IBA is mixed with talcum powder in the powder form and with alcohol in the liquid form. Either form works for herbaceous plants as long as the active ingredient is 0.1 percent or less. When propagating woody plants, the liquid form is highly effective. It penetrates the bark quickly, and a handful of cuttings can be dipped at one time.

The timing of cuttings can be critical for some species and unimportant for others. The general rule is to take herbaceous cuttings from mid-May through July 15, when the shoots are actively growing. In general, take stem cuttings before the plant begins to flower. Some plants, such as garden phlox and monardas, do not root well once flower buds begin to form. Plants have hormones to stimulate flower formation, and once the balance tips from rooting hormones to flowering hormones, root growth is greatly reduced. Removing buds and flowers will help but won't reduce the flowering hormone already present in the stem if the cutting is taken too late.

Root cuttings perform best when taken six to eight weeks before stem-and-leaf growth appear above ground. Root cuttings might be taken in mid-March in Tennessee, in February in central Alabama, or in January in lower Louisiana. Folks in the Upper South will be able to dig in thawed spring soil by the time they need to dig roots for cuttings.

Types of Stem Cuttings
Tip Cuttings

Most herbaceous stem cuttings are taken at the terminal end of a new shoot that has become slightly firm. The cutting is usually 3 to 5 inches long and will have about four leaf nodes.

Leaf Node Cuttings

On many plants, you can take several cuttings from one stem, not just one from the tip. These are called leaf node cuttings, as opposed to tip cuttings, when just the terminal end of the stem is used. These cuttings may have just two to three nodes, one that goes below the soil level and one or two that retain leaves above the soil. The only trick is to keep the up end up on erect plants. Creeping, prostrate plants often root at any leaf node and can grow up, down, or sideways.

Mallet Cuttings

Mallet cuttings usually refer to a woody plant cutting but can also describe a cutting of a herbaceous plant. Using a sharp knife, cut a one-inch piece of the stem with a side shoot positioned in the middle. The resulting cutting has the shape of a croquet mallet. The main stem piece is the striking head, and the side shoot is the handle.

Heel Cuttings

Using a sharp knife, carve a side shoot off, retaining a triangular bit of the crown (the portion where the stem and root join) along with the stem and leaf material.

Plants to Propagate From Stem Cuttings

Asters — *Aster* spp.
Beebalm, wild bergamot — *Monarda* spp.
Bluestars — *Amsonia* spp.
Boltonia — *Boltonia asteroides*
Carolina jasmine — *Gelsemium sempervirens*
Coreopsis — *Coreopsis* spp.

STEM CUTTINGS

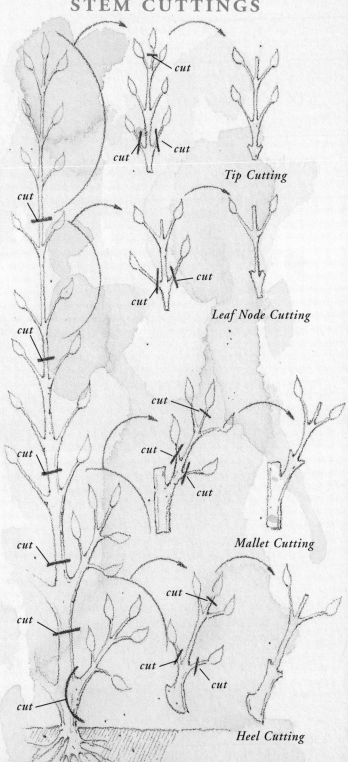

Tip Cutting

Leaf Node Cutting

Mallet Cutting

Heel Cutting

cut

Fire pink, catch flys ⁓ *Silene* spp.
Goldenrods ⁓ *Solidago* spp.
Hibiscus ⁓ *Hibiscus* spp.
Indian pink ⁓ *Spigelia marilandica*
Ironweed ⁓ *Vernonia* spp.
Lobelias ⁓ *Lobelia* spp.
Mountain mints ⁓ *Pycnanthemum* spp.
Obedient plants ⁓ *Physostegia* spp.
Partridgeberry ⁓ *Mitchella repens*
Phlox ⁓ *Phlox* spp.
Salvias ⁓ *Salvia* spp.
Scarlet honeysuckle ⁓ *Lonicera sempervirens*
Skullcaps ⁓ *Scutellaria* spp. (perennial ones)
Sneezeweeds ⁓ *Helenium* spp.
Sunflowers ⁓ *Helianthus* spp.
Thoroughworts ⁓ *Eupatorium* spp.
Verbenas ⁓ *Verbena* spp.
White snakeroot ⁓ *Ageratina altissima*
Wild ageratum ⁓ *Eupatorium coelestinum*
Wild indigoes ⁓ *Baptisia* spp.

RHIZOME CUTTINGS

Remove the terminal bud on a creeping rhizome, and lateral buds will form. This method applies to the rhizomatous members of the Liliaceae, which are slow or difficult to reproduce from seeds. In late spring, after the bloom fades but while the foliage is still firm, sever the rhizome about 0.5–1″ behind the terminal bud or active shoot. Place the cuttings in a tray of construction sand and perlite or some other medium with excellent drainage. Water sparingly. These cuttings rot easily.

PLANTS TO PROPAGATE FROM RHIZOME CUTTINGS

False Solomon's seal ⁓ *Maianthemum racemosum*
Merrybells ⁓ *Uvularia perfoliata*
Solomon's seal ⁓ *Polyganatum biflorum*
Wake robins ⁓ *Trillium* spp.
Wild ageratum ⁓ *Eupatorium coelestinum*

ROOT CUTTINGS

Many plants have dormant buds in the roots that can be induced to produce a leafy shoot. Whether the root is fibrous or fleshy, a leafy shoot will develop if one applies heat, light, and moisture at the right time of year. Root cuttings can be taken any time of day. Most root cuttings are taken from November through February.

A good example of a fleshy-rooted plant is butterfly weed. In February or March, dig a 3- or more year-old plant from the ground. Rinse the soil from the roots. Cut the roots into 1- to 2-inch segments, being careful to keep the end closest to the stem portion of the plant up. The plant is geotropic, and the root piece will rot if the stem end is down. Place the cuttings vertically in a flat of sand, or plant directly into containers of well-draining potting soil. If you forget which end is which, place the cutting horizontally on the medium. Cover with 1/4 inch of soil. Place in good light in the greenhouse and keep at 70 to 80 degrees. Water regularly but sparingly. Shoots will emerge in about six weeks.

In areas of the country where the ground freezes solid in the winter, one can dig mature plants from September through November. Remove excess soil from the roots and store the bareroot material in barely moist sphagnum moss in a ventilated plastic bag at 40 degrees. Check the bags regularly for fungus growth and provide more air if necessary. Take root cuttings any time from November on.

To preserve a "one of a kind" plant in the ground, cut a half circle around one side of the plant about 3 inches out from the crown and remove a few roots without disturbing the mother plant unduly.

Herbaceous perennials with fibrous roots (for example, garden phlox, Stokes aster, Culver's root) fill a pot quickly during the growing season. In the fall, select a few healthy plants to save for winter root cuttings. From January through March, invert the pot and knock the root ball into your hand. Lay the plant sideways on a cutting surface and cut the entire bottom off the root ball. You now have what looks like a Frisbee of roots and soil. The plaque of roots can be 1/4- to 1-inch thick. Cut this disc into quarters as you would cut a pizza, and tease the root pieces apart a bit if they form a solid mass. The root cuttings can be lined out in trays of well-draining medium (the same medium as for stem cuttings) or they can be tossed into a clear, ventilated plastic bag with a handful of moist bark chips and placed under the potting bench where the temperature is 45 to 60 degrees and a bit of light sneaks in. Be sure the bag has air holes. Check the cuttings every few days to be sure they have not dried excessively; add water as needed and watch for leaf formation. I like the "ignored bag" method because I have a tendency to over-water root cuttings in trays and cause them to rot. One tip about root cuttings developing in moist medium in trays is this: do not remove them to a pot as soon as you see leaves. Allow them to develop a second set of leaves. The cuttings from the bag can go into a pot of soil as soon as they begin to develop leaves. I can't explain this mystery. This is just my experience.

PLANTS TO PROPAGATE
FROM ROOT CUTTINGS

Anemones – *Anemone* spp.

Black-eyed Susans – *Rudbeckia* spp.

Coneflowers – *Echinacea* spp.

Culver's root – *Veronicastrum virginicum*

Dwarf coreopsis – *Coreopsis auriculata*

Garden phlox, prairie phlox – *Phlox* spp.

Lizard's tail – *Saururus cernuus*

Meadow beauties – *Rhexia* spp.

Milkweeds – *Asclepias* spp.

Rattlesnake master – *Eryngium yuccifolium*

Shooting star – *Dodecatheon media*

Thoroughworts – *Eupatorium* spp.

White snakeroot – *Ageratina altissima*

Wild indigoes – *Baptisia* spp.

Yuccas – *Yucca* spp.

BULB SCALES

As defined in the botanical term section, bulbs are tightly packed, reduced leaves attached to a basal plaque of stem material. You can remove up to a third of the scales on a mature bulb without interfering with flowering. To remove a scale, gently pry it away from the bulb using your fingers. Pull out and down. New bulbils develop at the injury site. Put all the scales in a plastic bag with a powder fungicide and shake the bag to coat the scales with the dust. Place the scales scar end down in a tray of gritty or sandy peat. Leave a third of the top of the scale exposed in the tray. Keep the tray in an unheated greenhouse. An ideal temperature range is 50 to 60 degrees, but scale cuttings will produce bulbils and then roots any time of year with some attention. (After the bulbil is removed from the scale, it must undergo a cold period.) The scales can be reused up to seven times. The scales can also be buried in the ground, 1 to 2 inches deep and ignored. Perform the procedure after the plant has flowered, and the bulbils will mature in the moderate temperatures of fall. The only plant profiled in this book that can be propagated using bulb scales is the Carolina lily *(Lilium michauxii)*.

CONTAINERS

Containers for cuttings can be anything from a molded plastic nursery tray to a plastic bulb pot or a recycled gallon milk jug. Soak recycled containers overnight in a 10 percent solution of household bleach before using them for seedlings. The container depth can be from 3 to 6 inches, depending on the length of the particular cutting. The one crucial feature is drainage holes; have plenty of them. The cutting needs to be stabilized by the medium in the container until it can produce roots. It does not need to absorb a lot of water. Daily misting maintains the fluid balance. The pot must provide good drainage or the cutting will rot.

MEDIA

The medium for stem or root cuttings needs to drain well also. It should be porous. It can be construction sand, horticultural vermiculite, perlite, or chipped pine bark, or any combination of these. Sand works well but is heavy. Vermiculite is heat-expanded mica and when young is a great light medium. Over time, it breaks down into a slippery, clay-like material. Perlite is light and retains less water than vermiculite, but it is unhealthy for birds. Large amounts of perlite are not conducive to plant health in the long run. When perlite breaks down, it becomes dusty and, in large quantities, can damage roots. Composted pine bark, the small chip variety sometimes called soil conditioner, is resistant to insertion of bruisable cuttings. Like everything in life, nothing is perfect. On the bright side, the cuttings will form roots in three to eight weeks and exit the medium before it decomposes. I use a mix of one-third vermiculite and two-thirds perlite when I use a standard, molded plastic, greenhouse flat. These flats need support by a second lattice tray, and even with support, can crack if one uses sand. In a flowerpot, I may use sand or a mix of ingredients.

METHOD

Take stem cuttings in the morning while the leaves are still moist and cool. Collect the cuttings in a white plastic bag and keep them in the shade or a cooler. Prepare and "stick" the cuttings as soon as possible. (To "stick a cutting" means to insert the cut end into a moist medium.)

Fill the tray or pot with medium. Level the contents and spray lightly with water. Poke a line of holes in the moist medium with a pencil. Pushing a tender stem directly into the medium can bruise the cutting.

Using a clean, sharp knife or pair of double-edged pruning shears, cut a 3- to 6-inch piece off the tip end of a stem. It should have two to five leaf nodes. Make the cut about 1/2″ below the lowest node. Remove one or two of the lower leaves or pairs of leaves, taking care not to strip the stem. Remove any bloom buds or flowers and soft new growth at the end. Reduce large leaves in size by cutting away half of each leaf. Dip the cut end in hormone. Tap excess powder or liquid from the cutting and insert it in the preformed hole in the rooting medium. Firm the medium around each row of cuttings before inserting the next row. The bottom one or two exposed leaf nodes should be surrounded by moist medium.

If you take cuttings all the way down a stem and get to an older, slightly woody section, gently scrape a bit of the brown woody material from a 1/2-inch strip on one side of the cutting at the bottom. This scarring of the semi-woody cutting allows the rooting hormone easier access to the living section of the stem and encourages a healing response in the cutting.

Rooted-cuttings, Verbena canadensis

SPACING

The cuttings need air circulation as well as high humidity. Space them so that the leaves do not overlap greatly. Small, tough-leaved plants like blue phlox can be crowded seventy to a tray. Joe Pye weed has large stems and leaves and may allow only thirty cuttings per tray.

MISTING

If you do not have a mist system in a shade house, place the flat outdoors in the shade. Using a mist head on a garden hose, sprinkle the cuttings once or twice a day, more often if the temperature is over 80 degrees. Or you can create a high-humidity chamber using an aquarium or a plastic tent. You must waft air through a closed space several times a day, so I prefer the great outdoors where humidity is high. Most of these cuttings will be taken from mid-May to mid-July (with a few in September through October).

Place the trays on a piece of snow fence or wire stretched over cement blocks or on a lattice-type table. If you place the flat on the ground, put slug bait underneath the flat. Slugs can decimate a tray of cuttings overnight.

FERTILIZING

Begin to apply one-third-strength balanced liquid fertilizer once the leaves begin to grow. Sprinkle this fertilizer on them once a week using an old-fashioned watering can, a mist bottle, or an injection system on a garden hose for large quantities.

POTTING

In four to six weeks, tug gently on the cutting. If it resists removal from the tray, lift a few cuttings to see if roots are present. An old fork is an ideal tool to insert under a rooted cutting to lift it from the tray. If you see no roots or only a doughnut-shaped callus, re-insert the test cuttings and wait a few more weeks. If roots exist, even a clump of short ones, you can pot the plants.

The medium for potting cuttings can be a commercial potting mix or amended soil conditioner (fine, composted pine bark). Homemade mixtures using pine bark need lime, trace elements, and a slow-release fertilizer containing N-P-K. Place the rooted cutting in the pot at the same level it was in the rooting medium. Gently firm the soil around the plant and water it to settle the soil. In the fall, plant the now well-rooted plant in the ground about one month before hard frost, or over-winter the plant in a cold greenhouse.

LAYERING

Many perennials form roots at a leaf node if the stem is pinned to the ground during active growth. Gently press a stem toward the ground and estimate where the leaf node will touch the earth. Scratch a patch of soil so it will be friable and receptive to new root growth. Prune the leaves from the leaf node,

cut here after roots develop

anchor the stem with a rock, and cover the denuded node with a light layer of soil. Roughly six weeks later, check for root formation. If the stem has new roots, cut it free from the parent plant.

When layering woody plants, scraping the bark lightly and applying a hormone may speed root formation.

PLANTS TO PROPAGATE BY LAYERING

Carolina jasmine ∽ *Gelsemium sempervirens*
Coral honeysuckle ∽ *Lonicera sempervirens*
Cardinal flower ∽ *Lobelia cardinalis*

PROPAGATION BY DIVISION

Most plants can be divided either in the spring or fall. A plant should be three or more years old before division is warranted. Divide a plant after bloom or when it is dormant. A loose rule of thumb is to divide spring-blooming plants in the fall and fall-blooming plants in the spring. Dig a large ball of soil with the plant in order to retain as many roots as possible. With a gun-type nozzle on the end of a garden hose, wash the soil from the plant so the entire root structure is visible.

Division of Stokesia laevis

While you are dividing the plant, keep the naked sections moist and in the shade. If you do not wish to disturb the mother plant, cut through the plant with a sharp spade and remove a wedge of the desired size.

Different types of underground structures require different techniques. Bulbs and corms can be pulled apart with the fingers. Clumping types can be pulled apart with the hands or may need a vertical poke with the point of a cheap paring knife. By cutting only the thickened stem area at points of natural division, most of the feeder roots can be left intact. Species with thick crowns require a more aggressive attack. A 10- to 12-inch serrated knife with a point is perfect for this job. Once again, the knife can be inexpensive. Look for buds on the crown and attempt to cut through the coarse, sometimes semi-woody material between buds. Cut or saw only through the crown. Stop before you slice through the feeder roots. Do not despair if you must cut through a few buds. The plant will live despite your heavy-handedness. Rhizomes tend to have many nascent buds and can be cut into 2- to 3-inch sections. On plants that have obvious "waists," break or cut the rhizome at that point. Tubers have fewer buds; each cut piece, which may be 3 to 6 inches long, should have an obvious bud swelling or leaves.

Dust the cut pieces with wettable sulfur powder if you have fungus problems in your garden. If you have not used fungicides in your garden soil, you will have beneficial fungi as well as potentially harmful ones, and the use of any fungicide is probably unnecessary.

Replant the pieces as soon as possible. Improve the soil with humus and drainage material if needed. Newly divided plants will need more pampering than established plants for the first year. Especially during the first two months, they need about 3/4 inches of water a week.

PLANTS TO PROPAGATE BY DIVISION
BULB OR CORM:

Green dragons, jack-in-the-pulpits — *Arisaema* spp.
Lilies — *Lilium* spp.
Spider lily — *Hymenocallis caroliniana*
Spring beauty — *Claytonia virginica*
Trout lilies — *Erythronium* spp.
Wild hyacinth — *Camassia scilloides*

CLUMP (CAN BE PULLED OR TEASED APART):

Allegheny spurge — *Pachysandra procumbens*
Alumroots — *Heuchera* spp.
Beardtongues — *Penstemon* spp.
Black-eyed Susan — *Rudbeckia fulgida*
Blue-eyed grass — *Sisyrinchium angustifolium*
Culver's root — *Veronicastrum virginicum*
Daisy fleabanes — *Erigeron* spp.
Dwarf coreopsis — *Coreopsis auriculata*
Fairy wand — *Chamaelirium luteum*

False aloe — *Manfreda virginica*
Golden alexander — *Zizea aurea*
Golden ragwort — *Senecio aureus*
Green and gold — *Chrysoganum virginianum*
Helmetflowers — *Scutellaria* spp. (perennials)
Lobelias — *Lobelia* spp.
Merrybells — *Uvularia perfoliata*
Mountain mints — *Pycnanthemum* spp.
Phlox — *Phlox* (shade spp.)
Pussytoes — *Antennaria plantaginifolia*
Sages — *Salvia* spp.
Shooting star — *Dodecatheon media*
Silkgrass — *Pityopsis graminifolia*
Spiderwort — *Tradescantia virginiana*
Sundrops — *Oenothera* spp.

CROWN (MUST BE CUT OR CHOPPED APART):

Asters — *Aster* spp.
Bird's foot violet — *Viola pedata*
Black snakeroot — *Cimicifuga racemosa*
Blue stars — *Amsonia* spp.
Boltonias — *Boltonia* spp.
Coneflowers — *Echinacea* spp.
Coreopsis — *Coreopsis* spp.
Garden phlox — *Phlox* spp.
Goldenrods — *Solidago* spp.
Green-headed coneflower — *Rudbeckia laciniata*
Ironweed — *Vernonia* spp.
Marsh mallows — *Hibiscus* spp.
Rosinweeds — *Silphium* spp.
Sneezeweed — *Helenium autumnale*
Sunflowers — *Helianthus* spp.
Thoroughworts — *Eupatorium* spp.
Wild indigoes — *Baptisia* spp.

RHIZOME OR TUBER:

Blazing stars — *Liatris* spp.
Bloodroot — *Sanguinaria canadensis*
Evergreen gingers — *Hexastylis* spp.
False Solomon's seal — *Maianthemum racemosa*
Iris — *Iris* spp.
Lizard's tail — *Saururus cernuus*
May apple — *Podophyllum peltatum*
Meadow beauties — *Rhexia* spp.
Mints — *Monarda* spp.
Obedient plant — *Physostegia virginiana*
Rue anemone — *Thalictrum thalictroides*
Solomon's seal — *Polygonatum biflorum*
Toothworts — *Cardamine* spp.
Wild ageratum — *Conoclinium, Eupatorium coelestinum*
Wild geranium — *Geranium maculatum*
Wild gingers — *Asarum* spp.
Yuccas — *Yucca* spp.

NATIVE GRASSES

DID YOU KNOW THAT GRASSES ARE FLOWERING PLANTS? Lacking sepals and petals, they do not have the huge blooms of a hibiscus, but in the fall, when the angle of the sun lowers on the horizon, the sparkle of light on seed heads and foliage is as attractive as the petals on insect seducers. Grasses deserve mention because they comprise 75 percent of the vegetation in a balanced meadow or prairie. Grasses feed wildlife and their fibrous roots prevent erosion and vastly improve the tilth of soil.

A meadow or prairie is any open area composed predominantly of grasses and flowering plants. In the West and Midwest, annual rainfall of 10 to 45 inches per year, soil factors, and maintenance burning keep woody plants from taking over open space. In the Southeast where rainfall is much higher, the land naturally supports forests (except where special soil conditions favor grasses and non-woody flowering plants). Periodic burning or mowing is still necessary to supplement naturally occurring fires.

The roots of native grasses probe deeply into the soil. New roots emerge continuously, and the old roots die and break down, adding to the humus and nutrient level in the soil. The pathways left by these decaying roots increase spaces for air, water, and beneficial soil organisms.

Commercial mixes of so-called wildflower seeds for instant meadows often contain annuals that are naturalized plants (whether from another country or the far western United States). These mixes often contain no grasses, and produce a flower garden, not a meadow. Germination is frequently poor, and if successful the show lasts for only one year. A few naturalized species like Queen Anne's lace may self-seed in successive years and coexist with the exotic weed seeds that are sure to germinate from the seed bank. Preparing, establishing, and maintaining a meadow are beyond the scope of this book. For more information on meadow gardening, see *Gardening with Native Wildflowers* (Jones and Foote, pages 99–119).

Grasses can be sod-forming or clump-forming. In recent years, buffalo grass *(Buchloe dactyloides)* has been recommended as a native sod-forming lawn grass. Unfortunately, it is intolerant of short mowing and heavy traffic.

Grasses are also categorized by the time of year in which they thrive and form seed heads. Cool season grasses form seed heads in cool weather. In the warm Southeast, we have many more warm season grasses than cool season grasses. Warm season grass seed germinates after the soil temperature rises above 60 degrees and forms seed heads during warm weather. They go dormant when serious frost arrives in the fall or winter.

GRASSES:

Beach panic grass – *Panicum amarum*
Beaked panicum – *Panicum anceps*
Bent awn plumegrass – *Saccharum contortum*
Big bluestem – *Andropogon gerardii*
Black-seeded needle grass – *Stipa avenacea*
Bottlebrush grass – *Hystrix patula*
Broomsedge – *Andropogon virginicus*
Bushy beardgrass – *Andropogon glomeratus*

Crinkled hair grass	*Deschampsia flexuosa*
Cutgrasses	*Leersia* spp.
Eastern gamma grass	*Tripsacum dactyloides*
Elliott's bluestem	*Andropogon elliottii*
Fowl meadowgrass	*Glyceria striata*
Giant cane	*Arundinaria gigantea*
Gulf Coast muhly	*Muhlenbergia capilaris*
Gulf Coast muhly	*Muhlenbergia filipes*
Indian grass	*Sorghastrum nutans*
Little bluestem	*Schizachyrium scoparius*
Longleaf uniola	*Chasmanthium sessiliflora*
Narrow plumegrass	*Saccharum strictum*
Northern wild rye	*Elymus canadensis*
Old field three awn	*Aristida oligantha*
Old witch grass	*Panicum capillare*
Panic grass	*Dicanthelium scabriusculum*
Poverty grass, June grass	*Danthonia compressa*
Poverty grass, white oat grass	*Danthonia spicata*
Prairie dropseed	*Sporobolis heterolepis*
Purple lovegrass, ticklegrass	*Eragrostis spectabilis*
Purpletop, greasegrass	*Tridens flavus*
River oats	*Chasmanthium latifolium*
Sea oats	*Uniola paniculata*
Side oats grama	*Bouteloua curtipendula*
Silver bluestem	*Bothriochloa laguroides*
Silver plumegrass	*Saccharum aloepecuroides*
Southern wild rice	*Zizaniopsis miliacea*
Split beard bluestem	*Andropogon ternarius*
Sugarcane plumegrass	*Saccharum giganteum*
Switch grass	*Panicum virgatum*
Toothache grass	*Ctenium aromatic*
Tufted hair grass	*Deschampsia caespitosa*
Two-seeded melic grass	*Melica mutica*
Wild rice	*Zizania aquatica*
Wild rye	*Elymus virginicus*
Wire grass, arrowfeather three awn	*Aristida purpurascens*
Wire grass, pineland three awn	*Aristida stricta*

Sedges and rushes are grass-like plants. Remember: Sedges have edges and rushes are round. The blade of a rush is round in cross section. The leaf of a sedge is often V-shaped, and the stem is triangular. Both groups tend to occupy wetter sites than grasses. The rush family has about 400 species, the sedge family about 4,000, and the grass family about 10,000.

Some sedges are weedy, like nut sedge or nut grass *(Cyperus esculentus)* and the annual low kyllinga *(C. tenuifolius)*. Some rushes are also weedy, especially path rush *(Juncus tenuis)*.

Other species can make good additions to wetlands. A good example is giant bulrush *(Scirpus validus)*, which is beautiful, stabilizes banks, and provides food for a wide variety of wildlife. Some species are also showy such as wool grass *(S. cypernus)*, clubrush *(S. expansus)*, and leafy bulrush *(S. polyphyllus)*.

POLLINATION, SEED DEVELOPMENT, AND DISPERSAL

THE ROLE OF INSECTS AND ANIMALS IN THE LIFE OF PLANTS

POLLINATION IS VERY IMPORTANT TO THE SURVIVAL OF a plant species. Since plants are anchored in the ground and cannot move about except to bend in the wind, they depend on wind, water, animals, and insects to carry their pollen to other plants. Although some flowers have both male and female parts, they are usually self-incompatible, meaning the stigma needs to receive pollen from the stamen of another flower of the same species. Through the pollination process, wind and fauna (all the animal life of a region) help perpetuate genetic diversity and thus the health and survival of the species.

Plants have evolved to enhance optimum pollination. Several features attract insects such as flies, beetles, gnats, bees, and butterflies. The color and shape of the flower, as well as the arrangement of the flowers in an inflorescence, stimulate visual receptors. Sweet liquid secreted by glands called nectaries is a tasty reward. The sugar and protein content of nectar varies from plant to plant, attracting different insects. Odors of substances from special modified cells stimulate the sense of smell. The fragrance secreted by a flower can be one of three types: a floral smell, a dung- or carrion-like smell, or a mimicry of insect pheromones. These different floral smells are made of many different compounds. Unpleasant odors come from substances produced during the breakdown of proteins. The pheromone mimic smells like the secretions of a female insect.

Flowers and their pollinators have evolved together. The length of the proboscis of the insect or the tongue of the bird has evolved to match the length of the floral tube of the flowers it visits. For instance, hummingbirds have a long tongue and see the red colors well. They visit American columbine, fire pink, scarlet honeysuckle, trumpet vine, and many other flowers, for sucrose dominant nectar. Hummingbird flowers have no obvious floral scent because they don't need it. They need only a strong display of the color hummingbirds can see. The flower parts are positioned in just the right spot for a hummingbird to place or retrieve pollen.

Flowers can be pollinated by more than one insect, or by both hummingbirds and insects, so it is difficult to make generalizations about which creatures pollinate which flowers. Flowers offer more than just pollen and nectar. Some produce oils and pheromone precursors desired by pollinators. The flowers also can offer warmth and a place to breed. A few broad guidelines can help you theorize about potential pollinators; personal observation is the best method to confirm the suspicion.

Moths have a long proboscis and visit flowers with long floral tubes such as false aloe and yucca. Night-flying moths have a good sense of smell and are attracted to white flowers with heavy, sweet fragrances. These flowers produce large amounts of nectar high in protein and sucrose.

Butterflies prefer erect flowers with radial, flat, open faces. They like to land on the flower face but will dangle if necessary, as they must with some lilies. A single row of petals or rays makes access to the hidden nectar easiest. They like bright flower colors such as orange and purple. These flowers usually have a weak but sweet scent. The nectar is high in protein and sucrose. Examples of flowers sure to attract butterflies are: phlox, milkweed, gayfeathers, Joe Pye weed and other *Eupatorium* spp., and yellow-fringed orchid.

Beetles blunder around in large flowers that are white or dull-colored and have lots of pollen. The flower usually has a sweet or fruity smell, as in magnolias and sweet shrub. Beetles are more attracted to pollen than nectar, so the production of nectar varies in beetle-pollinated plants, probably depending on what other insect visitors also assist in pollination.

Flies prefer small flowers that are symmetrical and flat with a short floral tube. The flower is usually white or dull-colored and has nectar guides, although the amount of nectar produced is not copious. The flower may have no odor or a foul odor. Both the pollen and nectar are readily accessible. Two examples of fly-pollinated flowers are bluets and star chickweed.

Wasps visit flowers of variable color, size, and shape. Their preference is sweet, high-octane nectar, the kind with lots of protein and sucrose. Potent, sweet fragrances draw them to the flowers. The pollen lies close to the nectar, positioned to hitch a ride. Wasps like goldenrods and plants in the snapdragon (Scrophulariaceae) family.

Bees are highly productive pollinators, and flowers reward them with large amounts of pollen and nectar high in glucose and fructose. The size of the flower is not very significant, but the floral color is often yellow or blue. Bees see color in an ultraviolet range that is different from the colors we see. Bee flowers are often bilateral in shape and have prominent nectar guides. Think about the shape and color of blue lobelia, violets, delphinium, and pale jewel weed. These are all bee pollinated. Odor, like flower size, is not very significant. If the bee has difficulty pushing its way into the flowers, it may chew a hole in the side of the floral tube to "steal the goodies" without collecting or dispensing any pollen. Bees even find shelter inside flowers in a storm or overnight.

Bees perform a fascinating dance on the flowers of shooting star. They grasp the flower and vibrate their abdominal muscles to stimulate the flower to release its pollen. This performance is called buzz pollination.

Flowers have various mechanisms to prevent self-pollination and encourage cross-pollination. The pollen on the male parts of a perfect flower may disperse before the sticky stigma splits open. In the case of golden Alexander, all the flowers in a head will be male at one point in time. A single spring beauty flower is male on its first day and then female for the next nine days. Some flowers respond negatively to the pollen or pollen tube from their own flower and stop its growth at some point before fertilization occurs.

Cross-pollination is only the first step in the development of a healthy seed. The nutrient and moisture supply must be good that year, and the temperature needs to be favorable. A late freeze destroys many a fruit crop. Chance is another factor in survival.

Plants tend to produce many more seeds than are needed to perpetuate a community because many seeds perish. When it falls to earth, a seed may settle in a spot that has suitable growing conditions or it may fall on an unfavorable site. By releasing copious numbers of seeds, plants increase their chance for survival. A few plants secrete a chemical from their roots to ensure that their own seeds will not develop too close to the parent.

Once the seed develops, the plant is still dependent on outside forces to disperse the seed. Clever appendages help transport some seeds. Silken parachutes float on a breeze, barbs hook into an animal's pelt, Velcro-like seed coats mobilize hitchhikers. An appetizing pulpy exterior makes a meal for a bird or animal, and the seed gets a free ride and a fertilizer boost.

PLANTS TO ATTRACT BUTTERFLIES AND MOTHS

Overall, butterflies feed on a wide variety of liquids or dissolved solids: nectar, sap, rotting fruit, dung, bird droppings, carrion, and aphid "honeydew." The butterflies that feed on material other than nectar from flowers tend to live in woodlands. The habitat for nectar feeders is open, sunny areas. The flowers that attract these butterflies are sun lovers, many of which bloom in the summer and fall. If you wish to see the largest number of butterflies, wait until about 10 a.m., after the sun has warmed the insects' bodies and they become active.

Butterflies prefer flowers that offer a platform on which to stand as they sip nectar. The composites, such as asters, have many flowers forming a convex disc. The butterfly can land and walk around on the inflorescence, drinking from many flowers before it must fly again.

Butterflies differ in tongue length. Monarchs and swallowtails have relatively long tongues and can drink from flowers with fairly long corolla tubes.

Butterflies collect nectar at many different flowers but usually lay their eggs on one specific plant species. The eggs are laid on the plant the larvae need to eat as they grow and eventually form a chrysalis. Most species of eastern butterflies feed on plants in their larval stage.

Nectar Plants:

American columbine – *Aquilegia canadensis*
Asters – *Aster* spp.
Beardtongues – *Penstemon* spp.
Beebalm, bergamot – *Monarda* spp.
Beggar ticks – *Bidens* spp.
Black-eyed Susans – *Rudbeckia* spp.
Blazing stars – *Liatris* spp.
Blue stars – *Amsonia* spp.
Boltonia – *Boltonia asteroides*
Carolina jasmine – *Gelsemium sempervirens*
Coneflowers – *Echinacea* spp.
Coral honeysuckle – *Lonicera sempervirens*
Coreopsis – *Coreopsis* spp.
False aloe – *Manfreda virginica*
Fire pink – *Silene virginica*

Fleabanes ⇀ *Erigeron* spp.
Goldenrods ⇀ *Solidago* spp.
Iris ⇀ *Iris* spp.
Ironweed ⇀ *Vernonia* spp.
Jewel weed ⇀ *Impatiens capensis*
Joe Pye weed, boneset, etc. ⇀ *Eupatorium* spp.
Lobelias ⇀ *Lobelia* spp.
Marsh mallows ⇀ *Hibiscus* spp.
Milkweeds ⇀ *Asclepias* spp.
Mountain mints ⇀ *Pycnanthemum* spp.
Passion flower ⇀ *Passiflora incarnata*
Phlox ⇀ *Phlox* spp.
Prickly pear cactus ⇀ *Opuntia humifusa*
Rosinweeds ⇀ *Silphium* spp.
Salvias, sages ⇀ *Salvia* spp.
Silk grass ⇀ *Pityopsis graminifolia*
Sneezeweed ⇀ *Helenium autumnale*
Spider lily ⇀ *Hymenocallis caroliniana*
Spiderworts ⇀ *Tradescantia* spp.
Sunflowers ⇀ *Helianthus* spp.
Trumpet vine ⇀ *Campsis radicans*
Turk's cap lily ⇀ *Lilium superbum*
Turtleheads ⇀ *Chelone* spp.
Verbenas ⇀ *Verbena* spp.
Violets ⇀ *Viola* spp.
White snakeroot ⇀ *Ageratina altissima*
Wild ageratum ⇀ *Eupatorium coelestinum*
Wild hyacinth ⇀ *Camassia sciloides*
Yellow-fringed orchid ⇀ *Platanthera ciliaris*

OTHER NATIVE PLANT NECTAR SOURCES NOT FEATURED IN THIS BOOK:

Black locust ⇀ *Robinia psuedo-acacia*
Buttonbush ⇀ *Cephalanthus occidentalis*
Crownbeards ⇀ *Verbesina* spp.
Indian blankets ⇀ *Gaillardia* spp.
Pickerelweed ⇀ *Pontederia cordata*
Salt marsh mallow ⇀ *Kosteletzkya virginica*
Sedums ⇀ *Sedum* spp.
Silverling or groundsel ⇀ *Baccharis halimifolia*
Summersweet ⇀ *Clethra alnifolia*
Thistles ⇀ *Cirsium* spp.
Turk's cap, sultan's turban ⇀ *Malvaviscus arborea*

BUTTERFLIES AND HOST PLANTS:

American painted lady ⇀ *Antennaria* spp. (pussytoes)
American painted lady ⇀ *Vernonia* spp. (ironweeds)
Black swallowtail ⇀ *Zizea aurea*
(golden alexander)

Buckeye ⟶ *Agalinis* spp. (false foxgloves)
Buckeye ⟶ *Penstemon digitalis*
(smooth beardtongue)
Buckeye ⟶ *Ruellia* spp. (wild petunias)
Buckeye ⟶ *Verbena* spp.
Coral hairstreak ⟶ *Amsonia* spp. (bluestars)
Diana, great spangled fritillary,
variegated fritillary ⟶ *Viola* spp. (violets)
Dwarf yellow ⟶ *Helenium autumnale*
(sneezeweed)
Eastern black swallowtail ⟶ Apiaceae (parsley family:
dill, Queen Anne's lace,
rattlesnake master,
golden alexander)
Falcate orange tip ⟶ *Cardamine* spp. (toothworts)
Gray hairstreak ⟶ *Pycnanthemum* spp.
(mountain mint)
Gray hairstreak, painted lady,
checkered skipper ⟶ *Hibiscus* spp.
Gulf fritillary, variegated
fritillary, zebra swallowtail ⟶ *Passiflora incarnata*
(passion flower)
Lynx flower moth ⟶ *Erigeron* spp. (fleabanes)
Monarch, sleepy orange,
queen, coral hairstreak ⟶ *Asclepias* spp. (milkweed)
Pearl crescent, American
painted lady, painted lady,
Silvery crescentspot ⟶ *Aster* spp. (asters)
Silvery crescentspot ⟶ *Echinacea* spp. (coneflowers)
Silvery crescentspot ⟶ *Helianthus* spp. (sunflowers)
Silvery crescentspot ⟶ *Rudbeckia laciniata*
(green-headed coneflower)
Variegated fritillary ⟶ *Podophyllum peltatum*
(may apple)
Wild indigo duskywing,
southern dogface, hoary edge,
occasionally orange sulfur ⟶ *Baptisia* spp. (wild indigoes)
yucca moth ⟶ *Yucca* spp.

BUTTERFLIES AND OTHER NATIVE HOST PLANTS NOT FEATURED IN THIS BOOK:

Eastern snout and hackberry ⟶ *Celtis* spp. (hackberries)
Baltimore ⟶ *Chelone* spp. (turtleheads)
Buckeye ⟶ *Linaria* spp. (toadflax)
Cloudless giant sulphur,
hackberry ⟶ *Cassia* spp. (sennas)
Dogface ⟶ *Dalea* spp. (prairy clovers)
Dogface ⟶ *Vicia* spp. (vetches)
Dogface ⟶ *Amorpha fruticosa* (leadplant)
Giant swallowtail ⟶ *Ptelea trifoliata* (wafer ash)

Giant swallowtail ⁓ *Zanthoxylum* spp.
(prickly ashes)
Goatweed ⁓ *Croton* spp. (goatweeds)
Mourning cloak, viceroy ⁓ *Salix* spp. (willows)
Palamedes swallowtail ⁓ *Persea borbonia* (red bay)
Palamedes swallowtail ⁓ *Sassafras albidum* (sassafras)
Pipevine swallowtail ⁓ *Aristolochia* spp.
(Dutchman's pipe vines)
Question mark ⁓ *Ulmus* spp. (elms)
Red spotted purple (uses many
other trees as host plants) ⁓ *Morus rubra* (red mulberry)
Red spotted purple,
mourning cloak, viceroy ⁓ *Populus* spp. (poplars)
Spicebush swallowtail ⁓ *Lindera benzoin* (spicebush)
Tiger swallowtail (uses many
other trees as host plants) ⁓ *Fraxinus* spp. (ashes)
Variegated fritillary ⁓ *Linum* spp. (flaxes)
Viceroy ⁓ *Malus* spp. (apples)
Viceroy ⁓ *Pyrus* spp. (pears)
Viceroy (uses many
other trees as host plants) ⁓ *Prunus serotina* (black cherry)
Zebra swallowtail ⁓ *Asimina* spp. (paw paws)

HUMMINGBIRD PLANTS

Hummingbirds collect nectar from a wide variety of plants, woody and herbaceous, native and exotic. They do not need a platform on which to stand, like the butterflies. They can hover in mid-air, and they have a long tongue so they can sip from tubular flowers that butterflies cannot access. (One butterfly, the cloudless giant sulphur, is an exception to the short-tongue rule. Huge numbers of these sulphurs visit salvias in the fall.) The color red attracts hummingbirds strongly, but they also visit yellow, pink, and white flowers. Nectar is not their only food. They also eat small insects on the plants.

NECTAR PLANTS
FOR HUMMINGBIRDS:

American columbine ⁓ *Aquilegia canadensis*
Beebalm, wild bergamot ⁓ *Monarda* spp.
Blazing stars ⁓ *Liatris* spp.
Butterfly weed ⁓ *Asclepias tuberosa*
Cardinal flower ⁓ *Lobelia cardinalis*
Fire pink ⁓ *Silene virginica*
Indian pink ⁓ *Spigelia marilandica*
Jewel weeds ⁓ *Impatiens* spp.
Marsh mallows ⁓ *Hibiscus* spp.
Phlox ⁓ *Phlox* spp.
Salt marsh mallow ⁓ *Kosteletzkya virginica*
Salvias, sages ⁓ *Salvia* spp.
Scarlet honeysuckle ⁓ *Lonicera sempervirens*
Verbenas ⁓ *Verbena* spp.

White Snakeroot
Ageratina altissima (Eupatorium rugosum)
Asteraceae (Aster or Sunflower Family)

This is one of many wildflowers that have a new botanical name. The *Ageratina* species resemble many of the *Eupatorium* species, but they have a different chromosome count. The name may have changed, but the plant hasn't. It now comes with designer-colored dark stems and leaves. It has the same white ageratum-type bloom that enlivens shady spots in fall, and it still can poison cattle and anyone who drinks their milk. Masses of fuzzy disc flowers combine to produce 4-inch blooms. White snakeroot is a relative of Joe Pye weed and boneset because none of them have petals (ray flowers).

Several different American Indian tribes used preparations containing the root of white snakeroot to treat fever, diarrhea, and problems of the urinary tract. They also used it as a stimulant and a tonic.

When cattle eat *Ageratina altissima*, they tremble and lose weight. The poison passes to people in milk and milk products, causing "milk sickness," which is reputed to have killed Abraham Lincoln's mother.

FLOWER: The inflorescence is a corymb of heads. It is made up of 3–5″ heads of clear white disc flowers. Each head contains tubular flowers, and there is no chaff between these disc flowers. The blooms look fuzzy, because the stamens project beyond the corolla tube. The receptacle bracts below the flower clusters do not overlap.

BLOOMS: 6 weeks between late July and October

LEAVES: Before it blooms, white snakeroot looks a bit uninteresting. The simple or branched stems, 1–3 per plant, arch haphazardly and bear large, sharp-toothed, pointed leaves. These simple, opposite, petiolate (petiole up to 2″) leaves are dull on top, ovate (2–7″ by 1.5–5″), and have hairs on the veins on the back.

UNDERGROUND STRUCTURES: White snakeroot has fibrous roots and rhizomes. Colonies increase quite rapidly by the rhizomes and by seeds.

SEEDS: The nutlets have slender ribs and a pappus of a single row of bristles.

HEIGHT: 2-4′

HABITAT: Rich, moist woods

CULTURAL TIPS (see page 62)**:** Tip prune to produce a bushier plant. The new dark-leaved cultivars maintain their dark leaf color best with a good dose of sunlight.

MOISTURE: Moist to average

PH: 5–6

EXPOSURE: Light shade to full sun

PROPAGATION (see page 66)**:** All methods are easy and successful.

SEED STORAGE: Store dry seeds in an airtight container between 40°and 70°.

SEED TREATMENT: Cold stratify at 40° for 1 month. Sow at 70°. Germinate in 1 week.

CUTTINGS: Spring to early summer on firm new shoots

DIVISION: Spring or winter

FAUNA: Many insects, including bees, wasps, and butterflies, visit white snakeroot.

OTHER SE SPECIES:
   Ageratina aromatica—This species has very short petioles, and the leaves are shiny on top. It inhabits drier sites than *A. altissima,* including dry woodlands and old fields.

BLUE STAR
Amsonia tabernaemontana
Apocynaceae (Dogbane Family)

The blue stars have a most unusual pale steel-blue color to their blooms. They bloom in mid to late spring, depending on the species. The leaf shape can vary from oval to thread-like but they all have graceful stems that recover quickly when burdened with rain. Neither pest nor disease mars the foliage.

The species name is derived from the names of two men. *Amsonia* honors Charles Amson, an eighteenth-century Virginia physician, and Jacob Theodorus Tabernaemontanus, a German physician and botanical author who died in 1590.

Apocynaceae comes from the Greek root word, *apocyn*, meaning "away dog." Members of this plant family were thought to be poisonous to dogs, but recent information finds them less poisonous than once thought. Tasting them is not recommended since one member of the family, oleander, is deadly.

FLOWER: Pale steel-blue flowers cluster in a terminal panicle. Each 1/2"-diameter flower is regular with all parts in fives. Pointed petals shoot from a fused tube, imbuing a star-like appearance. The outside of the corolla tube is pubescent.

BLOOMS: 3 weeks between March and May

LEAVES: Several smooth stems emerge from a central crown. The alternate, 4" long, simple leaves can be thin and lanceolate or ovate, depending on the variety. The stems exude milky sap when cut.

UNDERGROUND STRUCTURES: The crown and feeder roots become semi-woody over time.

SEEDS: The 3-4″ long seed pods project in groups of 2–3. Each looks like a very skinny green bean with only one seam. The cylindrical brown seeds are lined end-to-end in a single row inside the follicle. The seeds are ripe sometime between August and October when the follicle turns tan and begins to split.

HEIGHT: 2-3′

HABITAT: Rich, moist woods

CULTURAL TIPS (see page 62)**:** The variety of *Amsonia tabernaemontana* with ovate leaves loses its drab-colored leaves in September. The variety sold in the trade has willow-like leaves and thrives in sun or shade. The foliage turns a light-catching yellow in fall and persists until hard frost. Space 2′ apart. Division is not necessary for the health of the plant. Prune back by a third after flowering, for a bushier plant.

MOISTURE: Average

pH: 5–6

EXPOSURE: Filtered light to full sun

PROPAGATION (see page 66)**:** Easy from seed or stem cuttings

SEED STORAGE: Store dry seeds in an airtight container between 40° and 70°.

SEED TREATMENT: After a boiling-water soak; sow at 70°. Germinate in 3–4 weeks. Seedlings are easy to handle.

CUTTINGS (stem)**:** May through June; cut ends exude white latex that sticks to the hands. Wash with soap or a product like Goop™ to remove the tacky substance from your skin.

DIVISION: Spring or fall

FAUNA: Blue stars are butterfly nectar plants.

OTHER SE SPECIES:

Amsonia ciliata (fringed blue star)—The corolla is smooth on the outside, and the stem is pubescent. It has numerous linear leaves that give it a feathery appearance. It occurs naturally in sand hills and sandy woodlands.

CAROLINE DEAN

CAROLINA ANEMONE
Anemone caroliniana
Ranunculaceae (Crowfoot or Buttercup Family)

True anemones with single white-violet blossoms grace our roadsides and woodlands. These are not the exotic anemones sold as bulbs in the fall at garden shops, but native perennials with rhizomes or tubers. Frequently, the anemones have white sepals, but the 12″ Carolina anemone can be blue to rose to dark violet. In Greek, anemone means "daughter of the wind."

FLOWER: The showy, 1.5″ solitary flower sits atop a slender stalk. It has no petals, 10–20 sepals, and a generous puff of orange stamens.

BLOOMS: En mass for 6 weeks from February to April

LEAVES: The slender, erect stem is smooth but may have sparse long hairs. The dull green leaves are twice divided into slim segments. There are 1–3 petiolate basal leaves. A few sessile, stem leaves form a whorl just beneath the flower.

UNDERGROUND STRUCTURES: This drought-resistant plant has a rounded tuber and slender rhizomes.

SEEDS: The seed head is a dense, cottony mass surrounding a pointed conical receptacle. Each achene is flat, beaked, and pubescent. Seeds ripen about two weeks after bloom. Some flowers will still be blooming when others have ripe seed.

HEIGHT: 4-12″

HABITAT: Uplands (woods, fields, and prairies) with soil that drains rapidly

CULTURAL TIPS (see page 62)**:** In cultivation, Carolina anemone thrives in moist or dry sites.

MOISTURE: Average or moist with very good drainage

pH: 5.5–6.5

EXPOSURE: Full to partial sun

PROPAGATION (see page 66)**:** Division is easiest.

SEED STORAGE: Store seeds in an airtight container between 40°-70°.

SEED TREATMENT: Vernalize 4–5 months. Sow around Labor Day at 70°.

CUTTINGS: No

DIVISION (tuber)**:** Fall

FAUNA: *Anemone caroliniana* offers a pollen feast for small flies, bees, and beetles.

OTHER SE SPECIES:

    Anemone quinquefolia (windflower)—Windflower is a dainty 4″ spring ephemeral of rich, moist, acidic woods. It has single flowers with 5–6 petaloid sepals, deep green leaves with 3–5 lobes, and thin, fragile white runners just under the leaf mold. The seeds are greenish, elliptical in a half globe–shaped but angular aggregate. The seed is wet seed (see page 66). Sow fresh.

THIMBLEWEED, TALL ANEMONE
Anemone virginiana
Ranunculaceae (Crowfoot or Buttercup Family)

Anemone virginiana has many admirable qualities. It is an upright
plant of medium stature with simple white blooms. The dark
green, cut leaves have long stalks and cluster at the base of the
plant. The smaller, shorter-stalked leaves on the stem leave the
long, bouncy stems and flower stalks open to the action of the
slightest breeze. Thimble-shaped fruits adorn the plant in
summer. Thimbleweed merits the weedy appellation only when
sited inappropriately. The plant spreads by vigorous rhizomes as
well as seeds and can overwhelm a small garden or a moist, sunny
area. In its natural home, a woodland opening, it is a bright note.

Native Americans used thimbleweed to treat many different
problems, including whooping cough, tuberculosis, catarrh,
bewitchment, love, adultery, and boils. Except for a root poultice
applied to boils, a decoction of the root or of the stem and root
was the mode of delivery. Vomiting is the usual outcome.

FLOWER: Each stem has 3–9 long-stalked single flowers above a
clutch of leaves. The 12–14″ long peduncle (flower stalk) allows
the flowers to wave gently even on a hot still day. The 1″ simple

flower has no petals but it has 5 greenish-white sepals. Numerous green stamens surround a cone of pistils, also green.

BLOOMS: 2 weeks from May to July

LEAVES: The hairy stems are erect and unbranched. Most of the distinctly veined, hairy, dissected leaves are basal. They are dark green, irregularly 3-lobed, coarsely toothed, and have long petioles. The divisions taper to sharp points. The leaves below the flower cluster are similar to the basal leaves but they have shorter petioles.

UNDERGROUND STRUCTURES: Rhizomes with strong, fibrous roots run shallowly in the soil, creating colonies.

SEEDS: In its early development, the spiky "thimble" or seed head, is a bright green 3/4″ cylinder. In about 2 months, it turns tan. Over the next few weeks, it dries, expands, and evolves into an off-white woolly mass. Eventually, wind disperses the seeds.

HEIGHT: 2-3′

HABITAT: Rich, open woods.

CULTURAL TIPS (see page 62)**:** Dry shade helps keep thimbleweed in check.

MOISTURE: Moist to dry

pH: 5–6

EXPOSURE: Sun to shade

PROPAGATION (see page 66)**:** Seed or division is easy.

SEED STORAGE: Store dry seeds in an airtight container between 40° and 70°.

SEED TREATMENT: Stratify at 40° for 2 months; sow at 70°. Germinate in 2–3 weeks.

CUTTINGS: No

DIVISION: Early spring or fall

FAUNA: Await observation

Pussytoes
Antennaria plantaginifolia
Asteraceae (Aster or Sunflower Family)

Children love the soft, pinkish-gray bloom heads of pussytoes because they truly resemble small kittens' paws. The plants are dioecious, so one needs both a male and a female plant in order to have fertile seeds. For evergreen, gray, mat-forming foliage that attracts butterflies, the sex of the plant is unimportant.

Native Americans and colonists used pussytoes to treat dysentery, lung ailments, bruises, boils, strains, and snakebites.

FLOWER: Many small, white, tubular disc flowers combine to form a head that looks like a furry, pink-to-gray paw. They have no ray flowers. The tight flower heads form a corymb. Each head can contain 3-21 flowers. Female flower heads are taller and skinnier than male flower heads. A fresh corymb of male flowers looks like a miniature head of cabbage; 50-100 flower heads may wave above a mat of leaves.

BLOOMS: 3-4 weeks from March through May

LEAVES: The stems take the form of ground-hugging stolons. The 1-2″ long leaves are spoon-shaped, grayish-green, and have 3 veins. The undersides of the leaves are hairy. Rosettes of leaves are connected by runners. These offsets are prolific and form mats.

UNDERGROUND STRUCTURES: Each rosette has a mass of thin feeder roots that extend downward about 3″. Stolons connect the rosettes. These runners are the size of angel hair pasta. They can be torn by hand but are best cut with pruning shears.

SEEDS: The shiny brown nutlets are extremely small and have a piece of attached fluff, the pappus, that helps disperse the seeds in the wind. Male flowers have little pappus.

HEIGHT: The upright flower stalk ranges 2-10″. The stalk gets longer as the flower ages. Female plants have taller bloom stalks.

HABITAT: Dry, open woods

CULTURAL TIPS (see page 62)**:** Neglect it! It needs no fertilizer, mulch, or irrigation. Use as a year-round groundcover for the woodland edge. Male flowers are more attractive than the female but do not produce seeds.

MOISTURE: Average to dry

pH: 5–6.5

EXPOSURE: Filtered light or partial sun

PROPAGATION (see page 66)**:** Rosette division is easiest.

SEED STORAGE: Store dry seeds in an airtight container between 40° and 70°.

SEED TREATMENT: Vernalize 6 months. Sow heavily, and barely cover with grit. At 55–60°, germinate in 1–2 months.

CUTTINGS: No

DIVISION: Early spring or fall

FAUNA: The American painted lady butterfly lays her eggs on the leaves, and the larvae eat the leaves as they grow. When you see a patch of the silvery green rosettes, look for rolled leaves. Within that silk nest, a spiny black caterpillar hides while it munches the inside layer of the leaf. It has yellow stripes and white- or rust-colored spots. Its frightening appearance is deceptive—this caterpillar doesn't sting. If you unroll a leaf, do so gently and you may find the caterpillar or its gold-spotted, brown chrysalis.

OTHER SE SPECIES:
> ***Antennaria neglecta*—**This species has smaller leaves that are usually one-veined. It can be found in woods and open places. It seems to tolerate more sun than *A. plantaginifolia.*
> ***A. solitaria*—**The leaves of this species are similar to those of *A. plantaginifolia,* but the heads are solitary. It also inhabits woods.

JACK-IN-THE-PULPIT,

INDIAN TURNIP
Arisaema triphyllum
Araceae (Arum Family)

Jack-in-the-pulpit can become a jill-in-the-pulpit in a good year. Small, light corms produce flower stalks bearing male flowers on a spadix surrounded by the spathe. When the corm contains enough nutrition to support the development of a large seed head, the female flowers develop. A single corm first produces an asexual leaf in youth. In a few years, it produces male flowers. In another year or two and with good nutrition, it progresses to a female state. Following a drought year, the "jack" may once again bear only male flowers on the spadix. This changing sexual pattern is called paradioecious.

Native Americans ate the corm after drying it thoroughly. They drank a tea made from the dried, aged root to treat colds and coughs. Poultices of the root eased rheumatism, boils, and snakebites. The concentration of calcium oxalate, present in the entire plant, is particularly high in the corm. These sharp crystals cause burning of the mouth and tongue when ingested fresh. Drying reduces the danger.

FLOWER: The flower-bearing stalk of jack-in-the-pulpit is best enjoyed through the eyes of a child and from the height of a child. Get down on your knees and look under the leaf umbrella to see the spadix or "jack" alert beneath his overarching spathe or "pulpit." The upper part of the spadix and the spathe is usually green-and-white striped but may vary to shades of maroon. I call the heavily purple-pigmented jacks "black jacks." Female flowers, if present, are on the lower portion of the spadix; male flowers are on the middle portion of the spadix. Neither has petals or sepals. Rarely, female and male flowers may exist simultaneously. The very end of the spadix has no flowers.

BLOOMS: 4-6 weeks between March and May; seeds begin to turn red and decorative in July.

LEAVES: A single plant may have 1–2 leaves with long, sheathing bases. A flowering plant has 2 leaves. Younger or less vigorous plants may have only 1. The compound leaves have long upright petioles and 3–5 entire, ovate leaflets. Populations of jack-in-the-pulpit tend to have either 3 leaflets or 5 leaflets.

Taxonomists recognize the diversity within the species by describing four subspecies, which can hybridize.

A. t. ssp. *triphyllum*: Widest range, 1–2 leaves, 3 leaflets, green or purple spathe

A. t. ssp. *stewardsonii*: More northern, green spathe with white ridges on the outside

A. t. ssp. *pusillum*: Spathe completely green or completely purple, occasionally with thin green stripes

A. t. ssp. *quinatum*: Restricted range in the South, smaller plant overall, leaves 5-parted with a whitish "bloom" underneath, spathe green with no markings

UNDERGROUND STRUCTURES: The tan corms increase in size up to 2″ in diameter. Large corms produce offsets. Feeder roots emerge from the top of the corm at the base of the new shoot. Corms can be stored dry for a season.

SEEDS: In August and September, large clusters of red fruit litter a patch of jack-in-the-pulpit. The flower stalk collapses under the weight of the seed head, and the berries fall onto the moist, leafy seedbed below. Each red fruit may contain 1-6 seeds. The seeds look like small white-to-tan BBs. The red fleshy material contains a germination inhibitor. Seeds are ripe between mid-August and mid-October.

HEIGHT: Jacks can be 1–3′ tall, depending on the subspecies and on the conditions. In a rich, moist, woodland site, they can achieve a grand scale.

HABITAT: Flood plains, stream banks, low woods—anywhere moisture is plentiful during spring

CULTURAL TIPS (see page 62)**:** Incorporate copious amounts of humus into the planting bed. If you wish to fertilize, do so in winter before active growth begins.

MOISTURE: Moist to average; jack-in-the-pulpit thrives in cultivation if given plenty of moisture. Female flowers may not form every year if nourishment is inadequate.

pH: 5–6.5

EXPOSURE: Filtered light or heavy shade; excessive sunlight bleaches the leaves

PROPAGATION (see page 66)**:** Division produces a blooming plant sooner than seed propagation.

SEED STORAGE: Can be cleaned and stored dry, but dry storage can result in loss of viability and/or delayed germination.

SEED TREATMENT: Remove the red material from around the seeds. Sow promptly outside or stratify at 40° for 6–8 weeks in the refrigerator and then sow at 70°. The first method produces the healthiest plants. The first true leaves are the size of small fingernails and go dormant quickly. Caring for empty-looking pots is difficult. Let nature nurture the wee ones.

CUTTINGS: No

DIVISION: In fall or very early spring, remove offsets from large plants and replant to a depth equal to the diameter of the corm. Dig when the shoot is just emerging. Once the leaves unfurl from the sheath, the plant suffers from disturbance.

FAUNA: The red seed covering can rot away over time, or birds may eat the seeds and the red coating disappears during the digestion process. When the bird flies to a new area and eliminates, the seeds are scattered in a new site. Fungus gnats pollinate Araceae.

OTHER SE SPECIES:

Arisaema dracontium (green dragon)—Green dragons are larger overall than jacks. They have a compound leaf with 7–15 unequal divisions arranged in a semicircle. The spathe has rolled edges, and the end of the spadix is drawn out into a long whip, the "dragon's tongue."

WILD GINGER
Asarum canadense
Aristolochiaceae (Birthwort Family)

Before trees leaf out in the spring, flotillas of green sails rise from moist woodland plains. The green triangles unfold into furry, horizontal, heart-shaped leaves. They form a blanket that hovers above the ground, sheltering maroon-to-brown, primitive-looking, bell-shaped blooms. The blooms lie on the ground where insects can crawl or fly in and out of the blossom, transporting pollen in their search for brood sites.

Native Americans used wild ginger to flavor meat and fish. They thought it sanitized tainted meat. Hard candy made from a simple syrup makes a delicious cough drop. The rhizomes are the diameter of a pencil and are a bit tedious to clean.

Native Americans also used ginger to treat a variety of ailments: coughs, colds, fever, stomach upset, female ailments, and heart conditions. Ginger contains the anti-tumor agent aristolochic acid.

FLOWER: At the junction of each pair of leaves, the 1/2″-long, dark maroon bloom projects horizontally on a short stem. The regular open face of the bloom measures about 1″ across. This perfect flower has no petals, only firm, almost waxy, fused sepals with pointed lobes. Over its wide range, *Asarum canadense* is highly variable in color and shape of the bloom.

BLOOMS: 4-6 weeks between April and May

LEAVES: The simple, downy leaves rise in pairs from the creeping horizontal stems. There is no erect stem. Each 4-6″ wide, heart-shaped leaf has a 6–10″ long petiole, making these leaves excellent material for cut flower arranging. This ginger has unspotted, medium-green leaves that disappear completely in winter.

UNDERGROUND STRUCTURES: The aromatic, branching rootstocks have a massive network of feeder roots.

SEEDS: The leathery, 6-chambered capsule splits irregularly to release a generous number of shiny, humped, oval, brown seeds with a prominent aril (fleshy appendage). The aril looks like a mass of frog eggs on the flat side of the seed. In moist humus, wild ginger can self-seed with abandon. Seeds are ripe 2–6 weeks after bloom.

HEIGHT: 6-12″

HABITAT: Rich, moist woods

CULTURAL TIPS (see page 62)**:** Deciduous ginger is an aggressive groundcover. Do not plant it too close to botanical treasures. Sod-like patches help prevent soil erosion on creek banks.

MOISTURE: Thrives with good moisture but tolerates drought

pH: 5–7.5

EXPOSURE: Shade or morning sun

PROPAGATION (see page 66)**:** Division is easiest. From seed, 3 or more years to bloom.

SEED STORAGE: Can store temporarily in moist spaghnum at 40°.

SEED TREATMENT: Sow outdoors when ripe. They need rinsing, a warm/cold stratification, and temperature fluctuations.

CUTTINGS (rhizome)**:** 3″ with 2 leaves, after bloom, root in 4–5 weeks.

DIVISION: Spring or fall

FAUNA: Flowers in the genus *Asarum* emit a smell of decaying organic matter, which attracts fungus gnats and beetles. The flies think they will be able to lay their eggs in the site. They are fooled, but in the process they help pollinate the flower, and then go on their way (Proctor, et al, 1996). An individual plant may self-pollinate or cross with others of its species.

BUTTERFLY WEED,
PLEURISY ROOT, CHIGGER WEED
Asclepias tuberosa
Asclepiadaceae (Milkweed Family)

Thirty years ago, bright splashes of orange dotted roadsides, even
the edges of interstates, in summer. The dry full sun habitat along
road embankments is the perfect site for butterfly weed. Each year
the patches of color decline as highway maintenance depends
more and more on chemical herbicides. Increasing interest in
restoring roadside wildflowers gives hope that the butterfly weed
will continue to enliven our summers.

Butterfly weed gains fame from its association with the monarch
butterfly. The plant contains a cardiac glycoside, which passes
through the caterpillar into the butterfly and on to any bird feeding
on the insect. After one bout of nausea and vomiting, birds learn
to taste test a wing tip before consuming whole butterflies.

Another common name for butterfly weed is pleurisy root.
Poultices of the root soothed bruises, swellings, and rheumatism.
Native Americans and colonists made a tea from the root to
treat lung ailments. However, use caution—in large quantities
butterfly weed tea is toxic! These medicinal uses explain the
derivation of the genus name, *Asclepias,* from the name of the
Greek god of medicine, Asklepios.

Whether butterfly weed harbors chiggers is open to speculation,
but the grasses that associate with it are frequently home to the
irritating mite.

The magical flight device for milkweed seeds is a gossamer tail.
This silky material in milkweed pods has great buoyancy and was
used in flight suits in World War II. If the pilot crashed into
water, his suit, filled with milkweed down, would float.

FLOWER: The flower color can range from yellow to dark red but is usually a shade of orange. Individual flowers have 5 stamens and a reflexed, 5-lobed corolla. The sepals are also reflexed lobes but are hidden by the corolla. Above the corolla is a crown-type arrangement of petal-like hoods. Within each hood is a horn, which is short and hidden in butterfly weed. The pollen of milkweeds is enclosed in a sac. This sac of pollen (pollinia) is carried away intact by the pollinator.

BLOOMS: 6 weeks from May to September

LEAVES: The leaves are broadly lanceolate, sessile, alternate, 2-4″ long, and closely spaced. On branches at the tops of the erect stems, the leaves may be opposite. Both leaves and stems are hairy. The sap of butterfly weed is clear, unlike most milkweeds, which have milky sap.

UNDERGROUND STRUCTURES: The root is heavy, tuberous, and brittle. It extends deeply in the soil, helping the plant withstand drought.

SEEDS: The seed pods look like elongated footballs held upright. They are 4-5″ long and $1/2$–$3/4$″ in diameter. The pod turns from green to brown before splitting to release seeds that float on the slightest breeze. Seeds are ripe between July and September.

HEIGHT: 2–3′

HABITAT: Dry, open fields and roadsides

CULTURAL TIPS (see page 62)**:** When planting in clay, amend the soil with pea gravel and rotted pine bark. The thick taproot makes the plant difficult to move. Choose a permanent site before planting a new plant. Avoid heavy mulch, which can cause crown rot. New growth emerges in late spring, after the soil is warm. Label the plant to avoid slicing the crown in the flurry of spring planting. Removing spent flower heads produces a second flush of bloom. Fresh-cut blooms last a week in a flower arrangement.

Orange oleander aphids coexist with all milkweeds. One can spray with insecticidal soap, neem oil, or water. The aphids do not need to be assaulted unless the plants are already stressed by prolonged drought. In that situation, the sweet dew from the aphids encourages the growth of sooty mold, which can kill the plant. If you see a charcoal-black film on the plant or the ground beneath, grab the hose nozzle and blast away the insects. Use soap or chemicals as a last resort.

MOISTURE: Dry or average with good drainage; once established, butterfly weed is drought-tolerant. It may need supplemental water once a week for the first month after planting if no rain falls. During prolonged droughts (2–3 months), a young planting (up to 18 months) may need irrigation. Too much water is more of a problem than too little for this plant.

pH: 5–7

EXPOSURE: Butterfly weed prefers full sun but will tolerate a bit of shade.

PROPAGATION (see page 66)**:** Seed or root cuttings are easy methods of propagation.

SEED STORAGE: Store dry seeds in an airtight container between 40° and 70°.

SEED TREATMENT: Collect seeds just as the pod begins to split, usually in July or August. Hold the pod together with a rubber band until you can clean the seeds. To clean, grab the bundle of silks tightly between the thumb and forefinger of one hand, and push the seeds off with a thumb or fingernail of the other hand. Sow at 70°. Germinate in 2–4 weeks; bloom the first year.

Germination percentages can be quite variable. After 2–8 months dry storage, first-year seeds germinate well. Sow any time January through May. Older seeds that fail to sprout can be given 2 weeks in damp sand in a plastic bag in the freezer; this seems to jump start them.

Add sand or starter chicken grit (grade 2 granite rock) to the potting soil to enhance drainage. Contrary to some old-time advice, fertilizer does not harm the plants in pots. Time-release granules or liquid fertilizers are acceptable. Once in the ground, the plants need no feeding.

CUTTINGS (stem): 3–4″ tip cutting before flowering; roots in 4-6 weeks
CUTTINGS (root): 2″ pieces; keep the upper end upright; cover with 1/2″ of soil medium; roots, stems, and buds form in 10 weeks.

DIVISION: No

FAUNA: Hummingbirds and butterflies find nectar at this orange-red milkweed.

Many butterflies, such as the monarch, the red-spotted purple, and swallowtails, perch easily on the umbel of the milkweeds. They drink the nectar and carry pollen from plant to plant. The monarch lays eggs on the leaves of the milkweeds. The resulting larvae consume leaves and buds. They feed voraciously for 10–14 days and then crawl to a stiff horizontal stem or branch and form a gold-banded, green chrysalis. In a few weeks a butterfly emerges.

Butterflies prefer the swamp milkweed to the butterfly weed for nectar and as a host plant. I surmise the milky sap contains more of the toxin that protects butterflies from predation.

OTHER SE SPECIES: In these species, the lanceolate to ovate leaves are opposite or whorled, and the sap is milky.

Asclepias amplexicaulis (curly milkweed)—This species has stalked, burgundy flowers; 4–6 pairs of sessile; wavy-edged, blunt leaves clasp the unbranched stem. It can be found in sandy clearings and on roadsides. It is an indicator plant for acidic soils.

A. exaltata (poke milkweed)—This species has pale, greenish-pink stalked flowers in loose umbels. The long petiolate, broadly lanceolate leaves are smooth underneath. Poke milkweed is found in meadows and deciduous woods.

A. humistrata (sand hills milkweed)—This species has a lavender corolla with white hoods. The broad clasping leaves have pink coloration in the veins. The stems are unbranched but occur in clusters, and the plant has very milky juice. It is found in sand hills, dunes, and sandy, dry, open woods.

A. incarnata (swamp milkweed)—This species has pink or purple to white, short-stalked flowers and is found in moist areas. The stems are smooth or slightly hairy. The leaves have a short petiole. Cold-stratify the seeds for 2 months, and they will germinate in 1-2 weeks at 70°-80°.

A. lanceolata (few-flowered milkweed)—This species has bright red or orange flowers. The smooth, linear, or lanceolate leaves are often longer than 6″. Three to six pairs of leaves are widely spaced on a smooth stem. It is found in wet savannas and fresh or brackish marshes.

A. perennis (aquatic milkweed)—This species has small, white-stalked flowers, and horns longer than the hoods. It is found in swamps. The leaves are thin, lanceolate, and petiolate. The mature fruits are pendant, and the seeds have no silks.

A. syriaca (common milkweed)—This fragrant species has a greenish-purple to pink corolla and is found in fields and waste areas. The elliptical to ovate leaves are hairy beneath. The fruit is soft spiny.

A. variegata (white milkweed)—This species has dense, stalked, mainly terminal flower clusters. The white flowers have purple centers. The unbranched stem has 2–6 pairs of broad, petiolate leaves, which are pubescent beneath. It is found in thin, dry woods. In my experience, this species does not attract butterflies but does attract a wide variety of sizeable flying insects. Seed set is tenuous in this species, and seed fertility is low. Cold-stratify the dry seeds for 2 months at 40°. Sow at 70°-80°. Germinate in 2-3 weeks.

A. verticillata (whorled milkweed)—This species has stalked flowers in terminal and axillary clusters and is found in dry, thin woods and sand hills. It has greenish-white petals with white hoods and exposed, in-curved horns. The linear leaves are in whorls.

A. viridis (green milkweed, spider milkweed, antelope horn)—This species has a large, showy terminal flower cluster and is found in prairies and cedar glades. The petals are green and spreading (not reflexed). The hood is purple. The leaves are alternate to nearly opposite.

JESSIE HARRIS

SILKY ASTER,
EASTERN SILVERY ASTER
Aster concolor
Asteraceae (Aster or Sunflower Family)

There are more than 250 species of asters. About 60 of them grow in North America. Identification of the species is difficult in the best of circumstances. Several features can place a plant in the genus *Aster*. The simple leaves are alternate. The flower heads have both disc and ray flowers, although the rays may be inconspicuous in a few species. The involucral bracts (modified leaves) are in two or more rows. There is no chaff on the receptacle. The seeds have several ridges and bristly pappus.

Aster is the Greek root word for star, referring to the shape of the dried flower heads. *Concolor* means "of one color."

FLOWER: The heads are dispersed in a long, wand-like raceme. Each head has 8–16 blue or lavender rays and numerous yellow disc flowers. The involucral bracts on the underside of the flower head are whitish with green tips.

BLOOMS: 6 weeks from August to October

LEAVES: The arching, simple stems are lightly silky. The alternate, oblong, 1–2″ by ½″ sessile, slightly clasping leaves are silky with hairs. Older leaves may become leathery. The small leaves are closely spaced on the stems.

UNDERGROUND STRUCTURES: The plants have stocky, short rhizomes.

SEEDS: The brown, tapering nutlets are so densely silky that the ridges are hidden.

HEIGHT: 1–2′

HABITAT: Sandy soil, often among pines, flatwoods, and in old fields.

CULTURAL TIPS (see page 62)**:** In general, asters need division every 2–3 years. If grown in sandy soil, this species rarely needs division.

MOISTURE: Average to dry

pH: 5–6

EXPOSURE: Full or partial sun

PROPAGATION (see page 66)**:** All methods are successful.

SEED STORAGE: Store dry seeds in an airtight container between 40° and 70°.

SEED TREATMENT: Sow heavily (asters have low fertility). Cold-stratify at 40° for 3 months. Sow at 70° or sow in a flat in the fall and leave outside.

CUTTINGS (stem)**:** Spring or early summer; 1-2″ long, terminal cuttings with 2–3 leaves; roots form in 3 weeks.

DIVISION: Early spring or fall; remove outside portions of clumps.

FAUNA: Asters are good nectar and host plants for butterflies.

OTHER SE SPECIES (with short leaves that are silvery and silky on both sides)**:** *Aster sericeus* (western silvery aster)—This species has violet flower heads in a loose corymb on a 1–2′ branching stem and is found in dry prairies and open places. The seeds are smooth. The involucral bracts are silky on the back but do not have hairs on the edges.

SMOOTH ASTER
Aster laevis
Asteraceae (Aster or Sunflower Family)

One of the easiest asters to identify is the smooth aster. It blooms mid-summer to fall, has large blue flower heads, and smooth foliage with a decidedly blue tint to the green. The middle vein of the leaves is often red.

The specific epithet, *laevis,* comes from the Latin root word meaning smooth. Fox Indians used smoke from the whole plant in sweat baths and blew the smoke into the nostrils of a comatose person to revive him.

FLOWERS: The bloom is a 1″ diameter, radiate head of ray and disc flowers. There are 15–30 pistillate, fertile, pale, violet-blue ray flowers and numerous perfect purple tubular disc flowers. The style branches have a yellow hairy appendage. There are 2 rows of pointed bracts, which press against the base of the head of flowers. They have dark green diamond-shaped tips. (See page 111 for tips on identifying asters.)

BLOOMS: 6 weeks between July and October

LEAVES: The stems are stout, so the plant is erect whether single-stemmed or branched. The leathery, blue-green, clasping leaves are alternate, simple, entire, or with short, raspy teeth or bristles along the edge. The shape of the leaf is variable, but the leaves are widely lanceolate, strongly ribbed, tapering to a point at the apex and tapering to a petiole at the stem end. The stem leaves are broadest in the middle, up to 1.5″. The smaller leaves under the blooms are widest at their base, about 0.25–0.5″.

UNDERGROUND STRUCTURES: Smooth aster has short, thick rhizomes and smaller, creeping rhizomes. It is not invasive.

SEEDS: The ribbed seed is a smooth achene with reddish pappus hairs. The entire flattish receptacle is covered with seeds.

HEIGHT: 1–4′

HABITAT: Dry, open places

CULTURAL TIPS (see page 62)**:** Too much water and fertilizer and too little sun can turn an upright plant into a sprawler. Light fertilization and pinching back until mid-June produces a bushy, richly colored plant. Divide every 2–3 years.

MOISTURE: Average to dry

pH: 5–6

EXPOSURE: Full sun (at least 6 hours)

PROPAGATION (see page 66)**:** All methods are easy.

SEED STORAGE: Store dry seeds in an airtight container between 40° and 70°.

SEED TREATMENT: Sow at 70°–80°. Cover very lightly so light can reach the seeds.

CUTTINGS (stem)**:** From plants in the ground; terminal tips in spring; roots form in 3 weeks. In a propagation house, new basal tips can be rooted year-round.

DIVISION: Early spring

FAUNA: Asters have many insect pollinators: bees, bumblebees, butterflies, moths, wasps, beetles, and flies. *Aster laevis* is a host plant for the pearl crescent butterfly.

FLAT-TOPPED ASTER,
BAYGALL ASTER
Aster umbellatus
Asteraceae (Aster Family)

White asters often have many small flower heads. The flat-topped aster stands out, with its showy 4–5″ flower head clusters. It is a summer bloomer that fills the time slot between the milkweeds and the hibiscus and Joe Pye weeds. It can continue blooming for a long time into fall.

Trying to identify a white summer or fall blooming aster can be a daunting task. *Aster umbellatus* is one of the easier species to identify because it has a many-flowered, showy corymb. If you see a colony of white-rayed, aster-type flowers arranged in flat clusters on erect 4–5′ stems, especially in a moist area, check to see if it is the flat-topped aster.

FLOWER: Each bloom head has 7–14 white, female ray flowers and 16–40 yellow, perfect disc flowers. (Var. *latifolius* has fewer ray and disc flowers.) The rays are about 1/4″ long but less than 1/2″ long. A dense mass of 30–300 heads form a flat corymb-like inflorescence.

BLOOMS: 4 weeks between June and August (later for var. *latifolius*)

LEAVES: The medium-green, distinctly veined, thin leaves are alternate, simple, narrowly elliptical, and visibly veined. They have no hairs on top but feel a bit rough. They may have sparse hairs on the veins on the underside. The longest leaves are mid-stem, and they can be 1″ wide (wider in var. *latifolius*) and 4″ long tapering to a point. They have short petioles. There are no basal leaves when the plant is blooming, but the stem leaves persist all the way to the ground in a moist site. The stem is smooth except for occasional hairs.

UNDERGROUND STRUCTURES: This species is strongly rhizomatous.

SEEDS: The small, dark brown seeds are obovoid, hairy, and have a double row of pappus hairs at the wider end. The outer row is less than $^1/_{16}''$ long and is visible with a hand lens on a dry seed but not on a fresh green one.

HEIGHT: 4–5′

HABITAT: One of the varieties of *Aster umbellatus* occurs in all the physiographic provinces. The more inland variety inhabits meadows and wet-to-dry woodlands or bogs. The Coastal Plain species frequents bogs, creek banks, low thickets in pinelands, and open woodlands.

CULTURAL TIPS (see page 62)**:** Cut back by one-third to keep shorter but cease pruning before June 1 to allow flower buds to form.

MOISTURE: Moist to average

pH: 5–6

EXPOSURE: Full sun to half-day sun

PROPAGATION (see page 66)**:** Seed is easy.

SEED STORAGE: Store dry seeds in an airtight container between 40° and 70°.

SEED TREATMENT: Sow heavily in a flat that can stay outside over the winter to receive cold and fluctuating temperatures. If sown in January, they will begin germinating outside in 2–3 months.

CUTTINGS (stem)**:** May or June, when new growth stiffens

DIVISION: Early spring or fall

FAUNA: Butterflies seek nectar at asters and some use asters as host plants. A variety of bees and insects help pollinate the flowers for nectar and pollen rewards.

OTHER SE SPECIES(with 2 unequal rows of pappus)**:**
    Aster infirmus—This species is similar to *A. umbellatus* in that the rays are white, and the distinctly veined leaves are thin but not linear. Where *A. infirmus* differs is in the lack of rhizomes and in the smooth texture of the seeds. It is found in dry, deciduous woodlands.
    A. linarifolius (stiff-leaved aster)—This 2′ aster has violet rays and thick, needle-like leaves that have only 1 prominent main vein. It occupies dry, open woods.
    A. reticulatus (white-topped aster)—This 1–3′ aster has long (about $^1/_2''$) white rays and inhabits low pinelands. The leaves are downy on the back sides.

WHITE BAPTISIA,
WHITE WILD INDIGO
Baptisia alba
Fabaceae (Bean Family)

Baptisias come in many colors, usually white, cream, yellow, or blue. Every state in the Southeast has at least 2–3 species, usually in the white-to-yellow color range. The identifying (and most long-lasting) feature of these plants is the 3-part pea foliage. These handsome leaves usually have a blue cast. Putting a species name on all the whites is difficult, complicated by their tendency to hybridize. Currently many old species names are lumped into the category alba.

The genus name, *Baptisia,* comes from the Greek *baptistis,* a person who dyes things. The blue- and yellow-flowered species in particular were used for dye plants but produced inferior dyes.

Although the emerging stalks look like asparagus and some species have been eaten in New England, other southern species may be toxic. None should be eaten.

Native Americans used *Baptisia* spp. for many medicinal purposes, both internally and externally. The usual outcome of ingestion is diarrhea and vomiting. Current research focuses on the action of baptisia on the immune system. A bit of *Baptisia tinctoria* (shoofly) tucked into the hatband to repel flies is safe and probably efficacious.

FLOWER: The flowers are typical of the legume or bean family. The 5 petals vary: 2 fuse to form a keel, 2 are wings, and 1 is an unpleated fan behind the other 4. In the alba species, the flowers are white (see below for colors of other species); 10–30 flowers cluster in a terminal raceme on an upright stalk.

BLOOMS: 3 weeks between April and June

LEAVES: Each leaf has 3 elliptical leaflets. The leaves alternate on an upright stem. In spring, the shoots look like a stalk of asparagus emerging from the ground. The stems have a charcoal-colored "bloom." In the fall, the leaves blacken.

UNDERGROUND STRUCTURES: The ropy feeder roots supporting the heavy crown have swellings or nodules that produce nitrogen. They dive deeply into the soil, helping the plant resist drought but making transplanting difficult.

SEEDS: The kidney-shaped seeds are tan or dark brown when dry. The ellipsoid, inflated pod or legume has a short beak and turns black as it dries. The number of seeds in each pod is highly variable but there are usually 1–8. Seeds turn brown in 4–6 weeks.

HEIGHT: 2–3′, sometimes up to 6′

HABITAT: Thin woods and clearings, prairies, sand hills, post oak hills, and flatwoods

CULTURAL TIPS (see page 62)**:** White wild indigo tolerates light or heavy soil.

MOISTURE: Average (sandy soil preferable in areas with more than 55″ of rain per year)

pH: 5–6

EXPOSURE: Full to partial sun

PROPAGATION (see page 66)**:** Seed is easiest.

SEED STORAGE: Fumigate. Store dry seeds in an airtight container between 40° and 70°.

SEED TREATMENT (*Baptisia alba* in particular)**:** For best germination results, collect seeds while green, before they form a hard seed coat. Sow fresh at 70°–85°. Germinate in 1–2 weeks. If collected from dry, cracked pods, fumigate seeds. For old seeds stored for several years, use a boiling water soak.

CUTTINGS (stem)**:** When new growth firms

DIVISION: Possible, but not recommended

FAUNA: The seed capsules are zoos of insects and larvae. Bumblebees can push their way into the springy, hooded flower.

OTHER SE SPECIES:

Baptisia australis (blue wild indigo)—This upright, 3′ herbaceous multi-stemmed plant has deep blue flowers and occurs naturally in thin woods, edges, and glades. It is a lime-lover that is happiest in full sun in cultivation.

B. bracteata (cream wild indigo)—This baptisia rarely exceeds 2′ because it has a lax habit. It has cream-colored flowers on short pedicels (less than 1/2″). In winter, the entire dry plant breaks loose from its moorings and rolls like a tumbleweed. Plants are scattered here and there in dry, second-growth piney woods. To propagate, allow seeds to dry on the plant. Soak dry seeds in warm water for 24 hours. Cold-stratify at 40° for 2 months. Germinates in 1–2 weeks at 70°.

B. cinerea (sand hills baptisia)—This 1-2′ baptisia has rich yellow flowers in erect racemes. It occupies sandy soil in thin woods.

B. leucophaea (long-bracted wild indigo)—This baptisia resembles *B. bracteata*, with its cream color and lax habit. But in this species, the pedicels exceed 1/2″. It is wide-ranging in sandy soils.

B. nuttalliana—This upright, many-branched baptisia has bright yellow flowers and inhabits prairies, roadsides, and fields. The leaves are obovate.

B. perfoliata (gopherweed)—The yellow blooms of this baptisia are in the axils of the simple, perfoliate leaves. It inhabits sand hills and dry, open woods.

B. sphaerocarpa (yellow wild indigo)—This 2–3′, erect plant has intense, bright yellow flowers. This prairie plant turns black in late summer.

B. tinctoria (shoofly, yellow wild indigo, horsefly weed)—This 3′ bushy-branched plant has small yellow flowers. It is a common dye plant and repels flies. Horsefly weed is found in open woods and clearings throughout the Southeast.

Beggar Ticks,
Stick Tight,
Tickseed Sunflower
Bidens aristosa (B. polylepis)
Asteraceae
(Aster or Sunflower Family)

Yellow composites of Asteraceae abound in the fall. How can you tell one from another? The beggar ticks offer a useful identification clue. The seeds of almost all the species of *Bidens* are on the plant at the same time as the flowers, because most of the species are annuals. The seeds usually have 2 barbed awns that grab onto the fur or trousers of passing mammals. Although the seeds of beggar ticks may be a bit taxing, the flowers are truly beautiful and will be recognized by more and more people as their use in highway plantings increases. They thrive and perpetuate themselves in moist ditches and meadows, giving pleasure to thousands of passersby.

The flower heads of beggar ticks and coreopsis are similar, but the seeds differ. The seeds of coreopsis do not have barbs on the awns and are usually winged.

Bidens (from Latin) means two teeth. *Aristosa* (from Latin) means bristly. All of the common names refer to the barbed awns or teeth that are the dispersal mechanism for the seeds.

Bidens aristosa and *B. polylepis* have been treated as two taxa and as two varieties of one species. This treatment acknowledges the documentation by Lipscomb and Smith (1977), who found intergradation of the involucral and achenial characteristics of the two species over the whole range of the two taxa.

FLOWER: Each 1.5-3″ diameter flower head has its own stalk. The 8–10 yellow ray flowers—"petals"—are female. The perfect disc flowers are also yellow.

BLOOMS: August to frost

LEAVES: The opposite, toothed leaves may be smooth or hairy. They have a stalk and are pinnately or bipinnately divided into lanceolate segments. A plant may have single or multiple stems.

UNDERGROUND STRUCTURES: These annuals have a taproot as a counterbalance to the profusion of flowering heads.

SEEDS: The seed achene is dark brown, ¼″ long, twice as long as it is broad, flattish but with 4 sides, and has 2 barbed teeth. It is mature when it turns from green to brown, 2–3 weeks after it finishes blooming.

HEIGHT: 2–5´

HABITAT: Wet ditches and fields, meadows, borders, waste areas, and marshes.

CULTURAL TIPS (see page 62)**:** Seeds can be sown outdoors in fall, in open moist areas. These plants are lovely in drifts but need a good deal of space. Mow the area in fall or late winter, after the seeds have dispersed.

MOISTURE: Moist-average with supplemental moisture during drought

pH: 5–6.5

EXPOSURE: Full to partial sun

PROPAGATION (see page 66)**:** Seed is easiest.

SEED STORAGE: Store dry seeds in an airtight container between 40° and 70°. Seeds lose viability in long-term storage.

SEED TREATMENT: Collect seeds when they are dark green or brown. Can begin cold, moist stratification at 40° as soon as the seeds ripen (turn brown). Stratify 1–3 months; sow at 70°. Germinate in 1 week. If sowing outdoors, sow in fall.

CUTTINGS (stem)**:** Tip cuttings in spring root in 1 week.

DIVISION: No

FAUNA: *Bidens* spp. attract a variety of butterflies.

OTHER SE SPECIES:

Bidens bipinnata (Spanish needles, high brighties)—This annual species may or may not have ray flowers. The seeds are spindle-shaped and have awns that catch on animal pelts and peoples' clothing. They are not seriously painful or difficult to remove, but they travel in large groups. The Cherokee chewed the leaves to soothe a sore throat. A tea made from the leaves served as a vermifuge. Settlers cooked the young shoots and leaves into a potherb.

B. frondosa (devil's beggar ticks, boot jacks, rayless marigold)—This species has no ray petals. *Frondosa* means leafy.

B. laevis (smooth beggar ticks, bur marigold)—This 3´ perennial has smooth, unlobed, toothed leaves. The tips of the bracts between the disc flowers are red, giving the disc a dark appearance. It is found in fresh or brackish marshes.

B. pilosa (shepherd's needle)—This 6´ annual has white ray flowers and spindle-shaped seeds.

BOLTONIA
Boltonia asteroides
Asteraceae (Aster or Sunflower Family)

Given moisture and sun, boltonia covers itself with masses of daisy-like flowers in late summer and fall. It is almost as wide as it is tall, and the entire plant is covered with blossoms. As the species name *asteroides* suggests, it shines.

FLOWER: Numerous blossoms arranged in corymb-like clusters cover the entire plant. Individual 1″ heads have disc and ray flowers. The yellow disc flowers are perfect and fertile. The white (occasionally pink or lavender) ray flowers have only pistils, but are also fertile. The small, rounded receptacle bears no chaff between the flowers or seeds.

BLOOMS: 6 weeks between August and November

LEAVES: The smooth, blue-green leaves are simple, entire, lanceolate, elliptical, and alternate. They are 3-5″ long by 2″ wide and taper at both ends. They get smaller toward the top of the branching stems.

UNDERGROUND STRUCTURES: The rootstock is rhizomatous with fibrous feeder roots.

SEEDS: The flat, brown, oval seeds (achenes) have wings and a short, bristly pappus. Seeds are ripe about 3 weeks after the blooms fade.

HEIGHT: 5–6′

HABITAT: Common on alluvial soils and in marshes and pinelands

CULTURAL TIPS (see page 62)**:** This species is a floppy plant requiring staking. Cultivars perform well in the Piedmont but not in all the other physiographic provinces. Boltonia does best in moist organic soil but is highly drought-tolerant.

MOISTURE: Moist to average

PH: 4.5–6

EXPOSURE: Full sun

PROPAGATION (see page 66)**:** Either cuttings or division is easiest.

SEED STORAGE: Store dry seeds in an airtight container between 40° and 70°.

SEED TREATMENT: Sow heavily. Germinate at 70°-80° in 2–3 weeks

CUTTINGS (stem)**:** May through July; root in 4–5 weeks

DIVISION: Spring division of basal rosettes

FAUNA: *Boltonia* is a butterfly nectar plant.

OTHER SE SPECIES:

> ***Boltonia caroliniana***—This species has smaller flowers, is much more branched, and occurs in moist lowlands. The inflorescence is leafy. The stem leaves present at the time of bloom are ¹/₂″ wide.
>
> ***B. diffusa*** (doll's daisy)—Similar to *B. caroliniana* but has no leaves, only bracts on the inflorescence, which give it an airy appearance. Most of the linear stem leaves fall off before the plant comes into bloom. It grows in open areas, wet to dry.

WILD HYACINTH,
EASTERN CAMAS, QUAMASH
Camassia scilloides
Liliaceae (Lily Family)

The eastern wild hyacinth has a unique ethereal blue color. The flowers on the 2′ stalk open about the same time the native azaleas bloom, filling the garden or woodland with Easter egg pastels in celebration of spring's rebirth.

The genus name, *Camassia,* comes from the American Indian name quamash or camas. The eastern camas is one of five North American species. The four western species were so important in the diets of the Native Americans that war, the Bannock War of 1878, broke out in Idaho when white settlers introduced pigs that unearthed and ate the staple crop of the Native Americans. The eastern species, like the western, looks like a small white onion and is edible but rare in many states and should not be harvested.

FLOWER: Wild hyacinth has pale violet-blue, regular flowers arranged in a 6–18″ raceme on a 1–2′ stalk. The 6-parted, star-like flowers are perfect. Light yellow anthers blend subtly with the overall pastel effect. Flowers begin to open at the bottom of the spike first.

BLOOMS: 6 weeks between March and May

LEAVES: Most of the smooth, linear leaves arise from the bulb at the base of the plant. A few small leaves may appear on the flower stalk below the raceme of flowers. The leaves have a bright green appearance due to the absence of hairs, and they have the fleshy texture common among members of the lily family.

UNDERGROUND STRUCTURES: Wild hyacinth forms 1″ diameter white bulbs, which multiply by offsets as well as seed. The bulb may develop a brown coat in storage. This bulb has a high sugar content. White feeder roots extend downward 3–4″ from the bottom of the bulb.

SEEDS: Copious dry, shiny, black seeds develop inside 3-chambered, beige capsules. The seed is about the size of mustard seed (commonly used in cooking). It has a lopsided, round shape with a point. Seeds ripen within 4–6 weeks.

HEIGHT: The tip of the inflorescence may reach 2.5′. In a pressed herbarium specimen, the leaves can equal the flower stalk in length; but fresh, they are narrow (less than 1/2″ wide) and relaxed, curving gently earthward. The retiring leaves do not obstruct the view of the blooms.

HABITAT: Look for quamash in moist-to-wet, open woods; in glades; on rocky slopes; and on prairies. It is often found on limestone.

pH: 5–7

EXPOSURE: Full sun to filtered shade

CULTURAL TIPS (see page 62)**:** Wild hyacinth is extremely hardy and performs well in cultivation. It performs well in loam and moist, well-drained soil. Strong, filtered light encourages maximum bloom. Plant bulbs 3–4″ apart in October or November. Cover the bulbs with 1–2″ of soil.

PROPAGATION (see page 66)**:** Seed (sown in the ground) or division is easy.

SEED STORAGE: Store dry seeds in an airtight container between 40° and 70°.

SEED TREATMENT: Sow on moist ground in November or cold stratify at 40° for 2 months and sow at 55°-70°. Germinate in 5–14 weeks; rate of germination is high. Bulbs do not over-winter well in pots. Seed-grown plants bloom in 3–4 years.

CUTTINGS: No

DIVISION: Clumps can be divided in late fall.

FAUNA: Wild hyacinth is one of the nectar sources for the cobweb and dusted skippers.

AMERICAN BELLFLOWER
Campanulastrum americanum
(Campanula americana)
Campanulaceae
(Bellflower Family)

Imagine an erect, branched, 4′ plant with violet-blue flowers in terminal spikes and in each leaf axil. This cool-colored biennial blooms in late spring or mid-summer depending on its location. Although it is not perennial, it self-seeds at a satisfying rate, guaranteeing plants in future years.

Campanula means "looks like a small bell," but this flower does not have the bell shape of true campanulas.

Native Americans used concoctions of the leaves and roots to treat coughs.

FLOWERS: The flowers start opening at the bottom of the flower raceme. These buds look pleated right before the 5 petals spread open. Each perfect, regular flower has 5 sepals, 5 blue petals, and 5 off-white stamens. The violet pistil extends an inch from the base of the flower. As the flower matures, the end of the style splits into 3 parts, each of which curls backwards. The wavy petals join where they are clasped by the calyx (sepals). At this juncture the petals have a line of white which creates a pentagon in the center of the flower face.

BLOOMS: 3-4 weeks between June and September

LEAVES: The angled, green to slightly purplish stem has widely spaced branches in the upper two-thirds of the plant. The stem may be smooth or slightly pubescent. The leaves are lightly pubescent. Bellflower has 2 distinct types of leaves. First-year leaves are heart-shaped with a point, much like a non-waxy violet leaf. They are 1-1.5″ long, 1″ wide, and have a long petiole, which forms a dark green basal rosette. Second-year leaves on the elongating stem are alternate, simple, petiolate, serrate, elliptical lanceolate, and taper to a point. They are medium-green, visibly veined, and 1-3.5″ long by 0.25-1″ wide.

UNDERGROUND STRUCTURES: American bellflower has a weak taproot.

SEEDS: Tan capsules contain numerous small, shiny, brown, ellipsoid seeds. The papery, angled capsules are 3/8″ long and have pores near their apex. The seeds mature within a month after bloom. Seeds are available for collection for 2 months, because the fruit develops over time from the bottom of the stem up, the same order in which the flowers open.

HEIGHT: 2–5′

HABITAT: Rich woodland edges, river and stream banks

CULTURAL TIPS (see page 62): Plant height varies with the amount of light. Plants in partial sun stay shorter than plants in the shade. They do well in the woodland garden or rock garden. American bellflower occurs naturally on basic soils but tolerates acidic soils.

MOISTURE: Average to dry

pH: 5–7

EXPOSURE: Partial sun

PROPAGATION (see page 66): Seed is the only method. Start seeds in October or November, and the plant acts like an annual, blooming the following spring.

SEED STORAGE: Store dry seeds in an airtight container between 40° and 70°.

SEED TREATMENT: Stratify at 40° for 1 month. Barely cover the seeds (light requirement), and then place in 70°. Germinate in 2 weeks; will also germinate at lower temperatures but more slowly. If you stratify outside, watch for germination during winter. Year-old seeds that have been stored dry have higher germination rates than first-year seeds.

CUTTINGS: No

DIVISION: No

FAUNA: Bumblebees visit American bellflower, and deer may nibble on the leaves.

Cut-Leaf Toothwort,
Pepper Root
Cardamine concatenata (Dentaria laciniata)
Brassicaceae (Cruciferae), (Mustard Family)

As winter winds to a close, I eagerly await the reappearance of the toothworts. They are ephemeral (come and go in a few months) but, oh, the beauty of clusters of pinkish-white bells in the fresh light of spring. When their season is over and they have thrown their seeds about, they have the grace to go dormant quickly. The foliage looks tan and forlorn for a very few days and, poof, it is gone.

Cardamine comes from the Greek, *kardamon,* which was the name of a cress that reputedly strengthened the heart. *Laciniata* means cut leaves. Some taxonomic authorities prefer the genus name *Dentaria* to *Cardamine. Dentaria* refers to the canine tooth-shape of the roots of some species.

The Iroquois used a poultice of the root to treat headaches. They also used it for divination, as a hunting medicine (roots rubbed on traps and lines), and as a love medicine (root or plant carried in pocket or mouth).

The tubers of toothworts have a pungent, peppery taste and can be ground and mixed with vinegar to produce a condiment similar to horseradish.

FLOWER: The inflorescence is a loose raceme of white (may be a tinge of pink) flowers. Each perfect, regular, tubular flower has 4 petals, 4 sepals, and 6 yellow stamens.

BLOOMS: 3 weeks between March and May

LEAVES: The upright, smooth stem usually has 3 leaves. The petiolate, dark green leaves may be basal or nearly opposite. They are ter-nately or palmately dissected, and the narrow, lanceolate segments are toothed.

UNDERGROUND STRUCTURES: The slender tubers are cream-colored and jointed.

SEEDS: The brown, oval seeds form 2 lines in the 1-1.5″ long, linear, 2-chambered seed pod. The pod points upward and dehisces with an elastic snap, flinging the seeds a good distance. The seeds ripen about 4–5 weeks after flowering.

HEIGHT: 8–15″

HABITAT: Rich, damp woods and slopes

CULTURAL TIPS (see page 62)**:** Although toothwort occurs naturally in moist soil, it is drought tolerant during its dormant period. It is best not to test its tolerance and to improve the soil with plenty of organic material, which will retain moisture without rotting the root. Do not move this plant in spring. The entire stem snaps off at the root in a second. Mark the patch for fall division. It self-seeds admirably.

MOISTURE: Moist, especially in winter and spring

pH: 5–6.5

EXPOSURE: Shade of deciduous woodlands

PROPAGATION (see page 66)**:** Tuber division is the easiest. Each piece will produce a plant.

SEED STORAGE: Store seed temporarily in moist spaghnum at 40˚.

SEED TREATMENT: Sow fresh into an outdoor seed bed; germination is poor in sterile media. Expect flowers in 3–4 years.

CUTTINGS: No

DIVISION: Fall and winter

FAUNA: The toothworts are host plants for the falcate orange-tip butterfly, a small, white butterfly that appears very early in spring. Only the male has the orange patch on the tip of the forewings. The egg is a green-yellow to orange, segmented oblong. The caterpillar is green with white side-stripes and an orange back stripe. The chrysalis looks like a green thorn on the supporting plant stem. Falcate orange-tips live in woodlands; development can threaten their numbers.

OTHER SE SPECIES: (One of the trade-offs for all the bother of moving to a new part of the country is being able to grow plants that wouldn't thrive in the old location. I'm crazy about the green-in-winter *Cardamine diphylla*, a pest in some folks' gardens, if you can believe it, and *Cardamine douglassii*, a knockout species with especially pink flowers and especially large flower clusters and blue-green foliage.)
   Cardamine bulbosa (springcress)—The flowers are white, and the simple leaves are elliptical to roundish. It has tubers. Pull on your Wellingtons to get a close look at this cress. It inhabits alluvial woods, marshes, and wet ditches. The leaves and roots are edible.
   C. diphylla (crinkleroot)—This white-flowered species is only 3-15″ tall and makes a good winter groundcover in the South. It has 2 opposite, toothed, 3-part leaves and a brittle, white rootstock that creeps and branches to form colonies. It is edible after anaerobic fermentation for 4–5 days.
   C. douglassii—The flowers are pink. The stem leaves are dentate but not divided. The thick, bluish basal leaves are wavy-round. It has tubers. It is called mountain watercress, but it is very happy in Birmingham.

FAIRY WAND,
DEVIL'S BIT
Chamaelirium luteum
Liliaceae (Lily Family)

Fairy wand, or devil's bit, is an infrequent but unforgettable inhabitant of moist woodlands. The white spires are beacons that attract the eye. Male plants have a longer raceme than female flowers, and male flowers appear slightly off-white due to the presence of yellow stamens. Initially erect, the raceme elongates and assumes unpredictable curves over time.

The genus name, *Chamaelirium,* comes from the Greek *chamai,* meaning "on the ground" and leirion, meaning lily. The term *luteum,* refers to the yellowish color of the flowers of a dry, pressed specimen.

Legend holds that the devil bit a large piece of the fleshy rhizome from the plant to deprive man of its beneficial uses in treating gastrointestinal and gynecologic ailments.

FLOWER: Multiple small, white regular flowers mass on a 3–9″ spike. They are dioecious, which means individual plants are male or female. Plants of each sex must be in reasonably close proximity for the plant to produce fertile seeds.

BLOOMS: 4–6 weeks from March to May

LEAVES: The smooth, simple stems are round in cross section. The true green, smooth, spatulate basal leaves form a rosette. These leaves turn red and persist all winter in areas where the ground rarely freezes. The stem bears a few much smaller lanceolate leaves, more on female plants than on male plants.

UNDERGROUND STRUCTURES: The roots are fleshy. With age, the plant slowly develops rhizomes.

SEEDS: Seeds ripen over many months and are not ready for collection until mid-October or November. The capsules turn tan and begin to split when the seeds are mature.

HEIGHT: 1–3′

HABITAT: Moist, rich woods and bogs

CULTURAL TIPS (see page 62)**:** Enrich the soil with copious amounts of humus and bits of gravel.

MOISTURE: Moist to wet; tolerant of periods of drought

pH: 5.5–6.5

EXPOSURE: Shade or partial shade, depending on moisture

PROPAGATION (see page 66): Seed propagation is the most efficient method by which to produce large numbers of plants.

SEED STORAGE: Store these long-lasting, dry seeds in an airtight container between 40° and 70°.

SEED TREATMENT: Stratify at 40° for 1 month. Sow at 70°, covering the seed to its depth. Germinate within 1 month. Leave young seedlings in clumps when potting. Separate clumps after 6 months. Pot or plant. Bloom in 3 years.

CUTTINGS: No

DIVISION: Early spring or fall; not necessary for the health of the plant

FAUNA: Await observation

GREEN AND GOLD
Chrysoganum virginianum
Asteraceae (Aster or Sunflower Family)

Green and gold is a low-growing, semi-evergreen ground cover that sports an abundance of quarter-size blooms in early spring. It is a good example of a plant that may be uncommon or rare in the wild but that is seen frequently in gardens. It spreads rapidly and is easy to propagate so it is readily available commercially, by mail order if not in a local nursery. Gardening friends share the bounty of this healthy, but never thuggish, star of the woodland edge.

The Greek word *chrysos* means golden, and *gonu* means a knee or joint. The flower stalks emerge from a pair of leaves at a stem node.

FLOWER: Regular, 1–1.5″ gold discs nestle among furry leaf rosettes early in spring. As the season progresses, the flower stalk lengthens, and flowers rise above the leaves. The ray flowers are fertile, and the disc flowers are sterile. There are usually 5 notched rays. The gold of the central disc flowers is richer than the color of the ray flowers, and they have an additional color dot of dark stamens.

BLOOMS: 6–8 weeks between March and June (Good selections bloom on and off through the summer and fall, especially farther north.)

LEAVES: The opposite, hairy, toothed, ovate leaves are 1-3″ long with a petiole that lengthens from 1–4″ through the seasons. Var. *australe* is stoloniferous and forms mats. Var. *virginianum* (a more northerly plant) has a few upright stems and is clump-forming and more floriferous.

UNDERGROUND STRUCTURES: Fibrous roots fan from the base of each plant in the colony. Wherever a runner touches the ground at a leaf node, new roots form.

SEEDS: The dark brown, pubescent, oval seeds ripen 2–3 weeks after the bloom fades. Under a hand lens, a seed looks like a tiny keeled boat. Each ray flower produces 1 seed, so 1 head can produce only 5 seeds in the best of circumstances. Seeds are ripe from May through September.

HEIGHT: 3–12″ with a 12″ spread

HABITAT: Rocky, open woodlands

CULTURAL TIPS (see page 62)**:** Plant on a slope. Improve the soil with humus for any type of soil. Cut clay with small gravel. Do not mulch heavily and never cover the furry stems and leaves with mulch unless using removable pine boughs for protection during extreme temperature slides. In the Deep South, this plant is susceptible to mildew and fungal diseases, especially southern blight *(Sclerotium rolfsii)*. Good drainage and spare mulching should prevent problems. Local ecotypes are less likely to have disease problems. Green and gold self-seeds readily in gravel mulch.

MOISTURE: Adequate moisture with excellent drainage is essential for plants in the ground, in pots, or for cuttings.

pH: 5–6

EXPOSURE: Morning sun to filtered light; needs more shade farther south

PROPAGATION (see page 66)**:** Division is easiest.

SEED STORAGE: Store dry seeds in an airtight container between 40° and 70°.

SEED TREATMENT: Cold-stratify at 40° for 6 weeks (refrigerator okay). Sow at 70°.

CUTTINGS (mallet)**:** May through September, roots in 4–6 weeks

DIVISION: Early spring or fall; separate rosettes

FAUNA: Small flies pollinate green and gold.

Spring Beauty,
Wild Potato
Claytonia virginica
Portulacaceae (Purslane Family)

When it seems that winter will never end, we are nudged from our doldrums by the cheery pink and white blooms of spring beauty. Masses of small, star-like blooms nestle in tufts of grass-like foliage. Light kisses these faces open each day. Once we have been escorted safely from the season of darkness, spring beauty goes completely dormant until the next year, when its emergence reminds us that rebirth hastens.

The genus name *Claytonia* honors John Clayton of Virginia (1694–1773). He botanized in the state of Virginia for fifty-one years and sent specimens of plants to Johann Friedrich Gronovius, who organized the information and published it in the *Flora Virginica.*

"Wild potato" can be eaten after it is boiled 10–15 minutes. But each "potato" is about 1/4″ in diameter, so the quantity needed for a meal would require hours of collection and preparation.

FLOWER: 1 mature corm gives rise to several flowering stems. Each individual, regular, perfect flower has 5 petals, which are white or pink and streaked with pink veins. The flower has 2 sepals and 5 stamens with pink pollen. Each flower has a stalk, and 6–20 flowers form a raceme. The stamen emerges on day 1, and the pistil on days 2-10, which assures that the flower will be cross-pollinated.

BLOOMS: 3 months from February to May

LEAVES: Each bloom stalk has a pair of smooth, opposite, linear to lanceolate leaves. The leaves emerge as early as November but are often overlooked because they are maroon during most of the winter and turn green with the added light of longer days, warmer weather, and resumption of growth.

UNDERGROUND STRUCTURES: The feeder roots from the round corms are as long as the leaves and flowers are tall.

SEEDS: 6 round, flat seeds fill the 1-chambered, ovoid capsule. The seeds are the size of a deer tick; they are black, lustrous (as ebony), and have a small white aril. Seeds that look like amber may not be ripe. The seeds fall before the stems lie flat and "melt."

HEIGHT: 5–12″

HABITAT: Rich, moist woodlands; roadsides and lawns

CULTURAL TIPS (see page 62)**:** Spring beauty is ephemeral (goes dormant after seeding) so it leaves a void in a planned design. Interplant with other wildflowers and ferns. It self-seeds readily but neither shades out other neighbors nor loses to competition easily.

MOISTURE: Average to copious amount of water in spring; when dormant, it can tolerate drier conditions.

pH: 5–7

EXPOSURE: Shade of deciduous trees (full sun during bloom period)

PROPAGATION (see page 66)**:** Division is easiest.

SEED STORAGE: Store temporarily in moist spaghnum at 40°.

SEED TREATMENT: Sow fresh at 70° for 3 or more months. Switch to 40°. Germinate in 6–7 weeks.

CUTTINGS: No

DIVISION: Divide corms while the plants are dormant. Replant 1–2″ deep.

FAUNA: A small, ground-nesting bee *(Andrena erigeniae)* collects the pollen of spring beauty to feed to its larvae. It visits several flowers as it harvests, and in the process carries pollen from one flower to another. Other insects, including a long-tongued bee fly, also visit the flowers and transfer pollen.

Mouse-eared Coreopsis,
Dwarf Coreopsis
Coreopsis auriculata
Asteraceae (Aster or Sunflower Family)

If you find a short coreopsis blooming in early spring in a moist, shady spot, it is probably *Coreopsis auriculata*. Usually, coreopsis bloom in late spring or summer in sunny, open areas. This spring bloomer is a rebel sibling. Its strong gold-yellow color is a welcome spot of light in the dark environs it frequents.

Coreopsis literally means "resembling a bug." The reference is to the seeds of coreopsis plants. *Koris* is the Greek root word for bug and *-opsis* means "looks like." *Auricula* means ear in Latin.

FLOWER: The inflorescence has 1–5 flat, round, flowering heads, each of which is 1–1.5″ across. The leafless flower stalk (peduncle) rises 6–18″ above the rosettes of basal leaves. Both the outer ray flowers, or "petals," and the inner, fertile disc flowers are gold-yellow. The ray flowers are neutral (no functional stamens or pistils). The rays are toothed on the outer edges.

BLOOMS: 6 to 8 weeks between April and June

LEAVES: The 4–20″ stems can be hairy or smooth. Most of the leaves are at the base of the plant and form rosettes. Many stolons or runners extend in pinwheel fashion from each mother plant and produce baby plants. The 1–2″ petiolate leaves are furry and oval-shaped, with some small lateral lobes or auricles at the base. Due to its stoloniferous nature, eared coreopsis produces a solid groundcover. The foliage persists in winter in mild areas.

UNDERGROUND STRUCTURES: Many white-to-tan feeder roots descend from the base of each established leaf rosette.

SEEDS: The smooth, black seeds are elongated ovals, about the size of dill seeds. They have narrow wings. Seeds are ripe about 4 weeks after the flowers wither, sometime between May and July.

HEIGHT: 10–12″

HABITAT: Rich, moist woodlands and woodland edges

CULTURAL TIPS (see page 62)**:** Afternoon sun and dry soil cause a patch of dwarf coreopsis to shrivel and die in short order. Enrich the planting bed with copious amounts of humus.

MOISTURE: Requires consistent moisture supply; tolerates wet conditions in spring

pH: 5–6

EXPOSURE: Filtered light or morning light with afternoon shade

PROPAGATION (see pages 66)**:** All methods are successful.

SEED STORAGE: Store dry seeds in an airtight container between 40° and 70°.

SEED TREATMENT: Sow at 70°. Cover lightly. Germinate in 20–30 days.

CUTTINGS (root)**:** In February or March in a hot greenhouse, cut the bottom plaque of roots off a potbound rootball. Slice the plaque in quarters and invert each piece on the top of a pot full of potting soil. Cover lightly with soil and place in 50 percent light. New leaves appear in 6 weeks.

DIVISION: Separate offsets any time of year.

FAUNA: Butterflies visit coreopsis for nectar.

WHORLED COREOPSIS,
WHORLED TICKSEED
Coreopsis major
Asteraceae (Aster or Sunflower Family)

Coreopsis major is a common denizen of thin woods and woodland edges. Like all coreopsis, it has a long period of bloom. This
species is rarely found in home gardens and deserves attention.
It adapts well to many types of soil and exposure and is easy to
propagate from seed. The seeds resemble flat, brown ticks if the
ticks were stretched on a rack and had all their legs pulled off.

FLOWER: Multiple gold-yellow "flowers" float in a loose corymb.
Many small true flowers comprise the flower head. The outer ring
of flowers (the ray flowers) are yellow. The inner mass of flowers
(or disc flowers) are yellow or red. The ray flowers that we recognize as petals are female. The inner, disc flowers are perfect (male
and female parts). The combined ray and disc flowers form a symmetrical flower head that is a flat landing platform for butterflies.

LEAVES: Our eyes see 6 thin, lanceolate, dark green leaves arranged in
a whorl. In botanical reality, this coreopsis has opposite pairs of sessile leaves that are so deeply cut they resemble whorled leaves. The
paired leaves are spaced about 4″ apart on the stem, giving the plant
an airy effect. A mature plant with 5 stems maintains an upright,
open silhouette. The entire plant—stem, leaves, and seed heads—
turns black after the first frost, accenting the winter landscape.

HEIGHT: 2–3′

HABITAT: Dry or moist woodlands, thickets, and old fields

UNDERGROUND STRUCTURES: Long, slender rhizomes support the graceful stems.

SEEDS: The seeds are dark brown to black, shiny and oblong, about the size of dill seeds. They have no spines to grab clothing like the beggar ticks' seeds. The seeds begin to ripen in late August. The bracts blacken and hold the seeds in a tight, upright clump well into winter.

CULTURAL TIPS (see page 62)**:** Pampering not needed here. The height remains 2–3′ whether planted in sun or high shade. Provide good drainage.

MOISTURE: Average to dry; drought-tolerant

pH: 5–6.5

EXPOSURE: Filtered light to full sun

PROPAGATION (see page 66)**:** Seeds and cuttings are easiest.

SEED STORAGE: Store dry seeds in an airtight container between 40° and 70°.

SEED TREATMENT: Collect from September through February. Vernalize 6 months. Cover lightly. Germinate in 2–3 weeks when the temperatures are 70° (day) and 50° (night). They would probably germinate more quickly with temperatures in the 70–90° range.

CUTTINGS (stem)**:** Spring; root in 6 weeks

DIVISION: Divide mature plants in late fall.

FAUNA: Butterflies visit coreopsis for nectar, and finches and sparrows eat the seeds.

STAR TICKSEED
Coreopsis pubescens
Asteraceae (Aster or Sunflower Family)

Coreopsis pubescens is found throughout the Southeast in a wide range of sites, sunny or shady, moist or dry. It blooms like an annual from May to October and is evergreen in a normal winter. Because it has no rhizomes, it is a good neighbor with other plants. The highly floriferous clump requires no staking. Seeds germinate rapidly and produce a blooming plant in 3 months. To my knowledge, this plant is not available in the commercial trade. It should be!

FLOWER: The 1.5″ gold-yellow blossom has both disc and ray flowers. Both types of flowers are yellow. Each tiny disc flower has 5 lobes and 5 stamens, which, along with the non-rhizomatous nature of the plant, is the easiest way to identify the species. The disc flowers are perfect. The ray flowers have only pistils. The flowering stems are leafy; blossoms emerge from leaf nodes on leafless peduncles (stalks), which elongate as the buds open. Plants are covered with flowers and seed at the same time.

BLOOMS: May through October

LEAVES: Individual 1-1.5″ long leaves are simple, entire, elliptical, opposite, and may have 1–2 small basal divisions. These leaflets are identical in shape to the main leaf, just smaller. They make the leaf look compound but they are not on every leaf. Most leaves have short petioles. The species has at least two varieties: *C. pubescens* var. *pubescens,* with soft, hairy foliage; and *C. pubescens* var. *robusta,* with entirely smooth foliage and slightly more lanceolate leaves.

HEIGHT: 18″–3′

HABITAT: Roadsides, meadows, woodlands, gravelly or sandy stream banks and beds, alluvial thickets, and cliffs

UNDERGROUND STRUCTURES: Star tickseed has a fibrous, rooted crown.

SEEDS: The seeds are dark brown achenes. Under magnification, you can see bumps on the bodies of the seeds and a pair of thin, pale, spreading wings. Seeds can be collected almost any time of year, because the receptacle holds some seeds even through the winter. Seeds have been collected on plants in the Black Belt Prairie Region of Alabama at the end of May. They had been on the plant since the previous year.

CULTURAL TIPS: (see page 62): If planted in a continuously damp site, add lots of sand or gravel to the soil. Shearing makes the plants bushier but it is not necessary. Dead-heading prolongs bloom.

MOISTURE: Moist (with drainage) to dry

pH: 5–6.5

EXPOSURE: Sun to light-shade

PROPAGATION (see page 66): Seed; quick and easy

SEED STORAGE: Store dry seeds in an airtight container between 40° and 70°.

SEED TREATMENT: Sow at 70°–80°. Germinate in 11 days and ready to plant or sell in 10 weeks.

CUTTINGS (stem): Spring

DIVISION: Spring or fall

FAUNA: The open face of the coreopsis bloom is a perfect landing platform for butterflies. They can perch and sip nectar from many flowers on each blossom.

OTHER SE SPECIES:
C. tripteris—This is the only other coreopsis with 5 lobes and 5 stamens on the disc flower, but this species has rhizomes and is much taller, up to 6′. It is usually smooth and blooms for 3–4 weeks in late summer. The petioled leaves have 3–5 linear blades. It is found in moist, low places and in woodlands.

PRAIRIE LARKSPUR,
CAROLINA LARKSPUR, BLUE LARKSPUR
Delphinium carolinianum
Ranunculaceae (Crowfoot Family)

The garden delphiniums of Impressionist paintings wilt and sicken in the heat and humidity of the South, but we have our own home-grown varieties that thrive in various habitats. The one that has the widest range is *Delphinium carolinianum,* the prairie delphinium. It survives in exposed sites even along interstate highways. The luscious deep-blue blooms look like they have been dipped in sugar.

The genus name *Delphinium* comes from the Greek, *delphi,* meaning dolphin. When in bud, the spurred flower resembles a dolphin. Consider all species poisonous.

FLOWER: The 1″ perfect, spurred flowers are bright blue or violet, occasionally lavender. Multiple-stalked flowers form a narrow raceme. The spur on this species curves upward. The visible outer spur is a sepal. Within it are 2 nectar-bearing petal spurs.

BLOOMS: 3–4 weeks from April to July

LEAVES: The slender stem is hairy below the inflorescence. The alternate, 3″ wide leaves are deeply cut into linear segments.

UNDERGROUND STRUCTURES: The roots are long and firm.

SEEDS: The 3 chambers of the seed pod are erect and parallel. Each follicle ends in a sharp point. At maturity, they split apart to release the scaly, brown, winged seeds.

HEIGHT: 2–2.5′

HABITAT: Cherty limestone glades, prairies, and rocky or sandy openings in woods.

CULTURAL TIPS (see page 62)**:** Difficult in cultivation unless you happen to have a limestone outcrop or chalk prairie for your garden site.

MOISTURE: Dry

pH: 6–7

EXPOSURE: Full sun (at least 6 hours)

PROPAGATION (see page 66)**:** Seed is best.

SEED STORAGE: Store dry seeds in an airtight container at 70°.

SEED TREATMENT: Stratify at 70° for 3 months. Switch to 40° for 3 months. Switch to 70° dark. If using a layer of newspapers to create the darkness, check for germination each day after the first week and remove the paper layer as soon as germination begins.

CUTTINGS (basal stem)**:** Early spring

DIVISION (unlikely)**:** Early spring

FAUNA: Bees pollinate delphinium.

OTHER SE SPECIES:

 D. exaltatum (tall larkspur)—Like prairie larkspur, this rare species has an erect fruit follicle but is much taller (2–6′). The stem is smooth. The seeds are rough, and it blooms in the summer in openings or edges of rich woodlands.

 D. tricorne (dwarf larkspur)—Tricorne means 3-horned. The 3 chambers of the seed pod splay open and readily drop the smooth seed. It is 8–24″ tall, has fine hairs on the stem, thick roots, and flowers in the spring. Dwarf larkspur likes a calcareous soil with a pH of 6–7. Seeds germinate very slowly with alternating temperatures over many years.

SHOOTING STAR
Dodecatheon media
Primulaceae (Primrose Family)

Shooting star is a most appropriate name for this striking spring flower. The clean white petals point backward, completely exposing the stamens. Yellow anthers lead the trajectory of the star. Clusters of these pristine flowers dangle from an erect but gently arched flower stalk, emphasizing the cosmic effect.

Dodeka is the Greek root word for twelve. *Theos* is Greek for god. In Greek mythology, the primrose was under the care of twelve gods. The specific epithet, *media,* honors Richard Mead (1673–1754), an English physician who was a patron of botanist Mark Catesby.

FLOWER: Each regular, perfect flower has 5 pure white (rarely pink) petals united at the base at a burgundy ring. The petals are partially united and strongly reflexed. The reproductive parts form a cone tipped with yellow, pollen-encrusted anthers. A small flare of yellow behind the burgundy ring repeats the pollen color and gives the effect of movement.

BLOOMS: 6 weeks from February to May

LEAVES: The simple, lanceolate, smooth, 4–10″ leaves form a basal rosette. They have the pale green color and the watery texture of flat leaf lettuce. The petiole (leaf stalk) is winged.

UNDERGROUND STRUCTURES: The crown and roots of shooting star are white and succulent. It looks like a small octopus.

SEEDS: The 1/3″ ovoid capsule turns from green to brown, and then splits at the upper end. The minute, dry, brown seeds fall from the capsule slowly, because the capsule is upright and only spills bits of seeds when the wind blows and tips the container.

HEIGHT: 12–18″

HABITAT: Rich, moist, wooded slopes; wet meadows

CULTURAL TIPS (see page 62)**:** Rodents love them. Add starter chicken grit (small granite gravel) to the soil if underground rodents are a problem in your area. The warmer the climate and the sunnier the exposure, the more moisture this plant requires. Moisture is most important in spring. In mid-summer, the plant goes dormant.

MOISTURE: Moist with drainage

pH: 5–7

EXPOSURE: Light shade

PROPAGATION (see page 66)**:** Easy from seed or root cuttings.

SEED STORAGE: On collection, seeds may have some white, dusty material on them. Not to worry—it does not affect germination. Dry seeds store well in an airtight container at 40° to 70°.

SEED TREATMENT: Can cold-stratify at 40° for 3 months in the refrigerator and sow at 70°. Germinate in 2–14 days. Stratification in an outdoor seed frame is preferable to greenhouse growing, because first-year plants have only 1–2 leaves and go dormant in 6 weeks. Bloom in 3–4 years.

CUTTINGS (root)**:** In fall, dig a mature plant, rinse, and lift upward on a "leg" (it should dehisce from the crown with a bud or swelling at the top of the leg). Line out in a cutting tray or plant 1/4″ deep in potting mix. Remove only half the roots from the donor plant and replant it.

DIVISION: Early spring or fall

FAUNA: *Dodecatheon* species produce no nectar, only pollen. Bees, particularly worker bumblebees, collect the pollen. They assume a stance over the exposed cone of anthers, which allows "buzz polli-nation." (Vibration from the thorax muscles of the bee causes pollen to be released from the tips of the anthers.)

PURPLE CONEFLOWER,
ECHINACEA, HEDGEHOG CONEFLOWER
Echinaceae purpurea
Asteraceae (Aster or Sunflower Family)

Purple coneflower is one of the most popularized species of native plants. Few people see it in a natural setting, but it is a common garden plant in sunny perennial gardens. Its fame is well deserved. The large flower heads attract butterflies as well as people, and bloom for 2 months. It cuts well for flower arranging. Finches fight over the seeds in the fall. Lastly, it is an economically important plant in the international pharmaceutical trade. All parts of the plant stimulate the immune system. Native Americans taught the many uses of echinacea to early settlers. Whether cold, flu, spider bite, arthritis, sores, ulcers, venereal disease, mumps, toothache, or any other disorder, echinacea helped. The whole chopped plant was added to the feed of ailing cattle and horses. Today it is available in many different preparations in grocery and drug stores.

The demand for echinacea led to irresponsible collection of the many species in the genus. Entire populations were decimated, especially in the Midwest. It can be and is grown as a crop. With luck, farmers will be able to meet the needs of drug companies.

The genus name comes from the Greek, *echinos,* or hedgehog. The seed platform is cone-shaped and has sharp, black spines.

Purpurea is Latin for purple, a rather misleading term, because most of the ray flowers of the Southeastern coneflowers are pink.

FLOWER: Each 2-3″ wide, long-stalked, terminal "flower" has 12–20 ray flowers and numerous disc flowers. The pink "petals," the ray flowers, are female, but do not produce seeds. The dark purple, perfect disc flowers hide beneath orange spikes (the receptacle bracts). The receptacle is flat at the time of bloom and becomes conical when in fruit. The species is lightly fragrant. Selected garden cultivars have lost the fragrance.

BLOOMS: 6 weeks from June through August

LEAVES: The coarse, hairy leaves are alternate, simple, stalked, ovate, and toothed.

UNDERGROUND STRUCTURES: In a mature plant, the off-white roots are thick and fibrous.

SEEDS: The tan, quadrangular nutlets (achenes) are fat when fertile. Many seeds on a head may be infertile. Seeds are ripe in August and September.

HEIGHT: 1–4′

HABITAT: Prairies, rocky glades, and woodland edges

CULTURAL TIPS (see page 62)**:** Purple coneflower tolerates almost any site except underwater. Ensure drainage in moist sites.

MOISTURE: Dry to slightly moist

pH: 5.5–7

EXPOSURE: Sun to light shade

PROPAGATION (see page 66)**:** Seed is easiest.

SEED STORAGE: Store dry seeds in an airtight container between 40° and 70°.

SEED TREATMENT: Allow seeds to stay on the plant until they begin to loosen from the receptacle. Otherwise, they are difficult to remove from the spiny seed head even with the use of leather gloves and pliers. Stratify at 40° for 3 weeks; sow at 70°. Germinate in 9 days.

CUTTINGS (root)**:** Late winter; maintain polarity

DIVISION: Spring or fall

FAUNA: Coneflowers offer the landing platform butterflies favor. After the nectar is long gone, the seeds feed various finches in the fall.

OTHER SE SPECIES:
 Echinaceae laevigatae—This species is similar to *E. purpurea*, but it has smooth foliage and long ray petals. It blooms from April through June.
 E. pallida (pale purple coneflower, droops)—This species has long, thin, recurved ray petals and a strong taproot. The leaves are narrow and mainly basal. It blooms for 4 weeks from April through June.

DAISY FLEABANE
Erigeron philadelphicus
Asteraceae (Aster or Sunflower Family)

Daisy fleabane is a showy, long-blooming, short-lived perennial for roadside planting; it is an absolute pest in a planned perennial bed. When it gets started in the wrong place, it fits my definition of a weed, "any plant where you do not want it." The overall appearance of the plant is rather tough, but that toughness is what makes the plant so tolerant of the blazing heat of a roadside.

One might have difficulty telling a fleabane from an aster because they both have many fairly small flower heads with white, blue, or violet rays, and they both have alternate leaves. The season of bloom helps separate the asters and fleabanes. Asters bloom in late summer and fall, much later than the spring blooming fleabanes.

The genus name, *Erigeron,* derives from the Greek, *eri,* for "early," and *geron,* for "old man," referring to the hoary or white-haired appearance of the fluffy seed head. Fleabane literally means to keep away fleas.

Native Americans used a tea made from the root or whole plant of *Erigeron philadelphicus* to treat hemorrhages, kidney stones, coughs, headaches, and dim eyesight. The crushed plant causes dermatitis in some people.

FLOWER: The ¹/₂–1″, regular flower heads have both disc flowers and ray flowers. The tubular, perfect disc flowers are yellow, and the female ray flowers are pinkish-white. Both types of flower are fertile. The drooping buds are pink, and the rays become paler or white as the flower opens. This species has about 100 ray flowers. The 1–3′ bloom stalk is erect, hollow, corymbosely branched, and hairy. The flowers begin to bloom when the stalk is 3–4″ tall and continue opening as the stalk elongates.

BLOOMS: 4–5 weeks between March and June

LEAVES: The upright stems have alternate leaves that are dentate (coarsely toothed). The teeth are roundly pointed and angle forward. The 1–5″ basal leaves are spoon-shaped. The stem leaves clasp the stem.

UNDERGROUND STRUCTURES: Each plant has feeder roots and stolons that look like angel-hair pasta.

SEEDS: The greenish-tan, triangular, ribbed seeds can be lifted from the receptacle by pulling on the fuzzy pappus. They ripen within 2–3 weeks after the bloom period.

HEIGHT: 1–3′

HABITAT: Meadows, lawns, roadsides, or any disturbed site, including your garden

CULTURAL TIPS (see page 62)**:** This is an invasive plant difficult to remove due to the ability of the roots and stolons to form new plants.

MOISTURE: Moist or dry

pH: 4.5–6.5

EXPOSURE: Sun or light shade

PROPAGATION (see page 66)**:** Seed is easy.

SEED STORAGE: Store dry seeds in an airtight container between 40° and 70°.

SEED TREATMENT: Sow at 60°–70°. Fresh seeds germinate in 7–10 days. Older, stored seeds germinate in 3–4 weeks with lower germination rates.

CUTTINGS (stem)**:** New shoots in early spring before the stem becomes hollow

DIVISION: Right after bloom

FAUNA: Fleabane is the source of nectar for a wide variety of butterflies and the host for the lynx flower moth.

OTHER SE SPECIES:

Erigeron pulchellus (Robin's plantain)—This species is a 1–2′ hairy perennial and has a simple flower stalk and a larger flower than *E. philadelphicus.* The furry, serrate leaves form basal rosettes. It is stoloniferous, but less aggressive than *E. philadelphicus*, and is the best candidate for a small garden. *E. pulchellus* tolerates some traffic and forms a dark green, semi-evergreen groundcover. A cultivar called 'Meadow Muffin' has dark green, wavy leaves and short flower stalks.

E. strigosus—This annual species is similar in appearance to *E. philadelphicus* but is less hairy. It has narrow, non-clasping stem leaves.

RATTLESNAKE MASTER,
BUTTON SNAKEROOT
Eryngium yuccifolium
Apiaceae (Parsley Family)

This is the only genus of the parsley family that does not have an umbel-shaped bloom. The unusual spiked balls on 4′ stems give this plant an other-worldly look. When fresh, the flower heads are greenish-white, almost silver. With age, they become a dusty brown. Rattlesnake master may not fit the traditional image of a flower, but it is one tough plant and has had many medicinal uses over the ages.

Eryngus is a Greek root word meaning thistle, probably referring to the spiked balls of the inflorescence and the flexible spines on the leaf edges. *Yuccifolium* means "looks like a yucca."

Native Americans used preparations of the root to treat rattlesnake bites, whooping cough, kidney ailments, toothache, neuralgia, and rheumatism. They drank infusions of the root in preparation for war and in ceremonies involving the rattlesnake. Folk medicine continued these uses and added treatments for gynecologic problems and venereal diseases. As with so many plants, vomiting results from a large dose.

FLOWER: The erect stem branches at the top, displaying 5–30 greenish-white, spiked globes. Many perfect, regular flowers comprise each round head. Each 5-petaled flower has a bractlet beneath it, which creates the spiky look. Pointed bracts form a skirt beneath the head.

BLOOMS: 4 weeks between June and August. The bloom heads and seed heads are similar, so the period of bloom seems to last for months.

LEAVES: The 4′ tall, stiff stem has a few reduced, clasping leaves. Most of the leaves are at the base of the plant. They can be 2′ long. These leathery, medium-green leaves are linear, alternate, and parallel veined. Along the edges of the leaves are soft, white bristles every $1/2″$.

UNDERGROUND STRUCTURES: The aromatic taproot is white inside and heavily fibrous. The root smells like cilantro.

SEEDS: Each small flower produces 2 scaly fruits, which are lightly joined. Each one of them contains 1 seed about $1/4″$ long. The seeds are ripe in September and October.

HEIGHT: 2–4′

HABITAT: Edges of pine woodlands, woods, prairies, and roadsides

CULTURAL TIPS (see page 62)**:** The epitome of the "no care" plant

MOISTURE: Dry to average, or moist with good drainage

pH: 5–6

EXPOSURE: Partial to full sun

PROPAGATION (see page 66)**:** Seed is easy.

SEED STORAGE: Store dry seeds in an airtight container between 40° and 70°.

SEED TREATMENT: Stratify at 40° for 2 months; sow at 70°. Germinate in 1–2 weeks. Bloom the second year.

CUTTINGS (root, if taprooted)**:** March; maintain orientation of cuttings.

DIVISION: Possible in fall if plant has more than 1 rosette, but not recommended.

FAUNA: Many insects visit rattlesnake master, including shiny black wasps with white abdominal bands and white head slashes; also lilliputian bees.

OTHER SE SPECIES:

Eryngium aquaticum (eryngo)—This biennial or perennial has light-bluish silver flowers. The glaucous, oblanceolate leaves are more than 4″ long. They are pinnately veined and have wavy margins. Eryngo blooms from June through October in fresh and brackish marshes, drainage ditches, and occasionally in wet pinelands.

E. integrifolium (eryngo)—This species also has light blue flowers, but the leaves differ. They are less than 4″ long, smooth, elliptical, crenate, and net veined. It blooms from August to October in wet pinelands, meadows, and savannas.

E. prostratum (creeping eryngium)—This prostrate species has solitary pale to dark blue flowers in the leaf axils of simple, ovate leaves. It blooms from May to October in low meadows; moist, sandy ditches; and along pond and lake margins.

TROUT LILY
Erythronium spp.
Liliaceae (Lily Family)

Flood plains throughout the East Coast sprout a coat of glossy, speckled leaves in early spring. In a week or two, small lilies nod above the lawn of mottled leaves. When the sun shines, the buds open and glow yellow or white in response. Once the trees develop a canopy of leafy shade, the ephemeral lilies decline and disappear until time for the spring show the following year.

Native Americans drank a root tea to reduce fever, and applied a leaf poultice to skin ulcers and eruptions. The leaves and corms can be eaten after cooking but can cause vomiting.

FLOWER: Each flowering bulb produces a single, perfect, nodding flower. The 6 petals may flare or reflex (curve backward) at the tips. Two whorls of 6 stamens in colors such as cream, yellow, cinnamon, and violet add to the beauty of the bloom.

BLOOMS: 2–3 weeks between February and April. Blooms come and go in a 3-week period. Different species bloom sequentially: first, *E. umbilicatum,* then *E. albidum* and *E. rostratum,* and finally *E. americanum.* Some years, one jumps out of order just to keep you guessing. Nature abhors black-and-white thinking.

LEAVES: Each mature bulb produces 2 leaves and may have a small third leaf. The 2-3″ long, entire, lanceolate to elliptical leaf tapers to a petiole. Patches of green, brown, and purple speckle the smooth, green blade. The leaves may be in patches or colonies, depending on whether the species produces underground runners (stolons).

UNDERGROUND STRUCTURES: The bulb of trout lily is white inside, covered by a brown coat; 2–3 fleshy scales fuse together to form the narrow, ovoid bulb, which is pointed at the top and flat at the root end. The bulb shape is like that of a canine tooth, giving rise to the common name, "dog tooth violet." Some species have stolons *(E. americanum, E. rostratum,* and *E. umbilicatum* ssp. *monostolum).*

SEEDS: The softly triangular, obovoid capsule may be beaked, pointed, or indented. In late April or early May, it changes from green to yellowish and ejects many brown, crescent-shaped seeds that have a moist aril.

HEIGHT: 6–10″

HABITAT: Rich woods and bottomlands next to rivers and streams

CULTURAL TIPS (see page 62)**:** Do not try to transplant blooming-size bulbs of trout lily (except *E. umbilicatum* ssp. *umbilicatum,* a shallow-rooted clump former). As young bulbs grow to maturity, they bury themselves as much as 18″ in the earth. Efforts to dig those bulbs will just decapitate a nice plant. Dig small single-leaved bulbs and be patient for a year or two. You can enjoy the leaves while you await the reward of flowers. Trout lily needs plenty of water in the spring during active growth. The patch can dry somewhat in summer but should never become a dust bowl.

MOISTURE: Moist to average

pH: 5–6.5

EXPOSURE: Bright spring light of a deciduous woodland

PROPAGATION (see page 66)**:** Propagate this monocot by seed or division.

SEED STORAGE: Store temporarily in moist spaghnum at 40°.

SEED TREATMENT: Sow fresh. Begin stratification cycles at 70° for 3 months. Switch to 40°, then 70°, then 40°, then 70°, allowing 3 months in each stage. Bloom in 6–7 years.

CUTTINGS: No

DIVISION: Separate bulbs after the leaves go dormant (ideally in winter). To find the patch in winter, mark the site before the leaves disappear the previous spring.

FAUNA: Tiny flies visit the flowers and may act as pollinators.

OTHER SE SPECIES (Mathew, 1992; Parks & Hardin, 1963)**:**
    Erythronium albidum—White petals.
    E. americanum—Yellow reflexed petals (variable mottling); small auricle at base of petal; pollen yellow to brownish; many stolons; capsule held horizontally.
    ssp. *americanum*—Capsule round, truncate, or may end abruptly in a small pointed tip.
    ssp. *harperii*—Capsule ends abruptly in a small pointed tip.
    E. rostratum—Many more leaves than flowers; yellow petals (purplish or brown on backside); conspicuous auricle at base of petal; pollen always yellow; many stolons; beaked capsule held erect.
    E. umbilicatum—Yellow reflexed petals (variable mottling); pollen usually brown or purple; capsule indented and lies in leaf litter due to downward-arching fruit stalk.
    ssp. *umbilicatum*—No stolons.
    ssp. *monostolum*—1 stolon; fruiting stalk may hold capsule slightly off the ground.

WILD AGERATUM,
MIST FLOWER
Eupatorium coelestinum
Asteraceae
(Aster or Sunflower Family)

Have you ever whizzed by a moist ditch at 55 mph and wondered what that cloud of blue was? It was probably wild ageratum. When the first real heat of summer descends, the blossoms of the wild ageratum pop open; they continue to bloom for 6–8 weeks. The bloom period seems perfectly timed to meet the increasing nectar demand of the burgeoning butterfly population in summer.

Cono is Greek for "cone" and *clinium* means "slope (or bed)," referring to the receptacle for the flowers and seeds. *Coeles* is Latin for sky or heavens, referring to the blue color of the flowers.

FLOWER: The terminal, flat-topped corymbs of blue-to-lavender flower heads can be 3″ in diameter. On each conical receptacle rest 35–70 perfect, tubular disc flowers; 2 style branches extend beyond the end of the floral tube, giving the flower clusters a fuzzy look. This member of the aster family has no ray flowers.

BLOOMS: 6–8 weeks from June to October

STEM AND LEAVES: The medium-green, simple, round-toothed leaves are opposite on a square stem. They are lightly hairy. Each ovate leaf has a petiole about half as long as the leaf itself.

UNDERGROUND STRUCTURES: Aggressive rhizomatous roots quickly form a solid mat in moist soil.

SEEDS: The cylindrical, 5-ribbed, blackish nutlets have a short, whitish pappus.

HEIGHT: 1–3′

HABITAT: Woods, stream banks, meadows, borders, and fields throughout the Southeast

CULTURAL TIPS (see page 62): Mist flower is a good garden plant for a cool blue in mid-summer. It also cuts and dries well. But it is aggressive and should be given ample space. Fertilize with a balanced fertilizer in early spring to darken the green of the leaves. Too much fertilizer can cause lanky growth. Shearing encourages bushiness and new growth.

MOISTURE: Moist to wet; tolerates drought

pH: 5–6

EXPOSURE: Full to partial sun to high, filtered light

PROPAGATION (see page 66): All methods are quick and easy.

SEED STORAGE: Store dry seeds in an airtight container between 40° and 70°.

SEED TREATMENT: Stratify for 1 month at 40°; sow at 70°. Germinate in 1–2 weeks. Bloom that same year.

CUTTINGS (stem): May through July

DIVISION (rhizomes): Any time

FAUNA: Many butterflies seek nectar at wild ageratum.

JOE PYE WEED,
GRAVEL ROOT
Eupatorium fistulosum
Asteraceae (Aster or Sunflower Family)

At 6–10′, Joe Pye weed is hard to miss. It is a multi-stemmed perennial with dusty pink bloom heads clustered in a panicle as big as a bushel basket. The summer bloom period seems timed to the height of the butterfly season. Joe Pyes are sure to attract butterflies to your garden.

This is one of many *Eupatorium* species. Others are not as easy to recognize as the Joe Pye. The following identification guidelines help separate the *Eupatorium* species from other members of the aster family. First, they only have disc flowers. The seeds have a bristly pappus. There is no chaff among the flowers of each head. Beneath the receptacle of flowers are more than 4 bracts, which are in more than 1 row. The leaves are mainly on the stem. The stem and undersides of the leaves are not wooly-white. The flowers are perfect and fertile. Now we have arrived at the *Eupatorium* spp. They have 2 main leaf arrangements: whorled or opposite. This group, the Joe Pyes, have whorled leaves. White *Eupatorium* spp. with opposite leaves follow on later pages.

The genus name *Eupatorium* honors Mithridates Eupator, king of Parthia, 120–63 B.C. He was the first person reported to use a species of *Eupatorium* for medicinal purposes. *Fistula* is Latin for a pipe or tube, referring to the hollow stem.

The common name, Joe Pye, comes from two sources. Joe Pye was a medicine man (Native American or Caucasian), who used the root of one of the tall, pink, flowering *Eupatorium* spp. to bring about sweating to treat the fever of typhoid. In addition, the Indian word for typhoid, *jopi,* sounds phonetically like the name, Joe Pye.

Historical medicinal uses of Joe Pye weed are numerous. Teas made from the whole herb and the root relieved urinary tract problems. One common name for it is "little water medicine." Another name, gravel root, refers to the use of Joe Pye weed to treat kidney stones. Native American women drank an infusion of the root as a tonic during pregnancy. Various species were used to treat colds, aches, love problems, and crying children.

FLOWER: The large, convex, panicle-like flower heads are made up of many heads of perfect, pink disc flowers. Each head has 4–7 disc flowers with 5-lobed corollas.

BLOOMS: 6 weeks from July to October

LEAVES: The smooth, hollow stems become almost woody as they age. They support enormous weight when the leaves and blooms are wet, and they withstand wind and rain. The stems may be purple or green with purple spots. The 8-10″ long, toothed leaves are elliptical, lanceolate, entire, petiolate, and taper at both ends; 4–7 leaves form a whorl at a leaf node. The whorls are widely spaced so the plant has an architectural effect rather than a coarse massiveness.

UNDERGROUND STRUCTURES: Joe Pye forms a solid crown with large diameter, surprisingly brittle, feeder roots that counterbalance the imposing above-ground structure.

SEEDS: Clouds of purplish buff pappus float on the heads in the fall. Handfuls of ripe seeds can be plucked from the plant and placed in a collection bag or scattered in the wind. Seeds are ripe in September and October.

HEIGHT: 6–10′

HABITAT: Moist areas in sun or partial shade

CULTURAL TIPS (see page 62)**:** Joe Pye weed needs plenty of space and water. Add organic material to soil that is high in clay or sand.

MOISTURE: Moist to wet or average

pH: 4.5–6.5

EXPOSURE: Full sun to partial shade

PROPAGATION (see page 66)**:** Seedlings quickly outgrow a quart pot. Either plant in the fall or move up to a 2-gallon pot.

SEED STORAGE: Store dry seed in an airtight container between 40° and 70°.

SEED TREATMENT: Stratify for 1 month at 40°; sow heavily at 70°. Germinate in 1 week. Bloom the second year.

CUTTINGS (stem)**:** Firm terminal shoots in early June; roots form in 6 weeks.

DIVISION: Break open that can of spinach before digging a mature Joe Pye weed. Strong muscles are needed to dig and to chop apart the massive underground structure. Divide in early spring before bud break and keep a piece of root on each piece of crown.

FAUNA: Bees and butterflies and assorted other insects visit Joe Pye for nectar. Possible butterfly guests include:
Tiger swallowtail, great spangled fritillary, painted lady, viceroy, monarch, silver spotted skipper, leonard's skipper, little glassy wing, and southern golden skipper. Goldfinches love the seeds of Joe Pye weed.

OTHER SE SPECIES(with whorled leaves)**:**
Species with short leaves (less than 5″) that contract abruptly to the petiole:
Eupatorium dubium—This 3–5′ Joe Pye has short, thick, prominently 3-veined leaves. There are usually 6–9 flowers per head. It is found in acidic, moist to wet areas near the coast.
Species with long (can be more than 6″), evenly veined leaves that gradually narrow to the petiole:
E. maculatum—This species has convex corymbs with 9–22 flowers per head. It occurs in basic to neutral soils in moist woods or open areas.
E. purpureum—This species has convex corymbs with 4–7 flowers per head. The stem is solid or has a slim central pipe. The stem is purplish only at the leaf nodes. The crushed leaves are reputed to smell like vanilla. It is found in drier sites than *E. fistulosum*.

BONESET,
COMMON THOROUGHWORT,
AGUEWEED, FEVERWORT
Eupatorium perfoliatum
Asteraceae
(Aster or Sunflower Family)

Sorting out the white *Eupatorium*
species seems like a daunting task, but
they have distinguishing characteristics that make identification possible.
Of course they may hybridize and throw us a trick or two, but
we have to assume they generally mind their p's and q's. They tend
to be large (over 3'), coarse plants. Boneset is one of the best
known and easily identified species among the white species,
because the stem appears to perforate the paired and joined leaves.
The common name thoroughwort refers to the stem seeming to
pierce "through" the leaves.

The white *Eupatorium* spp. merit recognition for several reasons.
There is a white species for any site, wet or dry, sun or light shade;
and butterflies love them. So if you want to enjoy butterflies,
either take a field trip to "nature's table" or lay out a "butterfly
buffet" in your own yard.

The name boneset refers to its medicinal usage. Early
Americans gagged down large quantities of boneset leaf tea to
treat fevers and cold symptoms. It may actually stimulate an
immune response, but this treatment should be left in the annals
of folk medicine. In large doses, it causes vomiting and diarrhea.
I found only one reference of poultice application to a broken
bone. I think the name boneset refers to the treatment of a severe
fever called "breakbone fever."

FLOWER: The upright, hairy stem branches several times at the top,
giving rise to multiple-flower clusters. Each flat-topped grouping
contains many heads of perfect, regular flowers. Each head has
9–23 dull-white disc flowers. There are no ray flowers in the
Eupatorium spp.; 3 rows of overlapping bracts enclose the base
of the disc flowers like a cone of florist's paper.

BLOOMS: 3–4 weeks from July to October

LEAVES: Multiple erect stems emerge from the crown. The space
between leaves is about 3", resulting in a full plant. The 4-6" long,
hairy, opposite leaves are attached to one another at the base.
These simple, lanceolate leaves are coarsely toothed and pointed.
The hairs, plus a wrinkled texture, give the foliage a light gray-
green appearance.

UNDERGROUND STRUCTURES: Long basal offsets mass into a
thick crown.

SEEDS: The 4-angled seeds have a single row of pappus bristles. When they are ripe the pappus is fluffy white, and removing a pinch of fluff pulls a number of seeds from the flat receptacle. There is no chaff between the seeds.

HEIGHT: 3–5′

HABITAT: Moist, low areas

CULTURAL TIPS (see page 62)**:** Boneset grows best in a moist site but adapts well to average garden soil. Pinching back the plant to make it stockier is fine but not necessary. The plant does not require staking, even in partial shade. Drought can cause the loss of some of the lower stem leaves. More sun necessitates more water.

MOISTURE: Moist to wet; tolerates drought

pH: 5–6.5

EXPOSURE: Sun to partial shade

PROPAGATION (see page 66)**:** Seed is easy.

SEED STORAGE: Store dry seeds in an airtight container between 40° and 70°.

SEED TREATMENT: Stratify for 1 month at 40°; sow heavily at 70°. Germinate in 2–3 weeks. Bloom the second year. Cold stratification may be unnecessary if the dry seeds are stored 6 months at 40°.

CUTTINGS (stem)**:** Terminal shoots when firm in spring

DIVISION: Early spring, before shoots elongate, or in fall; requires a sharp spade and a strong back

FAUNA: All sorts of flying insects visit boneset, including butterflies such as the red-banded hairstreak, and shiny black wasps that have a white abdominal belt.

OTHER SE SPECIES (white flowered, most having 3–7 flowers per head)**:**
  Eupatorium capillifolium (dog fennel)—This 5–6′ tall annual or short-lived perennial has fine leaves that are dissected into thread-like segments. It is a noxious weed for southern nursery owners but is much better behaved and offers interesting textural design possibilities farther north. It does best in moist soils and is aggressively weedy in disturbed soil.
  E. glaucescens (E. cuneifolium)—This 3–4′ species has stems that branch at or near ground. The sessile leaves taper to a narrow base, and it has a crown, not rhizomes. It occurs in dry woodlands or sand hills.
  E. hyssopifolium—This 2–3′ tall species has 2–3 stiff stems with linear leaves. Native Americans applied crushed leaves to snakebites.
  E. rotundifolium (false hoarhound)—This is the first of 6 thorough-worts to bloom in my yard. It has hairy, sessile, roundish, 3-veined leaves, and occurs in dry woodlands.
  E. rugosum—*Ageratina altissima* (see page 93)
  E. serotinum (late-flowering thoroughwort)—This species has at least 9 flowers per head, bracts in 3 or more rows, and petiolate leaves. Some seedlings have wonderful burgundy tones in the stems and petioles. It thrives in moist or dry soil. The large, slightly convex inflorescence entertains myriads of small butterflies late into fall.

FLOWERING SPURGE
Euphorbia corollata
Euphorbiaceae (Spurge Family)

Flowering spurge is readily identifiable when in fruit because the 3-chambered capsule is enlarged and appears swollen. It splits open at 3 seams to reveal 3 round seeds as large as BBs in some annual species. The *Euphorbia* species also have a tropical look to the foliage. The leaves are bluish-green with red tones in the fall, and they are thick and smooth. Broken stems and leaves ooze a white latex that can be poisonous or at least irritating to the skin.

The genus name, *Euphorbia,* honors Euphorbus, the Greek physician to Juba, a king of Numidia, a Roman province in North Africa. *Corollata* comes from the Latin word for a small crown or wreath, referring to the ring of male flowers around the single female flower. The common name, spurge, comes from the old French word *espurgier,* meaning to purge.

Native Americans used preparations of the root to stop bleeding after childbirth, soothe skin sores and sore nipples, purge pinworms, and increase urination for various ailments.

Taxonomists recognize several varieties of flowering spurge. Differences exist in the amount of hairiness, looseness of branching, and size of flowers. The more floriferous variety is an excellent substitute for baby's breath in flower arrangements.

FLOWER: The cup-shaped, imperfect "flowers" have 4–5 petal-like appendages arising from floral glands. These glands may secrete an oil or resin that is the reward to the pollinator instead of nectar or pollen. A ring of 14–15 male flowers, each with 1 stamen, surrounds a female flower having 1 pistil. Terminal flower clusters crown the branches of this erect plant.

BLOOMS: 6–8 weeks from April to September

LEAVES: The dark green to red stems are erect. The simple, smooth, linear to oblong, blue-green leaves have a midrib that is whitish. The leaves are alternate on the lower part of the stem, form a whorl at the base of the inflorescence, and are opposite on the branches bearing flowers.

UNDERGROUND STRUCTURES: A torturous rootstock having few feeder roots and a semi-woody brown covering thrusts through gravelly soil to depths equal to the height of the plant.

SEEDS: Each 3-chambered capsule contains 3 small, white, round seeds. They ripen in late summer.

HEIGHT: 1–2.5´

HABITAT: Dry, open woods; roadsides; and fields

CULTURAL TIPS (see page 62)**:** This plant is extremely difficult to transplant. Use seed.

MOISTURE: Dry to moist (moist but draining)

pH: 4.5–7

EXPOSURE: Full to partial sun

PROPAGATION (see page 66)**:** Seed is easiest.

SEED STORAGE: Store dry seeds in an airtight container between 40° and 70°.

SEED TREATMENT: Stratify at 40° for 6 weeks; sow at 70°. Cover very lightly (light requirement). Germinate in 2–3 weeks.

CUTTINGS (basal shoots)**:** June through July

DIVISION: Early spring, if you must

FAUNA: Hay contaminated with spurge sickens livestock, but wild turkey grow fat on the flowers, fruit, and leaves. It is insect-pollinated. Monarch caterpillars can eat flowering spurge when they are desperate, but they much prefer milkweeds.

OTHER SE SPECIES:

Two annual *Euphorbia* species have showy bracts. The red bracts of *E. heterophylla* give it the common name wild poinsettia. The white bracts of *E. marginata* give it the common name snow-on-the-mountain. Like the perennial *E. corollata,* they have wide natural ranges in the eastern United States and the Midwest.

CAROLINE DEAN

CAROLINA JASMINE,
COW ITCH
Gelsemium sempervirens
Loganiaceae (Logania Family)

Even at 70 mph on an interstate highway, one cannot miss the
gaudy combination of the rich yellow of Carolina jasmine blooms
and the ruby tones of the maple samaras (seeds). The jasmine
flourishes in the extra light at the woods' edge. Maroon and
brown pigments in the foliage absorb light all winter long. After
2 months of lengthening days and increased light, the yellow
trumpets appear, heralding the arrival of spring.

Gelsemium comes from *gelsomino,* Italian for jasmine.
Sempervirens is from the Latin, *semper,* or always, and *vivus,* alive.

All parts of the plant are extremely poisonous and cause depres-
sion and paralysis. It is sometimes called cow itch, because juice
from crushed plant parts can cause contact dermatitis.

FLOWER: The 5 round-lobed, yellow petals join in a corolla tube.
The 5 sepals are separate. The 1–1/2″ regular, perfect, fragrant
flowers are often single but may be in cymes of 2–3 flowers. The
5 stamens adhere to the base of the floral tube. The style appears
to be divided into 4 parts.

BLOOMS: 4–6 weeks between March and May; may also bloom
lightly in fall

LEAVES: The vine has no gripper feet but twines, left to right, to
climb trees to reach for light. The smooth, evergreen, 2″ leaves
are opposite, lanceolate to elliptical, pointed, entire, and have
short petioles.

UNDERGROUND STRUCTURES: Thin, ropy feeder roots anchor the vine. When a vine touches the ground at a leaf node, more roots form at that point.

SEEDS: The numerous flat, brown, rough seeds are winged. The flat, oblong capsule is beaked and has a channel running down each side. The seeds are ready for collection September through November. The brownish, $1/2$–$3/4''$ capsule can be found beneath the leaves.

HEIGHT: 1–20′ vine

HABITAT: Woods, thickets, and roadsides

CULTURAL TIPS (see page 62)**:** It may not survive temperatures below zero. Train the vine on a fence and prune it after blooming to keep it from becoming leggy. Seedlings and mature plants respond to a balanced fertilizer. Mulch outdoor plants with compost or leaf mold. It blooms best in full sun but tolerates partial shade.

MOISTURE: Moist, well-drained

pH: 4.5–6.5

EXPOSURE: Full to partial sun

PROPAGATION (see page 66)**:** Cuttings are easiest.

SEED STORAGE: Store dry seeds in an airtight container between 40° and 70°.

SEED TREATMENT: Sow at 70°. Germinate between 2 weeks and 2 months.

CUTTINGS (softwood)**:** May through July, pot in 8 weeks.

DIVISION: Fall (wear gloves when handling broken roots to avoid contact dermititis)

FAUNA: Await observation

OTHER SE SPECIES:

> ***Gelsemium rankinii***—This species has pointed corolla lobes and is scentless; the seeds have no wings. It tolerates a wetter site and blooms a bit later in spring. *G. rankinii* is uncommon but easily propagated and grown. It has great commercial potential.

SOAPWORT
GENTIAN,
BOTTLE GENTIAN,
CLOSED GENTIAN,
MARSH GENTIAN,
ROUGH GENTIAN
Gentiana saponaria
Gentianaceae
(Gentian Family)

Soapwort gentian is truly a
southern plant. It does not
bloom until October or
September at the earliest—
in more northern areas it
would be stricken by early
frosts. The blooms are quite
unusual. At first, the united
petals appear to be a closed
vessel. As they mature, they
open at the top during the
middle of the day but they never open flat out. The rich blue of
these flowers is a visual treat whether in the wild or in the garden.

The genus name *Gentiana* honors Gentius, a king of Illyria in
the second century B.C. He is reputed to have discovered the
medicinal properties of *Gentiana lutea.* The specific epithet,
saponaria, comes from the Latin root word, *saponi,* referring to
the leaves that resemble soapwort or soap plant foliage.

The leaves of soap plants produce a slippery foam when rubbed
between the hands with water. A naturalized plant, *Saponaria officinalis* (bouncing bet or soapwort), was brought to the United
States from the British Isles for its excellent scouring action. The
active ingredient is a glucoside called saponin.

FLOWER: The tubular, violet-blue flowers cluster in tight groups at
the end of the stem and in a few to several leaf axils below the ter-
minus. The cylindrical corolla has 5 lobes connected by a thin tissue (pleats). The toothed pleats are about three-fourths the length
of the lobes. The calyx is also 5-lobed. At the height of their
bloom, the flowers open during the middle of the day, revealing
violet nectary guides. Flowers open sequentially over time, pro-
longing the period of bloom.

BLOOMS: 3–4 weeks from late September to November

LEAVES: The sturdy, smooth, round stem may or may not have short
branches near the top. Stems often appear in clumps. The
smooth, entire, ovoid, pointed, opposite leaves are fleshy and dark
green. Observed with a 10X hand lens, they have clear cilia on the
edges and on the midvein on the back of the leaf.

UNDERGROUND STRUCTURES: The fleshy, white roots are the size of cooked spaghetti.

SEEDS: Copious amounts of thin, elliptical seeds spill from the open beak of the papery, tan capsule. It is held erect but slowly splits open along side seams. The seeds are the color of a manila envelope and have a visible spot in the middle like the yolk of an egg. The larvae of some moth species feed on the embryo of gentians. Even when one collects the seeds slightly green, a weevil can often be found busy at work.

HEIGHT: 1–2′

HABITAT: Bogs, marshes, wet woodlands, glades, and swamps

CULTURAL TIPS (see page 62)**:** The only trick to growing the blue bottle gentians is constant moisture and rich, draining soil. Plants in cultivation are much more floriferous than those in the wild.

MOISTURE: Moist to wet

pH: 4.5–6

EXPOSURE: Light, high shade or morning sun

PROPAGATION (see page 66)**:** Seed is most successful. Leave seedlings in clumps when potting; divide them several months later.

SEED STORAGE: Store dry seeds in an airtight container between 40° and 70°.

SEED TREATMENT: Fumigate. Stratify at 70° in the dark for 6 weeks. Switch to 32° for 6 weeks. Sow at 70° (up to 94° is okay if misted frequently). Germinate in 11 days.

CUTTINGS (stem)**:** Terminal shoots in mid-spring, no later; roots develop in 8–12 weeks under regular misting.

DIVISION: Early spring

FAUNA: Bumblebees have to force their fat bodies into the opening between the corolla lobes. Sometimes, in frustration, they chew a hole in the side of the flower to get to the food they seek. In their search for food, the bees pollinate the flower and some chemical switch flips. Never again will bees visit that fertilized flower. Within a day, the petals begin to turn a dusty purplish color.

OTHER SE SPECIES:

Gentiana catesbaei (Elliott's gentian)—The rough, hairy stem may be single- or short-branched near the tip. The calyx lobes are longer than the tube. The corolla is bell-shaped. It blooms in late September to November in pocosins, savannas, and pine barrens in the Coastal Plain.

G. villosa (Sampson's snakeroot)—Greenish-white, closed flowers cluster in a terminal bouquet. Villosa means hairy, but this plant has smooth stems that are 6–20″ tall. It blooms from late August to November in dry, sandy areas in woods or along roads.

WILD GERANIUM,
CRANESBILL
Geranium maculatum
Geraniaceae (Geranium Family)

Splashes of the rich pink and dark green of wild geranium blend with the many pastels of the spring woodland garden. They bloom in chorus with blue phlox, rue anemone, wake robin, shooting star, and violets. Wild geranium may be the sturdiest of all these spring bloomers. It thrives in shade and tolerates a great deal of sun, except in the deepest South. When many spring wildflowers have gone dormant or look weary, the geranium is still fresh with decorative seed pods.

The genus name comes from the Greek, *gyranos,* or crane, referring to the beaked capsule. *Maculatum* means spotted. The common name cranesbill also refers to the beaked seed capsule.

Colonists used the root of geranium, or alumroot as they called it, to treat diarrhea and mouth ulcers and to stop bleeding. The root contains 10–20 percent tannin, making it highly astringent.

FLOWER: Pairs of perfect, regular, 1″ pink flowers wave on long stalks above the basal leaves. Each flower has 5 petals, 5 sepals, and 10 stamens.

BLOOMS: 3-4 weeks between April and June

LEAVES: The stems may be upright or recumbent. The mottled, hairy leaves are palmately lobed, and the lobes are deeply toothed. The basal leaves are long-stalked. Stalkless or short-stalked, smaller leaves subtend the inflorescence. The leaves assume wonderful shades of red in the fall and persist through most of the winter.

UNDERGROUND STRUCTURES: The knobby, brown, 0.5–0.75″ diameter rhizomes run just under the surface of the ground and climb all over one another in dense piles. The plants increase rapidly by branching of the rhizomes. Sparse brown feeder roots anchor the rhizomes.

SEEDS: The beaked capsule has 5 chambers, each containing 1 smooth, brown, oval seed. The seeds are attached to a springy filament that curls upward toward the tip of the beak. If they do not fall when the threads coil, they do so soon after. Seeds mature about 1 month after flowering. Geranium self-seeds readily in crumbly humus.

HEIGHT: 12–24″

HABITAT: Rich, moist woods

CULTURAL TIPS (see page 62)**:** Give geranium plenty of space. Division is optional but might be desirable in colder areas, where the top rhizome in a pile may be above ground.

MOISTURE: Moist, well draining; drought-tolerant

pH: 4.5–6

EXPOSURE: Morning sun or shade

PROPAGATION (see page 66)**:** Division is easiest.

SEED STORAGE: Store seeds for as brief a period as possible (4-7 days).

SEED TREATMENT: Collect capsules before they split and place them in a paper bag. Once the seeds ripen, sow them in an outdoor bed or stratify for 3 months at 70°. Switch to 40° for 3 months. Sow at 70°. Bloom in 2–3 years.

CUTTINGS (stem)**:** After flowering

DIVISION: Early spring or fall; rhizomes break apart at natural separations. Pieces without feeder roots will produce new roots. Plant every tiny bit.

FAUNA: Non-social wasps seek the partly concealed nectar. Dove and bobwhite quail eat the seeds.

SNEEZEWEED,
HELENIUM,
FALSE SUNFLOWER,
YELLOW STAR
Helenium autumnale
Asteraceae
(Aster or Sunflower Family)

The flower heads of helenium look like toy pinwheels. You never see just one blossom, but masses of bright, shiny faces. The flowers are long-lasting in cut flower arrangements.

The genus name *Helenium* applies to another plant that *H. autumnale* resembles, and that honors Helen of Troy. *Autumnale* means simply that the plant blooms in autumn. The use of the word *autumnale* in the name is somewhat misleading. They begin blooming in mid- to late summer, announcing the horde of sunflowers and goldenrods to follow.

Native Americans found many uses for sneezeweed. They used dried flower heads as a snuff to induce sneezing as a treatment for cough, cold, and headache. They soaked the leaves in hot water for 10–20 minutes and drank the resulting infusion for its laxative effect. Helenalin, the active ingredient in this and other *Helenium* species, shows promise as an anti-tumor agent against cancer. The active ingredient, helenalin, is poisonous to cattle, fish, worms, and insects. Some people get a contact dermatitis from handling helenium. Others may be allergic to the pollen, although that effect is not the origin of the name sneezeweed. Rather, its historical use as snuff gave it that common name.

FLOWER: The terminal, solitary, 1-2″ wide flower heads have perfect, yellow disc flowers and female (but infertile) yellow ray flowers. The corolla of the ray flowers—the part that looks like petals—widens at the end and has 3 lobes. The disc has no chaff—in other words, no receptacle bracts among the disc flowers.

BLOOMS: 4–6 weeks from July to October

LEAVES: The smooth or lightly hairy, upright stems branch at leaf nodes especially if the terminal tip is removed. The 4–6″ long, alternate, simple, elliptical to lanceolate, entire or toothed leaves taper to the stem. The leaf tissue extends down the stem, giving the stem a winged effect.

UNDERGROUND STRUCTURES: Perennial *Helenium* species tend to have fibrous root systems. Annual species often have a taproot.

SEEDS: The seeds form on a globose (earth-shaped) central disc. The seeds are dark brown and ribbed. Translucent scales sparkle along the ribs of the seeds and form a crown-like pappus. They ripen in October and November.

HEIGHT: 3–5′

HABITAT: Moist to wet fields, and waste areas

CULTURAL TIPS (see pagc 62)**:** *Helenium* gets bushier and requires no staking if the tips of the branches are removed in the spring. Fertilize lightly with a balanced fertilizer like 10-10-10.

MOISTURE: Moist to average

pH: 5–6

EXPOSURE: Sun to partial shade

PROPAGATION (see page 66)**:** All methods are easy.

SEED STORAGE: Store dry seeds in an airtight container between 40° and 70°.

SEED TREATMENT: Sow at 70°. Germinate in 7–14 days.

CUTTINGS (stem)**:** May to mid-July

DIVISION: Spring

FAUNA: I've seen butterflies visit the flowers of *Helenium* species.

OTHER SE SPECIES:

Helenium amarum—This upright, many-branched annual has very narrow, linear leaves and masses of yellow flowers from May until frost. The stems are not winged. It is a major pest in pastures and in plant nurseries. Grazing animals avoid the bitter weed but will eat it if other forage is scarce. The bitter taste transfers into the milk of cattle.

H. flexuosum—This sneezeweed is similar to *H. autumnale* but has reddish brown disc flowers instead of yellow.

SWAMP SUNFLOWER
Helianthus angustifolius
Asteraceae (Aster or Sunflower Family)

In late summer and fall, yellow flowers compete for attention in fields and along roads. Among the yellow swarms are the *Helianthus* species, or sunflowers. One of the tallest and most floriferous of these is the swamp sunflower, a common roadside plant that performs as well in the garden as in the roadside ditch.

The large, bright faces of many sunflowers follow the arc of the sun during the day. In art through the ages, these radial discs of yellow, red, and brown have been symbols for the sun. The genus name *Helianthus* comes from two Greek words, *helios,* or sun, and *anthos,* or flower.

Sunflowers can be annual or perennial and come in many sizes and shapes. Long-lived perennial species of sunflowers can be divided into two groups—those with red or purple disc flowers and those with yellow disc flowers. This first species, swamp sun-flower, has dark disc flowers. Ashy or downy sunflower, a species with yellow disc flowers, follows.

The seeds of sunflowers of all species are highly nutritious, whether for animals or man. Native Americans from South and North America made oil and flour from the seeds of various sunflowers.

FLOWER: Each stem bears a few radiate flower heads. The yellow ray flowers are infertile. The rays are 1.5″ long. The purplish-red disc flowers are fertile.

BLOOMS: 6 weeks from July to frost

LEAVES: Multiple erect stems rise from a cluster of rhizomes. The dark green, linear leaves feel rough. In mature plants, the leaves are mostly alternate and generally the same size all the way up the stem. The leaves are 10–30 times longer than they are wide and are rarely more than $^1/_2$″ wide. These long, relaxed leaves give the plant a willowy look.

UNDERGROUND STRUCTURES: Swamp sunflower has fibrous roots and very short rhizomes.

SEEDS: Many of the dark brown nutlets massed on the 1″ receptacle are fertile. They ripen in November.

HEIGHT: 4–7′

HABITAT: Ditches, wet meadows, savannas, and marshes

CULTURAL TIPS (see page 62)**:** Prune back by one-third prior to July 4 to create a bushier, wind-resistant clump.

MOISTURE: Moist to average; drought-tolerant

pH: 5–6

EXPOSURE: Full sun

PROPAGATION (see page 66)**:** All methods are easy

SEED STORAGE: Store dry seeds in an airtight container between 40° and 70°.

SEED TREATMENT: Sow at 70°. Germinate in 2 weeks or sooner if warmer than 70°.

CUTTINGS (stem)**:** When new growth gets firm, usually in June

DIVISION: In early spring, remove shoots from the outer edge of a clump or divide the entire clump.

FAUNA: Sunflowers are good nectar sources for insects, and seed sources for birds and rodents.

OTHER SE SPECIES (with purplish-red disc flowers):
   Helianthus atrorubens : This 3–5′ perennial has a loose corymb-like head of blooms. The opposite, ovate leaves are rough, hairy, and mainly basal. The few stem leaves are greatly reduced in size. The petioles are winged. It blooms July to October in dry, open woods and old fields.

ASHY SUNFLOWER
Helianthus mollis
Asteraceae (Aster or Sunflower Family)

Ashy sunflower is one of my favorite sunflowers for several reasons. Visually, the blue-green furry leaves contrast pleasingly with the golden yellow blossoms. The plant can reach 4′, but the unbranched stem never seems coarse. It spreads by rhizomes but in a non-irrigated site will not take over the farm. Lastly, *Helianthus mollis* is not fussy. I have seen it blooming in both a dry, open field and in a moist pine woodland. It is a midwestern and southern species that has been introduced in the Atlantic Coastal Plain.

The specific epithet *mollis* comes from the Latin root *moll,* meaning soft, referring to the texture of the leaves.

FLOWER: The flower heads are solitary on the erect, furry stems. There are 16–35 "petals," or rays. Each ray can be 1.5″ long. The ray flowers are infertile and produce no seeds. The disc flowers are fertile and produce generous amounts of seeds. Small bracts between the disc flowers give the disc a darker look than the rays.

BLOOMS: 6 weeks from June to August

LEAVES: The simple, ovate, toothed, opposite, sessile leaves are equally spaced along the erect stem about every 2–3″. All the green parts of the plant are softly hairy. The leaves have a distinct, whitish midrib. They are 3-4″ long and 1.5″ wide, getting a bit smaller toward the top of the stem.

UNDERGROUND STRUCTURES: Ashy sunflower has fibrous roots and long rhizomes.

SEEDS: The seed is contained in an achene, or nutlet, which is dark gray or black and just shy of ¼″ long. Seeds ripen 3 weeks after the flower fades.

HEIGHT: 3–4′

HABITAT: Prairies, woodland edges, and roadsides

CULTURAL TIPS (see page 62)**:** Ashy sunflower can spread aggressively by rhizomes. Dry, rocky soil slows it down.

MOISTURE: Average or dry

pH: 5–6

EXPOSURE: Sun or partial shade

PROPAGATION (see page66)**:** Any method is easy

SEED STORAGE: Store dry seeds in an airtight container between 40° and 70°.

SEED TREATMENT: Sow heavily at 70°-90°. Germinate anywhere from 3 days to 3 weeks. The higher the temperature, the faster the germination.

CUTTINGS (stem)**:** Take before flowering (probably in June); wait until new growth is firm

DIVISION: In early spring, remove shoots from the outer edge of a clump, or divide the entire clump.

FAUNA: Birds feast on the seeds in the fall.

OTHER SE SPECIES (with yellow disc flowers) **:**
  Helianthus hirsutus (rough sunflower)—This 3–4′ rough-stemmed sunflower has 1 or a few flower heads on short, stout stalks. The opposite, lanceolate to ovate leaves are rough and hairy on both sides. The base of the leaf is broadly rounded. It has very long rhizomes and blooms from late summer to fall in dry wooded or open places.
  H. microcephalus —The 3–6′ smooth, bluish-green stems support numerous 1″ flower heads. The lanceolate, petiolate leaves are rough on top and hairy and resin-dotted on the back side. It blooms in the summer in woods and open places.
  H. strumosus —The 3–6′ stem is smooth and bluish-green. The flower heads are 3″ wide and number a few to several per stem. The leaves are wide, firm, ovate to lanceolate, toothed, and have a long petiole. The leaves are rough on top and hairy underneath. The plant is aggressively rhizomatous. It blooms in the summer in woods and open places.

ALUMROOT,
ROCK GERANIUM
Heuchera americana
Saxifragaceae
(Saxifrage Family)

Alumroot is often overlooked because it has an inconspicuous flower. Yet it has many positive traits that warrant a second look. The geranium-shaped leaves form a tidy basal rosette, and they may be marbled in silver and rose. This species has a wide geographic distribution and is a member of several different plant communities because it thrives under a wide variety of conditions. Its adaptability and evergreen leaves make it a good candidate for cultivated gardens.

The family name Saxifragaceae comes from the Latin, *saxum*, a rock, and *frag*, to break. Members of this family often grow in rock crevices. The genus name honors Johann Heinrich von Heucher (1677–1747).

Native Americans used the powdered root as an astringent and antiseptic. They drank leaf tea as a general tonic and treatment for stomach and intestinal disorders, and put a poultice made from the powdered root on wounds, ulcers, and other skin lesions.

FLOWER: The flower stalk stands 2–2.5′ above the basal rosette; 15–20 very small flowers form a skinny panicle. Each individual, perfect flower has 5 petals, 5 sepals, and 5 stamens. The opaque, greenish-white (or pink or purple) petals are smaller than the surrounding sepals. The stamens extend beyond the calyx, and the pollen on the ends is bright orange. From a distance the effect is of yellowish flowers.

BLOOMS: 1 month between April and June

LEAVES: The simple, toothed, basal leaves are cordate with rounded lobes. They are 2–5″ long, rough, and have a long petiole. Both leaf and flower stalks have a glandular pubescence. (Under a 10X hand lens, the hairs have glistening balls on the ends.) Seedlings of alumroot show great variability in the depth of the lobing and in the pigment markings of the leaf. The leaf may be almost pure green or have silver or maroon streaks or blotches. Each flowering stem has 2 reduced leaves. In late fall, the basal leaves turn claret red and remain decorative until the plant finishes flowering the next spring. At that time, a new set of leaves emerges.

UNDERGROUND STRUCTURES: The dark, almost woody crown is a cluster of plants that pull or are cut apart with ease. The interior of the rootstock is white. The rhizomes have fibrous feeder roots.

SEEDS: Large numbers of tiny red/black oval seeds fill the brown, oval capsule. These seeds have no endosperm (food stores). They are ripe 2–4 weeks after the flowers fade.

HEIGHT: 2–2.5´

HABITAT: Rock outcrops, drainage slopes of rich woods, and dry woods

CULTURAL TIPS (see page 62)**:** Although the name implies that alumroot occupies a crack in a rock, it grows well in rich, high-organic garden soil as long as it drains well. Divide every 3 years, because each year's new growth piles up on the previous year's growth.

MOISTURE: Average moisture with good drainage; drought-tolerant

pH: 5–6.5

EXPOSURE: Light shade or morning sun

PROPAGATION (see pages 66)**:** Seed or division is easy.

SEED STORAGE: Store dry seeds in an airtight container between 40° and 70°.

SEED TREATMENT: Sow at 70°; cover very lightly (light requirement). Germinate in 16–30 days. Leave in clumps when potting.

CUTTINGS: Pieces of rhizome should be capable of producing shoots, but I have not tried this method.

DIVISION: Early spring or fall

FAUNA: Bees spend a great deal of time going from flower to flower of alumroot.

OTHER SE SPECIES:
> ***Heuchera parviflora***—In this species, the thin petals are longer than the sepals. The small, sharply toothed, rounded leaves have gently cut lobes. The leaf petiole is hairy. It blooms from July to September beneath shaded cliffs.
> ***H. villosa***—The calyx (fused sepals) is hairy, and the leaves have sharp lobes and teeth. It blooms from June to September on rocks and ledges in mountainous areas.
> To distinguish alumroot from foamflower *(Tiarella cordifolia)*:
> ***Tiarella cordifolia***—This alumroot look-alike has sharp, lobed leaves. The leaves and stems are densely hairy. The showy raceme of white-petaled flowers has 10 exerted stamens, giving the bloom a bottlebrush look. It blooms in early spring.

LITTLE BROWN JUG,
HEARTLEAF, EVERGREEN WILD GINGER
Hexastylis arifolia (Asarum arifolium)
Aristolochiaceae (Birthwort Family)

Plants in the birthwort family earned the name by having a flower resembling a swollen womb. The ground-hugging, reclusive flowers are not the most significant part of these evergreen gingers; their true beauty lies in their rich, shiny leaves. They are closely related to the deciduous ginger *Asarum canadense,* but in addition to being evergreen, they do not spread rapidly by rhizomes. To the dismay of gardeners, they tend to stay in slow-growing clumps. *Hexastylis arifolia* is the most common evergreen ginger.

The genus name *Hexastylis* comes from the Greek root words, *hexa* and *stylis,* referring to the 6 styles.

Native Americans made a tea from the leaves to treat pain in the chest, back, and stomach.

FLOWER: The solitary, leathery, perfect, jug-shaped flowers have no petals. Greenish-brown sepals form an urn-shaped calyx with a tightly constricted neck. One variety *(arifolia)* has spreading calyx lobes. Another variety *(ruthii)* has erect lobes. The flowers lie on the ground between 2 leaf clusters. Each flower has 12 stamens. Flowers exposed to light may be more brown than green or pink.

BLOOMS: 3 weeks from March to May

LEAVES: The 3-6″ long, smooth leaves are thick, evergreen triangles with long petioles. The bases of the leaves are lobed. They are usually mottled in shades of green in the spring and summer, taking on bronzy tones in the winter. Sometimes one will see 2–3 leaves; at other times, a cluster of leaves can form a mass 18″ across. All the leaves are basal. There is no stem above ground.

UNDERGROUND STRUCTURES: The stems can be on the surface or underground in the form of aromatic, forked rhizomes. The feeder roots are fleshy.

SEEDS: The round, fleshy capsule contains numerous flattened seeds.

HEIGHT: 3–6″

HABITAT: Moist to dry woods (deciduous or pine)

CULTURAL TIPS (see page 62): *Hexastylis arifolia* occurs naturally in a wide range of cultural situations. It seems to be more tolerant of dry soil than the other evergreen species. Enrich the site with humus.

MOISTURE: Moist to average

pH: 5–6

EXPOSURE: Shade to filtered light

PROPAGATION (see page 66): Any method is slow.

SEED STORAGE: Store seeds temporarily in moist spaghnum at 40°.

SEED TREATMENT: Sow fresh seeds outside or stratify for 2-3 months at 40°. Then sow at 70°.

CUTTINGS (mallet): Late spring or early summer; with high humidity, they should root in 5–6 weeks.

DIVISION: Early spring or late fall

FAUNA: Ground-feeding insects pollinate wild gingers. Among them are beetles, fungus gnats, and flesh flies.

OTHER SE SPECIES (in which the leaves are heart-shaped or roundish):
Hexastylis heterophylla—The short, (about 1/2″) cylindrical calyx tube has lobes 1/4″- 1/2″ long. The leaves are usually unmottled.
H. shuttleworthii (largeflower heartleaf)—The calyx is urn-shaped, wide at the bottom and constricted at the top. It can be more than 3/4″ wide and 3/4″long. The leaves have light green or white netting along the veins.
H. virginica (Virginia heartleaf)—This species has a short, (about 1/2″) cylindrical calyx tube with very short lobes. The leaves are often mottled.

CRIMSON-EYED ROSE MALLOW,
BREAST ROOT, WILD COTTON
Hibiscus moscheutos
Malvaceae (Mallow Family)

On the first day of summer, look for the 4-8″ wide showy flowers of hibiscus in moist areas. The bloom is a larger version of okra, cotton, or hollyhocks, which are also members of the mallow family. The flowers are usually white, pink, or red, but may be a pale yellow. All have a red or maroon center and a projecting column of stamens.

Hibiscus is the Greek name for mallow. *Moscheutos* means "scented like the musk rose."

Many of the hibiscus are called marshmallows because of their family relationship to *Althaea officinalis,* a plant introduced from Europe from which marshmallows were made. Today, marshmallows are made from corn syrup and gelatin.

All parts of the plant are viscous sticky. In folk medicine, a poultice of the leaves and roots was used on breast tumors and for gastrointestinal, lung, and bladder problems. The poultice has a locally soothing and softening effect.

FLOWER: The flowers develop in terminal clusters. Each regular, perfect flower has 5 petals, 5 stamens, and 5 sepals. The pink or white petals are rounded at the edges and have a translucent crepe-like texture. The base of each 4″ long petal is dark maroon, creating a bull's eye in the throat of the flower. The white stamens intertwine into an elaborate column that surrounds the pistil and then projects beyond the flower. The sepals are fused two-thirds of the way up their length; they continue to grow as the flower enlarges. They form a dry brown paper bag around the developing seed capsule. A whorl of bracts below the calyx looks like a ring of spider legs.

BLOOMS: 4–6 weeks from May to September; each flower blooms for only a day, but the flowers open sequentially over time.

LEAVES: The alternate, simple, toothed, petiolate leaves are softly pubescent underneath. They may be furry on top as well (ssp. *lasiocarpus*) or smooth on top (ssp. *moscheutos*). The leaves are highly variable but are ovate to ovate-lanceolate and may be shallowly lobed.

UNDERGROUND STRUCTURES: The heavy crown becomes almost woody with age. The roots are thick and fibrous.

SEEDS: The ovoid seed capsule looks somewhat like a hickory nut on steroids. It has 5 compartments full of smooth, roundish, brown seeds. The seed pod is hairy in ssp. *lasiocarpus* and smooth in ssp. *moscheutos.* Seeds mature 4–5 weeks after bloom, sometime in August or September. Insect larvae often eat the seed embryo. Sturdy stems hold clusters of capsules upright, but when the seams split, the 5 compartments lay open. As wind moves the stems, the dried seeds gradually shake loose and fall.

HEIGHT: 3–6′

HABITAT: Wet places, ditches, swamps, or marshes

CULTURAL TIPS (see page 62)**:** Remove the previous year's stalks in late winter or before new shoots begin to emerge in the spring. Japanese beetles can damage buds and leaves. They do not seem to attack *H. aculeatus* or *H. coccineus* as much as other species.

MOISTURE: Wet to moist to average

pH: 5–6

EXPOSURE: Full to half-day sun

PROPAGATION (see page 66)**:** Seed is easiest.

SEED STORAGE: Store dry seeds in an airtight container at 40°.

SEED TREATMENT: Collect as early as possible; clean and fumigate. Give seeds a warm-water soak for 24 hours; sow at 70°. Germinate in 1–3 weeks. A few may bloom the first year, but most wait until the second year to bloom.

CUTTINGS (stem)**:** Terminal shoots in mid- to late June; roots form in 4 weeks.

DIVISION: Possible, but requires a cleaver or machete and a person with a strong back.

FAUNA: Many species of butterflies and hummingbirds seek nectar from hibiscus. The cloudless sulphur and duke's skipper are recorded visitors. I have seen several kinds of swallowtails visit and linger.

OTHER SE SPECIES:
Hibiscus aculeatus (comfort root, pineland hibiscus)—The 6″ flowers are cream to yellow with a black-purple center. When fully open, the petals do not overlap. The 3-4′ stems and leaves have very rough hairs. The leaves have 3–5 palmate lobes. The calyx lobes have a nectary on the back.
H. coccineus (scarlet rose mallow, Texas star)—This species has crimson flowers on an 8′ plant with smooth foliage and deeply cut, palmate leaves. When fully open, the petals separate from each other.
H. grandiflorus (swamp rose mallow)—As the species name says, this species has large (10″ across) flowers. The leaves have large lobes and soft hairs on the back side. The seed pod is coarsely hairy. It is often found in standing water.
H. laevis (*H. militaris,* halberdleaf marsh mallow)—This wide-ranging species has smooth leaves and stems. The leaves are toothed with pointed basal lobes on bigger leaves. Small leaves may be unlobed. The flowers are usually pink with a maroon eye. The seed pod is smooth, but the seeds look like small brown hedgehogs.
H. syriacus (rose of Sharon)—This is a non-native, woody shrub or small tree with long-haired seed.

BLUETS,
QUAKER LADIES, INNOCENCE,
WILD FORGET-ME-NOT, VENUS' PRIDE,
BRIGHT EYES
Houstonia caerulea
Rubiaceae (Madder Family)

Chance upon a generous clump of bluets nestled in bright green moss on a woodland log hummock, and you'll think you've found a fairy wonderland. Bluets have a clean simplicity that has earned them common names like Quaker ladies and innocence.

The genus name honors William Houston (1695–1733), a Scottish ship's surgeon and plant explorer. *Caeruleus* is Latin for blue.

Cherokee mothers treated bedwetters with bluet leaf tea.

FLOWER: Each solitary flower is regular, perfect, and sky blue to white with a yellow eye. Bluets have 4 petals, sepals, and stamens. The petals are fused at the base into a short funnel from which the petal lobes flare into an open 1/4″ face. Some flowers have long stamens and short pistils, while some have long pistils and short stamens, which ensures that the plant does not pollinate itself and helps promote genetic diversity. The cross-shaped flowers are translucent, like a fine porcelain teacup.

BLOOMS: 2–3 months between February and May

LEAVES: Inconspicuous basal tufts of spoon-shaped leaves form an olive green backdrop for the erect flower stalks. A pair of tiny, ovoid leaves graces the stem.

UNDERGROUND STRUCTURES: A shallow fan of thin rhizomes anchors the clump.

SEEDS: The 2-lobed capsule looks like a side-by-side double scoop of ice cream on a single cone. Each rounded lobe contains 4–20 brown, pitted seeds, which look like button mushroom caps under magnification. They are ripe when the capsule turns brown, sometime between May and June.

HEIGHT: 4–6″

HABITAT: Bluets can be found in meadows, pastures, open woods, along roadsides, and on banks of streams.

CULTURAL TIPS (see page 62)): Bluets self-seed in patches of moss and in gravel. They transplant easily in early spring and make a superb rock garden plant.

MOISTURE: Moist but well-drained soil

pH: 5–7

EXPOSURE: Full sun to filtered light

PROPAGATION (see page 66): Challenging, but division of self-seeded plants is easiest.

SEED STORAGE: Store temporarily in moist spaghnum at 40°.

SEED TREATMENT: Place a pad of moss in a shallow flat that has drainage holes. Sow fresh bluet seeds over the moss. Place the flat outdoors in the shade, and water lightly every day. The seeds will germinate the following spring.

CUTTINGS (stem): Take after flowering

DIVISION: Divide in early spring.

FAUNA: Tiny flies pollinate bluets. Butterflies, such as the eastern-tailed blue, also visit.

OTHER SE SPECIES:
Houstonia procumbens (trailing bluet)—A white-flowered creeper that prefers sandy forests and dunes. It blooms in February, March, and April.
H. purpurea—A 6–10″ perennial with pale violet blooms that have a long corolla tube. It tends to grow along woodland edges and blooms in April and May.
H. pusilla—A 2–4″ annual with 1/4″ magenta violet blooms. It prefers open areas and blooms in February, March, and April.
H. serpyllifolia—A 4″ perennial with blue or purple-blue blooms. It is found along waterways and road shoulders at high elevations and in grass balds.
H. tenuifolia—A 7–9″ perennial that bears loose cymes of tiny, violet blooms. It inhabits dry woodlands and blooms in May, June, and July.

SPIDER LILY,
BASKET LILY
Hymenocallis caroliniana (H. occidentalis)
Liliaceae (Lily Family)

Spider lilies look so exotic and tropical, one suspects they came by mail, bareroot in a plastic bag. They are true natives of the Southeast. They open their fragrant, moth-pollinated flowers in the evening and remain open through the next day.

The genus name *Hymenocallis* comes from the Greek, *hymen* and *kallos,* meaning "beautiful membrane," which refers to the flower's white corona.

FLOWER: A group of 2–7 pure white flowers top each leafless stalk. The 3 petals and 3 sepals are similar. They are long and strap-like and join at the base in a long floral tube. Above the ring of straps is a flaring cup of white tissue connecting the bottom half of the stamen filaments. This corona resembles a morning glory. All the previously described parts are white except for the yellow, pollen-bearing anthers. An abrupt color change occurs between the white floral tube and the green ovary.

BLOOMS: 3 weeks from April through August

LEAVES: The upright, smooth, basal, linear, entire leaves are present when the plant flowers.

UNDERGROUND STRUCTURES: Seedlings have white fleshy roots. After 3 years a large, flat-bottomed, globular bulb develops. A black coat covers the bulb. Bulbs produce offsets.

SEEDS: The fleshy capsule has 3 compartments, each of which can contain 1–6 seeds. Individual seeds look like a fresh green olive. They are ripe in September and October.

HEIGHT: 2–2.5′

HABITAT: Moist to wet woods, stream banks, and roadsides

CULTURAL TIPS (see page 62)**:** Although spider lilies occur naturally in moist areas, they grow quite nicely in cultivation, in rich soil having average moisture with supplemental moisture during prolonged drought.

MOISTURE: Average to wet

pH: 5–6.5

EXPOSURE: Light, filtered shade to sun (if moist to wet)

PROPAGATION (see page 66)**:** Seed is easy.

SEED STORAGE: Store temporarily in moist spaghnum at 40°.

SEED TREATMENT: If you wish to watch the process, place fresh seeds in moist sand in a resealable plastic bag on a windowsill. When root radicles emerge in 3–4 months, gently sow the seeds in the top of 3″ pots in a cold greenhouse. Alternately, place the seeds in pots or flats outdoors. Leave the seeds exposed to some light but ensure constant moisture. Seeds in pots in a cold greenhouse need no special attention over the winter. The high humidity of the greenhouse is ideal for this seed. The house also offers protection during late freezes when spider lilies in pots above ground are vulnerable. Bloom in 3–4 years.

CUTTINGS: No

DIVISION: Separate bulbs in the fall. Small bulbs take 2 years to bloom.

FAUNA: Hawk moths pollinate spider lilies.

OTHER SE SPECIES:
(Note: Taxonomy and nomenclature are confusing and changing.)
Hymenocallis coronaria (Cahaba lily)—The corona is especially large and frilled. It lives in the middle of flowing streams, its roots anchored in the rocks. Their numbers have been greatly reduced by the damming of streams and rivers and other activities of man.
H. floridana (*H. crassifolia*)—This denizen of the outer Coastal Plain has 1–3 flowers in a cluster. It occurs commonly in freshwater marshes and infrequently in brackish marshes and swamp forests.
H. galvestonensis (*H. eulae*)—Like some of the *Lycoris* spp., this lily can be called a naked lady because the leaves are dormant during the flowering stage. The flower stalk is round. It is an upland plant that needs moisture during the leaf stage in spring but drainage during the rest of the year.
H. liriosome (spring spider lily)—This flower has a frilled corona and a yellow center. The 8-30″ long, dark green leaves emerge at the same time as the sharp-edged flowering stalk. It grows well in clay and standing water and blooms in March or April.

Jewel Weed,
Spotted Touch-Me-Not, Balsam, Brook Celandine, Ear Jewel, Kicking Colt, Silverleaf, Snapdragon, Hummingbird Tree
Impatiens capensis
Balsaminaceae (Touch-Me-Not Family)

The orange, crimson-spotted flowers of jewel weed are rich in color, and the leaves sparkle with dew. Sadly, some call it a weed because it self-seeds so vigorously. In moist areas, fields of this watery, hollow-stemmed plant appear as if overnight. It is one of the few annuals covered in this book because it is so common and because it is a nectar plant for hummingbirds. The plant is worth knowing for one other reason:

A mash of the leaves and stems will take the itch out of a poison ivy rash. This remedy can be used in the field or at home, and you can freeze the concoction in ice cube trays and have a ready supply of cool comfort in the freezer.

The silverleaf's name describes the look of a leaf held under water. A white film covering the leaf seems to repel water.

Young shoots of jewel weed can be eaten as a cooked green.

Native Americans used a poultice of the leaves and stems to treat a wide variety of skin problems, such as burns, rashes, sores, cuts, insect bites, warts, liver spots, and eczema.

FLOWER: Clusters of crimson-spotted, orange blooms dangle in the leaf axils. The l″ long, perfect, irregular blooms have 3 sepals, the lower one forming a sac with a curled spur; and 5 petals, the lateral ones looking like a 1-lobed petal. The anthers of the 5 stamens unite over the stigma.

BLOOMS: 4 months from May until frost

LEAVES: The 1-4″ long simple alternate leaves are ovate and coarsely toothed. They are soft, both in color of green and in texture, and bruise easily. The 4′ hollow stems are erect, but the plant has a loose aspect due to the 4″ long petioles on the leaves.

UNDERGROUND STRUCTURES: This annual has no heavy crown or tap root. The roots spread more widely than deeply and release their hold on the earth easily.

SEEDS: The 7/8″ long, 5-chambered seed capsule explodes when ripe, throwing seeds a great distance.

HEIGHT: 2–5′

HABITAT: Any moist area, such as a woods edge, marsh, or stream bank

CULTURAL TIPS (see page 62)**:** Seedlings of this exuberant plant pull easily.

MOISTURE: Moist to average

pH: 4.5–6

EXPOSURE: Partial sun, full sun, or shade

PROPAGATION (see page 66)**:** Seeding in situ is best.

SEED STORAGE: Store dry in an airtight container at 40°.

SEED TREATMENT: Sow in situ in the fall or stratify for 3 months at 40° and sow at 70°.

CUTTINGS: No

DIVISION: No

FAUNA: Ruby-throated hummingbirds get giddy in a patch of jewel weed. The spicebush swallowtail and the cloudless sulphur both have the long proboscis necessary to get nectar from tubular flowers like jewel weed.

OTHER SE SPECIES:

Impatiens pallida (pale touch-me-not)—This 5′ annual has light yellow flowers. It has a slightly more northern distribution than *I. capensis* and grows well in calcareous soils.

BLUE FLAG
Iris virginica
Iridaceae (Iris Family)

This is southern blue flag, which is difficult to differentiate from northern blue flag *(Iris versicolor)*. Both have a wide range of color, from blue to violet to white. The southern one may be slightly shorter and less erect, but both are garden worthy plants if sited in a moist spot. They bloom at a convenient time, after the spring flora fades and before the sunny summer plants begin their festival.

Iris was the Greek goddess of the rainbow, referring to the wide range of colors of various *Iris* species. The flag of the common name refers to the Old English word, *flagge,* which meant rush. The connection must be that they both tend to grow in damp places and have erect rush-like leaves.

The Cherokee used a poultice of the root of southern blue flag to treat skin ulcers. The plant should not be taken internally. Most irises are poisonous to some degree.

FLOWER: Terminal, regular, perfect flowers are lavender, violet, or white with purple veins. The sepals have a yellow pubescent blotch at the base and are longer than the petals. Each smooth, round flower stalk has several blooms that open sequentially. The bloom stalk stands above the leaves.

BLOOMS: 3–4 weeks between March and May

LEAVES: Upright, entire, smooth, true green, linear leaves are mostly basal from the rhizome. The leaves are about 1″ wide.

UNDERGROUND STRUCTURES: Blue flag has thick, long, straight rhizomes growing on the ground surface. Feeder roots anchor the plant.

SEEDS: The seeds look like brown, flat kernels of corn and are stacked in 3 compartments in the capsule. Larvae frequently bores holes in the seeds and eat everything inside, leaving a hollow shell.

HEIGHT: 2–3′

HABITAT: It can be found in wet areas in pine savannas and flatwoods, pastures, roadside ditches, marshes, and swamps.

CULTURAL TIPS (see page 62)**:** Rust (a leaf fungus) frequently attacks the leaves of iris in cultivation or in the wild. It does not seem to cause permanent damage, only marred foliage. If you don't cotton to chemical warfare, collect seed and grow new plants or just remove the affected foliage and send it to the landfill.

MOISTURE: Blue flag needs a good moisture supply year-round. Periods of drought can stress the plant and leave it susceptible to rust.

pH: 5–6.5

EXPOSURE: Full to partial sun

PROPAGATION (see page 66)**:** Seed or division is easy.

SEED STORAGE: Store fumigated, dry seeds in an airtight container between 40° and 70°.

SEED TREATMENT: Beginning in November, soak seeds 24 hours in tepid water. Sow the seeds and put the flat outside for temperature fluctuations. Allow to germinate naturally outside. An adequate period of cold is essential. In the Deep South, you may need to stratify in the refrigerator. Give the seeds at least 3 months at 40° and put the plastic bag of seeds out on the kitchen counter for a warm 6–8 hours every 2 weeks. This simulates the temperature fluctuations that seem to be necessary for germination. Bloom the second year.

CUTTINGS: No

DIVISION: From August through October, divide rhizomes into pieces that each have a leaf or leaves.

FAUNA: Iris are insect nectar plants.

OTHER SE SPECIES:
   Iris brevicaulis—This iris has a zigzag stem and pale blue flowers which nestle in the leaves.
   I. hexagona—This species is similar to *I. virginica* but has bigger flowers, a zigzag stem, and the lowest foliar bract reaches the topmost flower.

DENSE BLAZING STAR,
GAYFEATHER,
BACKACHE ROOT,
COLIC ROOT,
MARSH BLAZING STAR,
THROATWORT
Liatris spicata
Asteraceae
(Aster or Sunflower Family)

Most people have seen blazing star and don't know it. Every time you pass the florist shop in the grocery store, you probably pass spikes of this stalwart of the commercial bouquet. The showy inflorescence is intense rose-purple with flowers opening from the top of the spike down. In the wild, various species of blazing star inhabit many different sites. Some live in moist meadows, others favor dry prairies, rocky roadsides, or sand dunes. The common condition is sun—at least a half-day of good light.

Arthur Cronquist (see Bibliography page 288) lists 22 species of blazing star for the southeastern United States. They are divided into 2 groups by the type of pappus (the bristly or feathery brush) on the seed. Look at the pappus with a hand lens. If it has side hairs less than 0.3 mm, it is in the first group, and the pappus is called barbelate; 18 of the 22 species belong in this group. If the side hairs on a single feather are 0.5–1 mm, it is in the second group, and the pappus is termed plumose or feather-like. *Liatris spicata*, dense blazing star, belongs in the first group.

The Cherokee used a preparation of the root to relieve intestinal gas, increase urination, and relieve backache. It has been used in folk medicine to treat sore throats, kidney stones, and gonorrhea.

FLOWER: The inflorescence is an 8–12″ unbranched spike of crowded, sessile (no stalk), rose-purple (occasionally white) blossoms. Each rayless blossom has numerous (6–18) perfect disc flowers; 4–6 overlapping rows of oblong bracts clasp the base of the rounded involucre (flower holder). The corolla tube is smooth inside. The flowers begin to open at the top of the spike first.

BLOOMS: 1 month between June and August

LEAVES: Both the erect stem and the leaves are smooth. The 2–16″ linear leaves are alternate, simple, and entire. They are longest at the bottom of the stem.

UNDERGROUND STRUCTURES: Seedlings quickly develop a globose underground structure that looks like a corm. Technically, this is a stem base enlargement or rootstock. Feeder roots anchor the plant but they wither in winter and new roots grow in spring.

SEEDS: The floral receptacle is flat or slightly convex. The brown, ribbed achene is pointed at one end and flat at the end bearing the pappus (barbed bristles).

HEIGHT: 2–6′

HABITAT: Wet to moist soil

CULTURAL TIPS (see page 62): Too much fertilizer or not enough sunlight leads to a floppy flower stalk.

MOISTURE: Wet to moist to average

pH: 5–6

EXPOSURE: Full sun

PROPAGATION (see page 66): Seed is easy.

SEED STORAGE: Store seeds dry in an airtight container between 40° and 70°.

SEED TREATMENT: Stratify for 4 weeks at 40°; sow at 55°-70°. Cover seed well. Germinate in 7 days.

CUTTINGS: No

DIVISION: Spring or fall; the rootstock can be cut into pieces as long as each piece has an eye. Apply fungicide to the cut edges.

FAUNA: Many butterfly species favor blazing star.

OTHER SE SPECIES (with short barbellate pappus, that generally bloom in summer):

Liatris aspera—This is a 4-6′ tall gayfeather with broad flower heads, each having more than 16 flowers. It has rounded bracts that are thin and have pink to white margins and tips. The leaves are 0.5–1.5″ wide. It blooms anytime from August to November in dry, sandy, or rocky open areas.

L. graminifolia (grass-leaved blazing star)—This species has 3′ slim arching spikes. The sessile heads of flowers are longer than broad (or nearly so). The corollas are hairy inside. The bracts are flattened at the apex. It has very thin, cauline (non-basal) leaves. It favors dry spots, especially the edges of pine woods, salt marshes, and dune hollows, and blooms in late summer (August, September, and October).

L. scariosa (button blazing star)—This 1–4′ species can have lavender or white flowers. Each raceme can contain 4–30 largish, round, stalked flower heads. The bracts are thick, rounded, and green or purplish with spreading tips. The corolla tube is hairy inside. It blooms in late summer and early fall in dry woodlands.

SCALY BLAZING STAR
Liatris squarrosa
Asteraceae
(Aster or Sunflower Family)

If the stalk of rose purple flower heads doesn't stop you in your tracks, the continuous butterfly show surely will. Blazing stars must produce plentiful amounts of nectar because they seem to have a lepidopterous guest of one sort or another from 9 a.m. to dusk on sunny days. Even after the blooms have faded and the butterflies move on, the plant has decorative fluffy seed heads.

Squarrosa means recurved at the tip (of the bracts). The visual prominence of these bracts beneath the flower heads gives the plant the common name scaly blazing star.

FLOWER: A small number of flower heads on stiff erect stalks dot the upright raceme. Each head is made up of 20–45 disc flowers, but there are no ray flowers. The top flower may have as many as 60 disc flowers. The rose-purple flowers have hairs on the inner surface of the corolla. The plant is hairy, in general, at least in the area of the inflorescence. The green to purple, overlapping bracts are firm and taper to a recurving sharp tip.

BLOOMS: 1–2 months between June and September

LEAVES: The erect, solitary stem bears simple, firm, dark green, alternate leaves which are 2-10″ long and 1/8-1/2″ wide. The leaves near the base almost sheath the stem. Some of the lowest leaves are very small and fall off before the flowers bloom.

UNDERGROUND STRUCTURES: The thickened stem base looks like a corm but is more properly called a rootstock. It has fibrous feeder roots emerging from its base. The roots wither in fall and the rootstock can be stored dry for a few months. New roots emerge in spring.

SEEDS: The gray-black, 10-ribbed, pointed seeds have long hairs with feathery side hairs. This feathery pappus of hairs places this species of *Liatris* in the second taxonomic grouping, those with plumose pappus. The side hairs on a single hair measure 0.5–1 mm. Large numbers of seeds pack, point down, on a flat to slightly convex receptacle.

HEIGHT: 12–30″

HABITAT: Scaly blazing star can be found in rocky sites, in dry, open places, and in thin woods.

CULTURAL TIPS (see page 62): Do not tip prune *Liatris* spp. They will not replace the lost bloom.

MOISTURE: Average to dry

pH: 5–6

EXPOSURE: Full to partial sun

PROPAGATION: (see page 66): Seed is easiest.

SEED STORAGE: Store dry seeds in an airtight container between 40° and 70°.

SEED TREATMENT: Stratify for 2 months at 40°; sow at 70°. Germinate in 10 days. Bloom the second year.

CUTTINGS (rootstock): Large pieces with more than 1 bud can be cut into pieces, each having a bud. Dust the cut edges with fungicide.

DIVISION: The rootstock can be divided in the spring or fall.

FAUNA: Butterflies and bees get a nourishing reward for dispersing the pollen of blazing stars.

OTHER SE SPECIES (with feathery or plumose pappus):
   Liatris elegans—Each rose-purple flower head has only 4–6 smooth-throated disc flowers. The petal-like inner bracts are pink or white. This 1–4′ species blooms for 1 month from August to October. It also inhabits dry, open places.

CAROLINA LILY
Lilium michauxii
Liliaceae (Lily Family)

Hike in an upland deciduous woodland in spring and you may see some smooth, fat, 6″, pale green leaves nestled in last year's layer of fallen leaves. You may see 1 or 2, maybe 3, leaves. At first, you might think you have found an orchid or fairy wand, but come back in the summer. Brave the heat and poison ivy and return to experience the glory of our native spotted orange lilies.

Lilium michauxii honors Andre Michaux (1746–1802), a French botanist who, with his son, explored North America and catalogued the continent's plants.

Most native lily bulbs are edible but should not be squandered in this manner. They are not everyday roadside plants. Development and the burgeoning deer population of the East Coast threaten their existence. They are collected by unscrupulous plant dealers, and one should inquire about the source of the plants when purchasing them.

FLOWER: Each perfect, regular, drooping flower has 6 reddish-yellow reflexed petals with dark spots at the base. The 6 white stamens project 2.5–3″ from the lily. Brush the purplish-brown anthers on the pendulous flowers, and you will have a long-lasting stain from the pollen. Each terminal panicle consists of 1–6 (up to 15, rarely) flowers.

BLOOMS: 3 weeks between May and August

LEAVES: Whorls of 4–15 smooth, dark green, entire leaves march up the unbranched, erect stem. The leaves on Carolina lily are obovate (widest near the apex). Other species with drooping flowers and whorled leaves have lanceolate leaves.

UNDERGROUND STRUCTURES: Whitish bulbs with overlapping scales increase in size each year and put out a stolon, from which a new young bulb develops.

SEEDS: The upright, green capsule is 2″ long and 0.5–1″ in diameter. When it turns brown and splits at 3 seams, the seeds are ripe (6–8 weeks after flowering, August to October). The flat, brown, triangular seeds stack neatly in 6 compartments in the capsule.

HEIGHT: 1–4′

HABITAT: *Lilium michauxii* inhabits rich, upland woods, especially at the edges of pine and oak woods.

CULTURAL TIPS (see page 62)**:** Plant Carolina lily in rich, moist, but well-draining humus. Mulch with shredded leaf compost each year. Divide the bulbs when the stems of the plants get thin and crowded. Deer and voles seem to eat lilies before any other plants. Fence against deer and add sharp gravel to the soil to deter rodents.

MOISTURE: A good moisture supply produces a more robust specimen.

pH: 5–6.5

EXPOSURE: Open shade with an hour or two of good sunlight each day

PROPAGATION (see page 66)**:** Scale cuttings are easiest.

SEED STORAGE: Store dry, fumigated seeds in an airtight container at 40° to 70°.

SEED TREATMENT: Stratify in 3-month periods starting at 70°, switching to 40°, and then back to 70°. Bloom in 5 years.

CUTTINGS (bulb scales)**:** After blooms fade

DIVISION: Fall division of bulbs; late summer or fall

FAUNA: The sticky stigma of lilies is right out in the open where pollen from its own anthers can adhere, but it recognizes its own pollen and blocks self-fertilization. Bees, especially bumblebees, transfer pollen. Butterflies, especially swallowtails, visit lilies.

OTHER SE SPECIES:
   Lilium canadense (Canada lily)—This lily is very tall, 5–10′. The petals are spotted, red-yellow, slightly reflexed; and the flowers are pendant in groups of 4–10. It likes a lot of moisture.
   L. catesbaei (Pine lily)—A 2–3′ species with 1–2 red, upright flowers and grasslike leaves; it inhabits moist, acidic sites.
   L. superbum—Turk's cap lily is similar to Carolina lily but taller (up to 11′) and with more flowers in the head. It grows in moist areas at higher elevations.
   L. tigrinum—An exotic spotted orange lily, the tiger lily, is common in gardens and can escape. It is easy to distinguish from the natives because it has shiny, dark bulblets in the leaf axils. Tiger lily often carries the mosaic virus that can spread to other cultivated lilies.

CARDINAL FLOWER,
RED LOBELIA
Lobelia cardinalis
Campanulaceae (Bellflower Family)

The brilliant red of the flowers of cardinal flower distinguishes it from all the other species of lobelia. When colonies of this erect plant, with its large showy raceme, bloom in midsummer in moist roadside ditches and along waterways, it is a breathtaking sight. Hummingbirds and butterflies add to the spectacle.

The genus name, *Lobelia,* honors Matthias de l'Obel (1538–1616), a Flemish botanist, also physician to King James I. The specific epithet, *cardinalis,* means scarlet, the color of cardinals' robes.

All of the *Lobelia* spp. have had historical use by Native Americans and in folk and herbal medicine. They were used for multiple disorders, but can be toxic and even deadly. Modern herbalists discourage their use.

FLOWER: The 1–2″ flowers are perfect, bilaterally symmetrical, and subtended by leafy bracts. The corolla has 2 lips. The erect upper lip has 2 short lobes. The spreading lower lip has 3 lobes. The 5 stamens unite around the style which extends from the mouth of the flower.

BLOOMS: 4 weeks between July and October

LEAVES: The smooth (or sometimes sparsely pubescent), upright, unbranched stems may be thin or very thick and sturdy. Before and after flowering, a rosette of basal leaves photosynthesizes even during the winter. At the time of flowering, the basal leaves are gone. Leaves can be 2″ wide by 7″ long. The pointed stem leaves are alternate, simple, elliptical to lanceolate, toothed, and taper to a petiole. Upper stem leaves are sessile.

UNDERGROUND STRUCTURES: Sturdy white feeder roots extend radially from the plant crown, which develops offsets. These baby plants form their own sets of roots by fall.

SEEDS: The capsules are chock full of brown, elliptic to round, rough seeds. Seeds in the lowest capsules are ripe while the upper flowers are just opening, and others continue to ripen for 7 weeks after the flowers fade. They remain in the squat, round capsules in their tiffany settings for a long time and gradually sift out through pores in the top.

HEIGHT: 2–6′, usually 3′

HABITAT: Cardinal flower pops up in swamps, flood plain forests, bogs, and meadows, and beside streams and rivers.

CULTURAL TIPS (see page 62)**:** The basal leaf rosette photosynthesizes in winter and should not be covered with mulch. *Lobelia cardinalis* is susceptible to mustard seed fungus and can be short-lived, but usually replaces itself with seedling plants if the site is moist. The more sun it has, the more water it needs. If you see frass at the base of the stem, a larva is feeding inside the stem. This is a serious problem for which I know no organic solution. I suggest taking one of the larvae to your local extension agent for treatment recommendations.

MOISTURE: Moist to wet

pH: 5.5–7

EXPOSURE: Filtered light or morning sun only

PROPAGATION (see page 66)**:** Seed is extremely easily.

SEED STORAGE: The capsules often have a white powdery substance on them at the time the seeds are mature and ready for collection. This material is not part of the plant but does not seem to affect the viability of the seeds. Store dry seeds in an airtight container between 40° and 70°.

SEED TREATMENT: Sow lightly, and cover very lightly (light requirement). At 70°, germinate in 2 weeks. Some bloom the first year. Another method is to place a flat of surface sown seeds outside in January or February and cover the flat with a piece of glass. Seeds germinate when the weather is conducive for growth.

CUTTINGS (stem): Young firm shoot tips in spring or juvenile growth anytime.

DIVISION: Pull apart basal offsets in early spring or fall; use a sterile knife if you must cut into the crown to avoid spreading fungus to all the plants.

LAYERING: In midsummer, bend a stalk to the ground, stake it, and cover it with 1/4″ of soil. New plants, which form at the leaf nodes, can be moved in the fall.

FAUNA: Cardinal flower is pollinated by hummingbirds but is also visited by bees and butterflies, especially the swallowtails. The insects like the blue-flowered lobelias as well as the red.

OTHER SE SPECIES (these have blue to white flowers):
Species in which flowers plus calyx are 3/4-11/2″ long:
Lobelia amoena—This smooth-stemmed species has a loose raceme of a few to 40 flowers. The calyx margins may have a few teeth. The leaves are elliptical to ovate.

L. elongata (longleaf or purple lobelia)—This 5′ species is similar to *L. amoena,* but the lanceolate leaves are narrow and taper at both ends. It is common in the Coastal Plain.

L. puberula (downy lobelia)—This hairy-stemmed species has 20–100 bright blue flowers. The calyx margins may have a few teeth; it is common throughout the Southeast.

L. siphilitica (blue lobelia)—This 2–3′ species has 1″ bright blue flowers with a white throat stripe. The calyx is pubescent. There are no basal leaves at the time of bloom, but the stem is covered with pointed leaves. Native Americans and early settlers thought (mistakenly) that *Lobelia siphilitica* cured venereal disease. It is common throughout the Southeast.

Species in which flowers plus calyx are 1/4-3/4″ long:
Lobelia inflata (Indian tobacco, gagroot, emeticweed, pukeweed, vomitroot)—Leaves in the middle of the stem are at least 1/4″ wide. The oval bracts right under the flowers are leafy. The lower stem is pubescent, and the seed capsule is inflated. The common name, Indian tobacco, comes from the tobacco taste of the leaves. In fact, no record of its use as a tobacco product by Native Americans exists. The leaves, when chewed, cause profuse sweating, headache, and vomiting. Widespread use in folk medicine in the early to mid-1800s led to numerous deaths. It is common throughout the Southeast.

L. spicata—Like *L. inflata,* the median stem leaves are more than 1/4″ wide, but the stem is generally smooth. It may be slightly pubescent near the base. It is common throughout the Southeast.

CORAL HONEYSUCKLE,
SCARLET HONEYSUCKLE,
MAILBOX HONEYSUCKLE
Lonicera sempervirens
Caprifoliaceae (Honeysuckle Family)

One of the first plants to sustain hummingbirds on their journey north in the spring is coral or scarlet honeysuckle. The thin trumpet-shaped blooms hang in large clusters, providing a banquet for weary avian travelers. This native vine covers a fence steadily but slowly, unlike the romping, invasive Japanese honeysuckle that chokes woodlands and borders over the entire East.

The genus name *Lonicera* honors Adam Lonitzer (1528–1586), a German herbalist. *Sempervirens* is from the Latin, meaning "everliving."

In the middle to lower South, where the leaves of this vine can be evergreen, it is commonly planted at the base of mailboxes, giving it the common name, mailbox honeysuckle.

FLOWER: Each 2″, regular, perfect, tubular flower has 5 lobes and 5 stamens. The corolla is coral or scarlet, and the stamens are yellow. The flower clusters form at the leaf axils (where the leaf meets the stem). Sadly, the flowers are not fragrant.

BLOOMS: 8–12 weeks beginning in April or May

LEAVES: The opposite, simple, 1-3″ leaves are a smooth, rich green on the top side and whitish-green below. Most of the leaves are ovate to obovate and have no pedicel (or a very small one). The pair of leaves at the terminal end of a shoot, right behind an inflorescence, unite to enclose the stem and are more rounded in appearance than the majority of the leaves. The vine twines to climb. Old growth becomes woody. It is not evergreen in the upper South.

UNDERGROUND STRUCTURES: Fibrous, yellowish-tan feeder roots anchor the vine. New roots form wherever a leaf node touches the ground.

SEEDS: The sparse berries are red and 1/4″ in diameter. They ripen in late summer.

HEIGHT: 10–20′ vine

HABITAT: Occurs naturally in open woods and at woods edge

CULTURAL TIPS (see page 62)**:** Needs good air flow to avoid mildew. With attention, it can be grown in a large pot. Prune after flowering. Treat aphids with insecticidal soap, neem oil, or prune tips when they look deformed. Drought can cause stress, and stressed plants are more susceptible to mildew.

MOISTURE: Moist but draining

pH: 4.5–6.5

EXPOSURE: Full to partial sun

PROPAGATION (see page 66)**:** Cuttings are easiest.

SEED STORAGE: Store clean (remove pulp), dry seeds in a closed container between 40° and 70°.

SEED TREATMENT: Stratify for 3 months at 40°; sow at 70°. Watch for germination during the period of cold; bloom in 1–2 years.

CUTTINGS (stem)**:** New growth, May–July; root in 6 weeks

DIVISION: Avoid disturbing established roots

LAYERING: Any time during the growing season

FAUNA: The long-tongued hummingbird is able to lap nectar from the long floral tubes and, in exchange, pollinates the flowers with the pollen he carries on his face and bill. The sticky pistil projects from the flower, and the hummer brushes past it as he pushes into the flower to get nectar. As he gets deeper into the flower tube, pollen from the anthers clings to his face, and he carries it on to other honeysuckle plants.

OTHER SE SPECIES:
> ***Lonicera japonica***—This fragrant but invasive exotic has lightly hairy leaves and black berries all along the vine. The yellow floral tube is shorter than the tube in coral honeysuckle. This flower is pollinated by the evening-flying sphinx moths.

FALSE SOLOMON'S SEAL,
SOLOMON'S PLUME, SNAKE CORN
Maianthemum racemosa (Smilacina racemosa)
Liliaceae (Lily Family)

False Solomon's seal resembles true Solomon's seal *(Polygonatum biflorum)* in leaf shape and arrangement, but the flowers and fruit are all at the end of the single leafy stalk instead of scattered along the stem. Each year's dying stem leaves a scar on the rhizome that is reputed to look like the 6-pointed star on the seal of King Solomon.

The genus name *Maianthemum* comes from the Greek for May flower. In the South, false Solomon's seal peeks from the ground in late March, blooms in April, and is setting seeds by the end of May. It is a common inhabitant of many different woodland habitats over the eastern United States and into Canada.

Native Americans fed the rhizomes to hogs to prevent hog cholera. They also mixed the rhizomes with oats to fatten ponies. Humans can eat the young shoots in salads or prepared like asparagus. The berries are edible but mildly cathartic. Before consumption, the rhizome must be soaked in lye for 3–10 hours and parboiled; the cooking water must be discarded.

Many records of medicinal uses by Native Americans exist. The Cherokee used a cold infusion of the rhizome as a wash for sore eyes. Smoke from the rhizome was inhaled to treat insanity and to quiet a crying child. Rhizome tea was used to treat constipation and rheumatism, as a general tonic for people with stomach disorders, and for pregnant women. Tea prepared from the leaf was used as a contraceptive and for coughs. A poultice made from the leaf was used externally for bleeding, rashes, itching, and swelling. Various parts of the plant prepared in different ways seem to constitute a complete pharmacopoeia.

FLOWER: As the column of round, white flower buds emerges from the ground, it is sheltered by a partially open sheath of leaves and looks like a miniature ear of corn, thus the common name snake corn. The regular, perfect flowers are white or greenish. Each one is small, 6-parted, and starlike. The stamens are petal-like and showy. Up to 40 small flowers comprise each panicle of racemes. This slender grouping of flowers is reminiscent of a plume or feather.

BLOOMS: 1 month between April and early June

LEAVES: The leaves alternate on the 2–3′, upright, unbranched, arching stems. The sessile, dark green leaves are 2-3″ wide and 4-6″ long. They lie almost horizontally to the stem. They have 3–5 visible ribs, and the leaf edges may be flat or wavy.

UNDERGROUND STRUCTURES: The pale brown to whitish rhizome is thumb-sized and fleshy. These underground stems branch as they creep, creating great colonies of the graceful plumes. Feeder roots develop from the rhizome.

SEEDS: Each berry contains 1–3 ovoid, pale tan seeds. The fleshy, pea-sized berries change color from green to speckled blush to bright red as they ripen. They mature from August to October.

HEIGHT: 2–3′

HABITAT: False Solomon's seal can be found in rich humus in rocky, moist woods and in thickets below 3,500′ elevation.

CULTURAL TIPS (see page 62): Plant in an area without heavy tree root competition.

MOISTURE: A rich, moist site will help keep the leaves looking fresh into the fall.

pH: 4.5–6.5

EXPOSURE: Filtered shade of a deciduous woodland

PROPAGATION (see page 66): Division is the most reliable and quickest method.

SEED STORAGE: After removing the pulp from the seeds, they appear to be dry seeds, but they lose viability in dry storage. Store temporarily in moist spaghum at 40°.

SEED TREATMENT: Sow fresh, cleaned seeds outdoors. Cover the seeds with 1/4–1/2″ soil (possible dark requirement). Germinate in 2 years. Stratification using alternating 6 week periods of warm and cold shorten the time to germination, but the seedlings grow best if the seed germinates in the ground.

CUTTINGS (rhizome): Dig rhizomes after the bloom fades but while the foliage is still firm. Divide into 3″ sections, being sure each piece has a latent bud.

DIVISION: Fall or spring

FAUNA: Birds (ruffed grouse, gray-checked, and olive-backed thrushes) and the white-footed mouse eat the seeds of false Solomon's seal.

FALSE ALOE
Manfreda virginica
(Agave virginica)
Agavaceae
(Century Plant Family)

During a woodland ramble, you may stumble upon a green rosette of leaves that looks remarkably like a household aloe plant. Like the yuccas, it looks as if it should be in a desert setting in the Southwest, but it truly is an eastern woodland native. The succulent leaves and small flowers are curious, but rarely elicit a second glance. Anyone who has smelled the intoxicating evening fragrance develops an appreciation for the wiles of this unassuming flower.

Do not attempt to treat burns with the juice of this aloe. The plant juices cause dermatitis or skin irritation in some people. Native Americans drank a tea made from the root of *Manfreda virginica* as a diuretic.

FLOWER: Inconspicuous, fragrant, 1″ tubular flowers form a raceme at the top of a tall stalk. The purplish stamens with yellow anthers project way beyond the fused green petals to create a spiky, brush-like effect.

BLOOMS: 3 weeks between May and August

LEAVES: This agave family member has a basal rosette of smooth, lanceolate, pointed leaves from which the nearly naked flower stalk arises. The semi-evergreen, fleshy leaves are light green, occasionally speckled with maroon spots. Leaves can be 4-12″

long. Young leaves begin life upright. Older, outer leaves may lie on the ground. Water is stored in the succulent leaves.

UNDERGROUND STRUCTURES: The underground base of the plant is a white bulb-like swelling. A limited number of thick white feeder roots emerge from the swollen rootstock.

SEEDS: Flat, black semicircles are massed in a 3-chambered capsule. An individual plant rarely has more than 4–5 capsules, but I've never seen a colony of false aloe. Perhaps pollination levels are low when plants are scattered in the woods. The seeds ripen between September and November.

HEIGHT: The flowering stalk reaches 4–6′, giving rise to the family grouping in the Agavaceae. *Agave* comes from the Greek word meaning noble.

HABITAT: Aloe inhabits upland woods, dry and rocky woods, woodland edge, prairies, and partially shaded drainage areas.

CULTURAL TIPS (see page 62)**:** False aloe may inhabit fairly dry, sterile woodlands but it is perfectly happy in the well-draining loam of a perennial garden. When moving plants, dig a sizable root ball. The roots detach easily from the base. Until the plant is established (1 year), water during periods of drought. Once established, no additional water is necessary.

MOISTURE: Average to dry

pH: 4.5–6.5

EXPOSURE: Light shade or partial sun

PROPAGATION (see page 66)**:** Seed is easy.

SEED STORAGE: Store dry seeds in an airtight container between 40° and 70°.

SEED TREATMENT: Stratify for 6 weeks at 40° (refrigerated or outside); sow at 70°. Germinate in 3–4 weeks. Seedlings are easy to handle.

CUTTINGS: No

DIVISION: Spring or fall; plants very slow to produce offsets.

FAUNA: Moths are attracted to the airborne perfume in the evening and they pollinate the flowers.

PARTRIDGEBERRY,
TWINBERRY
Mitchella repens
Rubiaceae (Madder Family)

Partridgeberry forms an evergreen ground cover in woodlands
throughout the eastern United States. It even crosses the
Mississippi River into the Big Thicket of east Texas. It occurs in
several different types of forests: moist beech-oak; drier oak-pine;
maritime; and seasonally wet, sweet gum-oak flood plains. The
mat of dark green leaves is handsome all by itself, but the plant
also has lovely white flowers and bright red berries. It adapts well
to home gardens and does not choke out neighbors like so many
of the introduced ground covers commonly used in landscaping.

The genus name honors Dr. John Mitchell (1711–1768), a
Virginia physician and botanist who also prepared maps of North
America that helped resolve boundary disputes in later years.

Among many common names for *Mitchella repens* are running
box, twinberry, tea berry, squaw plum, squaw berry, and squaw
vine. Native American women of numerous tribes drank tea made
from the leaves and/or berries before and during childbirth for
pain relief. The tea was used as a general tonic for any condition
affecting the uterus, and also as a diuretic and astringent.

FLOWER: Paired pink buds open into fragrant, white salverform
(funnel-shaped) flowers with a united ovary. The corolla has 4
recurved bearded lobes. The flowers develop at leaf nodes and terminal ends of the trailing stems. Occasionally, blooms reappear in
the fall, and flowers and drupes can be seen simultaneously.

BLOOMS: 3–4 weeks between May and June

LEAVES: The opposite, evergreen, smooth, leathery leaves have short stalks. They are almost round and vary from $1/8$-1″ in diameter. The creeping stems root at the leaf nodes and form large mats.

UNDERGROUND STRUCTURES: The leathery feeder roots are golden.

SEEDS: The $1/4$″ red fruits are really globelike drupes containing 4–8 hard seeds. The fruit has 2 dark spots where the paired flowers dehisced.

HEIGHT: 2–8″

HABITAT: Partridgeberry inhabits moist and dry woodlands.

CULTURAL TIPS (see page 62): In the South, sod-like patches can be transplanted in the winter. Gardeners in more northern areas can move patches in the spring or fall.

MOISTURE: Moist to fairly dry

pH: 4–6.5

EXPOSURE: Deep shade, filtered light, or partial sun (morning only; leaves yellow in full sun in the afternoon)

PROPAGATION (see page 66): Cuttings best in the South

SEED STORAGE: Store clean seed 3-4 months in moist spaghnum at 40°.

SEED TREATMENT: In November, remove red fleshy covering and sow outdoors or stratify for 6-12 weeks at 40°. Sow at 70°.

CUTTINGS (stem): Root any time of year; 6–8″ pieces; hormone unnecessary; roots in 3 months

DIVISION: Fall or winter

FAUNA: Grouse, bobwhite, turkey, and the white-footed mouse eat the berries.

WILD BERGAMOT,
HORSE MINT
Monarda fistulosa
Lamiaceae (Mint Family)

Wild bergamot shares its beauty and bounty with insects and animals. It is still a common roadside plant on county roads, even in this age of herbicides. It thrives on steep rocky sites in full sun or partial shade, just beyond the reach of the spray wand. *Monarda fistulosa* earned the common name wild bergamot, because the oil from the leaves smells like the wild bergamot (*Citrus aurantium* var. *bergamia*) used to flavor Earl Grey tea.

The genus name honors Nicolas Monardes (1493–1588) a Spanish botanist and physician. He wrote the first European book on American medicinal plants. In Latin, a *fistula* is a pipe or tube and refers to the hollow stems.

Native Americans used a poultice of the leaves for headaches and colds. They also drank a tea made from the leaves for stomach aches and insomnia.

To make tea from any of the *Monarda* spp., steep the leaves in hot water for 10 minutes. Mix with other teas or sweeten if desired.

FLOWER: The terminal inflorescence is a 2″ diameter poof of irregular flowers. The flowers are usually lavender but may be pink or white. A ring of white to pinkish bracts encircles the underside of the flower cluster. Each 1-1.5″ long, finely hairy corolla has an arched upper lip with a tuft of hairs and a 3-lobed lower lip with dark purple spots. Two stamens extend beyond the corolla mouth. The flowers open from the center of the cluster outward, giving the bloom a "Friar Tuck" look toward the end of the bloom period.

BLOOMS: 4 weeks between May and September

LEAVES: The 2-4″ long, lanceolate leaves are opposite, simple, petiolate (stalked), and toothed. They are rounded or blunt at the base. Oil-bearing glands on the foliage exude a minty fragrance when crushed. The square stems of the plant can be smooth or hairy and green to dark purple. It can be branched or unbranched.

UNDERGROUND STRUCTURES: With the enthusiasm typical of a mint, wild bergamot rapidly forms mats of square, white rhizomes.

SEEDS: The dry, brown flower contains 4 nutlets, each of which can contain a shiny, ovoid seed. They ripen from July through October

HEIGHT: 3–4′

HABITAT: Woodland edges, roadsides, and prairies

CULTURAL TIPS (see page 62)**:** All of the *Monarda* spp. are prone to mildew on the leaves. Full sun, plenty of moisture, plus good drainage and adequate air flow are the best preventive measures. Plants get mildew when they are stressed, not when the humidity is high. Divide the plants every 3 years.

MOISTURE: Average to dry; tolerates moisture if drainage is good

pH: 5–6.5

EXPOSURE: Full to partial sun

PROPAGATION (see page 66)**:** Division of rhizomes is easiest.

SEED STORAGE: Store dry seeds in an airtight container between 40° and 70°. Viability decreases rapidly over 3 years.

SEED TREATMENT: Sow at 70°. Cover very lightly (light requirement). Germinate in 7–10 days.

CUTTINGS (Stem)**:** Young shoots in early spring as soon as they harden a bit; poor root formation to none, once the hormone for flowering begins to circulate and once the stems become hollow

DIVISION: Early spring or fall

FAUNA: Hummingbirds, butterflies, bees, and many other insects visit *Monarda* spp. for nectar and pollen. Bees are the most efficient pollinators. Goldfinches and field sparrows eat the seeds in winter.

OTHER SE SPECIES:

Monarda citriodora (lemon mint)—This annual species has showy flowers in 2 or more whorls at the top of the stem. Each flower has a lavender corolla with purplish spots. The pointed bracts can be purple, lavender, or white. It is found on calcareous outcrops and prairies.

Monarda didyma (beebalm)—Beebalm has red flowers and bracts in a large terminal head. It occurs mainly in the mountains in seepage areas.

M. punctata (spotted horsemint)—Spotted horsemint has showy flowers in 2 or more whorls at the top of the stem. The corolla is yellow spotted with purple. The bracts are white or purplish. It is found in sandy, dry, open woods and fields.

SUNDROPS
Oenothera fruticosa
Onagraceae (Evening Primrose Family)

Members of the evening primrose family have showy flowers in shades of yellow, white, pink, and red. Sundrops have yellow flowers that open during the day and will close on a cloudy day. Some species have flowers that open at night and close about noon the next day. Species like *O. fruticosa* are considerate neighbors in a cultivated garden. Others, like the yellow biennial and the pink showy primrose, romp all over the garden—the proverbial guest who won't go home.

Onager is the Greek word for wild ass. These beasts threw stones with their hind legs when agitated. In ancient times, a stone-throwing catapult became know as an onager. The first plant to be given the genus name was the weedy biennial sundrop, which flings its seeds far and wide.

Oeno is a Greek combining form meaning wine. The roots of some members of the evening primrose family were combined with wine, adding to the merry mood.

FLOWER: The flowers are sulfur yellow, 2″ in diameter, regular, perfect dollops of sunshine. They have 4 notched petals and 8 stamens. They gather in erect, terminal clusters with a few singles in the leaf nodes directly below the tip.

BLOOMS: 6–8 weeks between April and August

LEAVES: The smooth lanceolate to lance-elliptical, 2–3″ leaves alternate on the ruddy stem. The leaves are smooth and petioled. The stem has hairs that lie nearly flat and point upward. *O. fruticosa* ssp. *glauca (O. tetragona)* is nearly identical to *O. fruticosa,* except the hair on the stem is short and spreading and the hair on the capsule is glandular (knob-tipped). Lower leaves have a pair of small leaflets in the axil. After the flower fades, basal leaves emerge and form a rosette that turns red in winter. Dots of maroon pigment appear haphazardly in the leaves.

UNDERGROUND STRUCTURES: Fast-growing rhizomes support the original rosette and quickly produce new rosettes. Colonies of basal rosettes form a solid groundcover over time.

SEEDS: Nonglandular hairs hug the seed capsule and point in one direction. The 4-chambered capsule is extremely woody. The tiny brown seeds have little or no endosperm.

HEIGHT: 1–2′

HABITAT: Wet to dry rocky places, moist or dry thin woods, fields, or salt marshes

CULTURAL TIPS (see page 62)**:** Looks great with dark blue spiderwort. Sundrops will tolerate some drought but grow best in deep, highly organic soil, which retains moisture.

MOISTURE: Moist, well-drained

pH: 5–6

EXPOSURE: Full to partial sun

PROPAGATION (see page 66)**:** Division is the easiest method. I find few seeds in the capsules, and the seeds have little endosperm to nourish the germinating plant.

SEED STORAGE: Collect when hard capsules split open at end. Store dry seeds in an airtight container between 40° and 70°.

SEED TREATMENT: Sow at 70°. Germinate in 7–10 days

CUTTINGS (stem)**:** After flowering

DIVISION (rosettes)**:** Fall

FAUNA: Await observation

OTHER SE SPECIES:

   Oenothera biennis—These yellow, fragrant flowers open in the evening in sync with the nocturnal habits of their pollinators, sphinx moths. The plant is upright to 4–6′, and blooms between June and October. This common, weedy plant seeds vigorously in fields, roadsides, rocky woods, and gardens throughout most of the United States. Oil from the seeds has historical and current medicinal use.

   O. speciosa—These lovely pink to white roadside flowers on sprawling 1–2′ plants are naturalized from the Midwest, from Texas and Mexico eastward. They bloom continuously from March to August and tolerate heat, exposure, and a wide pH range (5–6.5 or higher). But beware, they will take over your garden.

PRICKLY PEAR CACTUS,
DEVIL'S TONGUE, INDIAN FIG,
OLD MAN'S HAND
Opuntia humifusa
Cactaceae (Cactus Family)

A cactus in the eastern deciduous forest? Yes, indeed. This dangerously barbed plant is common all over the East Coast. It has gorgeous, huge, yellow flowers and edible fruit. Since the pads remain alive above ground over winter, it is technically a woody plant, but it is short in stature and is used in landscaping like a flowering perennial. Since you will surely encounter it, and it may look out of its habitat, it has earned a place in this wildflower book.

The genus name *Opuntia* is a result of mistaken identity. The American plant resembled a plant that grew near the city of Opus in Greece. Pliny the Elder had named the Greek plant *Opuntium* in his book, *Natural History*. When prickly pear was first used by herbalists in Europe, it was thought to be the same as the Greek *Opuntium. Humifusa* means spreading.

Native Americans peeled the pads and placed the mucilaginous inner material on wounds and warts. They also drank a tea made from the pads for lung problems.

The fruit and the pads are edible. The flesh of the fruit can be eaten uncooked. The dried seeds can be ground into flour and used for baking or thickening. The flesh of young stems (pads) can be eaten like green beans once peeled. Use a small propane torch to remove the spines before peeling the fruit or stems.

FLOWER: The pure yellow sepals and petals are nearly identical, forming a showy, 3″ diameter floral cup. Numerous stamens form a ring around the pistil. This would be a good interstate roadside plant—indestructible, visible, and identifiable at 70 mph.

BLOOMS: 3 weeks between May and July

LEAVES: The jointed pads of prickly pear are actually the stem of the plant. They have the shape of a ping pong paddle and can reach 10″ long. They are fleshy and about ¹/₂″ thick. Stubby cactus fingers extend from the end of mature blades, and a bloom opens on the end of one or more of the stubs. Tiny leaves below the clumps of hair-like spines (glochids) fall early; 2-3″ long spines may or may not be present among the smaller hairy barbs. The long spines can cause a serious puncture, but it is the bristles that cause the longest lasting injury. The little barbs break off in the skin, causing itchy, painful dermatitis.

UNDERGROUND STRUCTURES: Remarkably small feeder roots support this prostrate mat. The fleshy, wax-covered stems store water, thus deep, water-absorbing roots are not necessary.

SEEDS: The decorative fruit is a shiny reddish-brown berry about the size and shape of a large, smooth date. It is edible after the tiny spines are removed.

HEIGHT: 3–4′

HABITAT: Sandy or rocky open areas

CULTURAL TIPS (see page 62): Cactus spines readily penetrate rubber or leather gloves. To handle the pads, enfold them in a thick layer of newspaper. Site the plants carefully. Only a very determined gardener, a bulldozer, or repeated fire will defeat this plant.

MOISTURE: Dry to average

pH: 5–6

EXPOSURE: Full to partial sun

PROPAGATION (see page 66): Cuttings are easiest. Handle pads with thick layers of newspaper or tongs.

SEED STORAGE: Store clean, dry seeds in an airtight container between 40° and 70°.

SEED TREATMENT: Wash and clean the seeds well before storage. Vernalize 6 months. Sow at 70°-80° in a soil mix of half outdoor "dirt" and half seed-starting mix. Germinate in 2-4 weeks. Bloom in 3–4 years.

CUTTINGS (stem): Insert a pad into sand in a container or directly into a sandy garden site. It will root in 3–4 weeks.

DIVISION: Spring or fall

FAUNA: The dotted skipper visits prickly pear cactus for nectar. Deer and rabbits eat the fruit and pads. Wild turkey, some songbirds, squirrels, and other rodents eat the fruit and seeds.

GOLDEN CLUB,
BOG CANDLE, NEVER WET
Orontium aquaticum
Araceae (Arum Family)

Unlike some other members of the arum family, this spring
bloomer flaunts its bright spadix for all the world to see. In bogs
and in the middle of woodland streams, the 2′ yellow-and-white
candles of golden club subtended by large, dark green leaves grab
your attention. You won't confuse it with any other plant.

Orontes was a character in the Aeneid by Virgil. He went down
with his ship when Juno convinced the winds to sink the fleet of
Aeneas. The seed of golden club sinks in its vessel also. The *Or* in
Orontium adds another layer of meaning to the genus name—it is
French for gold, the color of the flowers. *Aquaticum* is simply
Latin for "growing in water."

Both the berry and the roots are edible, but must be thoroughly
dried or boiled and rinsed before eating. They contain an acrid
compound that is offensively peppery.

Native Americans used the dried ground root for flour and the
boiled fruit as a pea-like vegetable.

FLOWER: Many bright yellow, regular flowers cap the upper end of the spadix. The spadix is about 1/4″ in diameter, thickening when in fruit. The lax or erect scape (leafless flower stalk) is white to red below the yellow flowers. The lower flowers are perfect, and the ones toward the tip of the spadix are more likely male. The sheath (the hood in the jack-in-the-pulpit) encloses the stalk of the budding inflorescence but either falls away or loosely wraps the base of the elongating stalk. The scape arches when the tip is heavy with berries.

BLOOMS: 3 weeks between March and June

LEAVES: Water beads and rolls right off the 6–12″, basal, elliptical, entire, dark green leaves. When the plant is in a stream, some of the leaves float on the water and wave back and forth on their long petioles. They are parallel-veined with no obvious midrib.

UNDERGROUND STRUCTURES: Thick rhizomes with fleshy feeder roots are amassed in the mud.

SEEDS: The fruit is a blue-green, gummy utricle (a bladder-like container that does not split open when the seed is ripe). The single seed inside is a flattish round seed and has no endosperm. The fruit falls from the stalk and sinks into the mud. The seed germinates 2 weeks later.

HEIGHT: 2–3′

HABITAT: Bogs, shallow streams, and swamps

CULTURAL TIPS (see page 62): Golden club is slow growing and does best in rich soil. Leaves persist year-round in areas with little frost.

MOISTURE: Plant in water 2-6″ deep, standing or flowing

pH: 4.5–5.5

EXPOSURE: Full to partial shade

PROPAGATION (see page 66): Seed is easy and quick.

SEED STORAGE: The fruit can be stored at 70° in moist spaghnum in a plastic bag for a few days.

SEED TREATMENT: Sow fresh in mucky soil in a nondraining container and leave outside. Germinate in 4–15 days; bloom in 3 years.

CUTTINGS: No

DIVISION: Possible, but a slow method of propagation

FAUNA: Await observation

ALLEGHENY SPURGE
Pachysandra procumbens
Buxaceae (Box Family)

Unlike the ubiquitous Japanese pachysandra, our native pachysandra species changes with the seasons. It has showy flowers in spring, fresh green leaves in summer, and mottled foliage in winter. Unfortunately, this native is fussy about where it lives and will not adapt to any old shady site as the exotic species will.

The Greek *pachys* means thick, and *andros* means male, describing the stamens.

FLOWER: 1–5 fragrant flower spikes nestle at the base of a petiole of a recumbent winter leaf. The flower has no petals but is quite showy. The spike is 4-5″ tall, and the white stamens are large and in groups of 4. There are many male flowers at the top of the spike and a few female flowers at the base. The sepals are green or purplish.

BLOOMS: 3 weeks between March and April

LEAVES: 4–6 oval, slightly furry, stemmed, 3–5″ leaves gather near the end of a thick stem that rises straight up in spring but gradually elongates and becomes recumbent as it elongates as the season progresses. In spring, the new leaves are bright lime green. In late fall, brown pigments mottle the leaves in a camouflage pattern.

UNDERGROUND STRUCTURES: The plant slowly increases in size by creeping stolons. A modest number of feeder roots support the stolons.

SEEDS: Each 3-chambered capsule can contain as many as 3 seeds.

HEIGHT: 6–10″

HABITAT: Rich, calcareous woodland slopes

CULTURAL TIPS (see page 62)**:** Consider this plant a specimen, not a ground cover. It spreads slowly. Divide to create a ground cover. Add humus! Avoid direct sunlight.

MOISTURE: Moist, but must drain

pH: 6–7

EXPOSURE: Light to heavy shade of a deciduous woodland

PROPAGATION (see page 66)**:** Division is easiest. Stem cuttings form new roots slowly and rot easily. The cutting medium must drain very well.

SEED STORAGE: Collection difficult; store temporarily in moist spaghnum at 40°

SEED TREATMENT: Sow fresh in an outdoor bed.

CUTTINGS (mallet)**:** Early summer; cuttings with a piece of the stolon or crown still attached

DIVISION: February or September

FAUNA: Await observation

PASSION FLOWER,
MAYPOPS, APRICOT
Passiflora incarnata
Passifloraceae (Passion Flower Family)

The showy violet flower of the passion flower, also called passion vine, looks like a tropical blossom. Many of its relatives do hail from the tropics. Almost all have edible fruit. Some gardeners consider these fast-growing vines "too weedy." In my experience, natural forces control its enthusiasm. The vine emerges fairly late in the spring, after all danger of frost is over. It grows and blooms rampantly all summer, then often disappears in October and November under the voracious grazing of the caterpillars of fritillary butterflies.

Passiflora literally means passion flower, not in the sense of eroticism but referring to the Christian passion. All the parts of the flower are in fives, so symbolism abounds. The combined sepals and petals could represent the apostles. The column of the ovary resembles a cross. The vine tendrils might be scourges. The 3 stigmas could be nails.

The fruit is edible fresh or cooked into juice or jelly. Many commercial fruit juices have passion fruit as an ingredient.

The common name maypop comes from the sound the fruit makes when stomped on the ground.

The Cherokee used a poultice of the root on boils and other inflammations, and they dripped a warm solution of the root extract into the ear for earaches.

Extracts of the dried plant are used in Europe to soothe anxiety, promote sleep, and lower blood pressure. But please exercise caution; it may be harmful in excess.

FLOWER: The perfect, regular, stalked flower is 2″ in diameter. 5 whitish sepals form the base of a cup. Next, the 5 blue to purple petals add a layer to the cup. A fringe called the corona forms the sides of the cup. 5–6 bands of violet pigment line the corona. A fountain of stamens and stigmas rises in the middle of the cup.

BLOOMS: 3 months between May and September; individual flowers last 3 days.

LEAVES: The slightly hairy, 3-lobed leaves are finely toothed and have a petiole. The 3–6″ leaves alternate on the vining stem and single flowers dangle from the axil of the leaf. At the base of the leaf blade are two glands that contain nectar. The vine climbs by tendrils.

UNDERGROUND STRUCTURES: The "roots" are creamy colored and fleshy. They must be a type of underground stem since cut pieces can produce a shoot. They lie in the soil until the temperature stimulates them and then they give rise to rapidly growing foliage.

SEEDS: The black seeds look like small, rough watermelon seeds. A clear gelatinous bubble (aril) encloses each seed. The unripe fruit looks like a pale lime. When ripe, it is wrinkled and yellowish.

HEIGHT: Vine can climb 10–20′ if it has support. Otherwise, it functions as a ground cover.

HABITAT: Fields, roadsides, open woods, often in sandy soils

CULTURAL TIPS (see page 62)**:** Passion vine is particularly beautiful when climbing a lattice or fence.

MOISTURE: Average to dry

pH: 5–6

EXPOSURE: Full to partial sun

PROPAGATION (see page 66)**:** Cuttings or division is more predictable than seed propagation.

SEED STORAGE: Removing the clear material around the seeds is difficult when first collected. Put the whole fruit in the refrigerator for 2–3 months. The jelly will have lost its glutinous quality and will have disappeared or be easy to remove when dessicated.

SEED TREATMENT: After the fruit has dried in the refrigerator, clean the seed and sow at 70°-90°. Germinate sporadically over a long period, as much as 2 years.

CUTTINGS (stem)**:** 6–8″; June

DIVISION: Dig suckers in early fall.

FAUNA: *Passiflora* spp. are host plants for variegated and gulf fritillary butterflies. Hummingbirds and bees visit the flowers. Deer and rabbits may eat the fruit.

OTHER SE SPECIES:

    Passiflora lutea—This vine has 1″ inconspicuous yellowish-green blooms. The leaves are shallowly lobed, and it has a black berry. It is shade-tolerant.

SMOOTH
BEARDTONGUE
Penstemon digitalis
Scrophulariaceae
(Snapdragon or
Figwort Family)

There are over 250 species of
North American beardtongues,
but the majority of them are
western plants. The eastern
species have white, pinkish,
or lavender blooms and are
usually found on well-lit and
well-drained slopes. Showy
clusters of lipped flowers make
identification in the spring
easy, but even when neither
flowers nor seeds exist, one can
identify the genus by the basal
rosette. In the fall, it changes from green to orange or burgundy.
Did you ever wonder where textile designers get their ideas about
appropriate seasonal colors? Before their winter dormancy, plants
lose the chlorophyll (the green pigment) before they lose the
anthocyanins (the blue and red pigments). The red and maroon
tones appear in the fall and increase in cold weather.

The genus name comes from the Greek, *pente,* meaning five,
and *stemon,* meaning stamen. *Digitalis* comes from the Latin
digitus, for finger, referring to the shape of the flower. The
common name beardtongue comes from the hairs on the sterile
stamen in some species.

In England in the seventeenth century, other members of the
Scrophulariaceae or figwort family were used to treat scrofula, the
King's Evil, and hemorrhoids, commonly referred to as figs. (See
explanation of wort under *Tradescantia virginiana,* spiderwort.)

FLOWER: Smooth, white beardtongue has an open panicle of flowers
in white or purple with a white interior. Each flower has a long
floral tube that flares into 5 irregular lobes. The upper lip has 2
lobes. The lower lip has 3 lobes. The floral tube swells abruptly in
the middle, which distinguishes it from some other species. The
single feathery pistil extends from the mouth of the flower; 1 of
the 5 stamens has no functional anther and is sterile. The 4
functional anthers are dark brown. Pink or purple guidelines on
the floor of the flower direct pollinators to the nectary.

BLOOMS: 3 weeks between April and June

LEAVES: Beardtongue has 2 kinds of leaves. The basal leaves are oval
and stalked. The stem leaves are opposite and clasp the upright
stem. *Penstemon digitalis* is smooth except for thin lines of hairs

on the underside of the leaves. The leaves are simple, toothed, and medium green. The reddish basal rosette lasts most of the winter.

UNDERGROUND STRUCTURES: A fan of white, fibrous roots anchors the crown.

SEEDS: A shiny brown or maroon, ovoid, hard seed capsule contains a large number of round, brown seeds. Crushed capsules have a distinctive smell, which resembles the smell of boxwoods (if you are like me—and about half the population—you think a boxwood smells like a cat just visited). Collect seeds in July or August.

HEIGHT: 2–3´

HABITAT: Open woods, meadows, and prairies

CULTURAL TIPS (see page 62)**:** Beardtongues can be short-lived perennials. Seed-grown plants from a local ecotype (a plant of the same species can be slightly different from one geographic area to another) are more likely to thrive and persist in the garden.

MOISTURE: Dry to average, with good drainage

pH: 4.5–5.5

EXPOSURE: Full to partial to lightly filtered sun

PROPAGATION (see page 66)**:** Seed is easiest.

SEED STORAGE: Crush the capsules with a rolling pin to release the seeds. Store dry seed in an airtight container between 40° and 70°.

SEED TREATMENT: Stratify for 3 months at 40°; sow at 70°. Germinate in 1 week. Start the cold treatment in April to produce a blooming plant in 1 year.

CUTTINGS (stem)**:** After bloom

DIVISION: Fall or early spring

FAUNA: The shape and color of the flowers suggest pollination by bees or wasps. *Penstemon digitalis* is one of the host plants for the buckeye butterfly.

OTHER SE SPECIES:

Penstemon australis—This species has lightly hairy stems and stem leaves. The infertile stamen is golden and extends beyond the flower opening. It is found in dry pinelands, sand hills, and fields.

P. canescens—In this species, the stems and oval stem leaves are hairy. The infertile stamen is yellow and does not extend beyond the floral tube. It is found in dry, sandy, or rocky soils in thin woods and fields and along roadsides.

P. hirsutus (hairy beardtongue)—As the names suggest, this plant has hairy stems. The stem leaves are lanceolate. The flowers are purple to violet with white lobes and a nearly closed throat. It is found in dry woods and thickets.

P. laevigatus—In this species, the stem is smooth. The leaves have no teeth. The flower starts white, then turns purple or violet. The floral tube is swollen. It is found in moist, sandy soil in rich woods and meadows.

P. pallidus—Pale beardtongue has hairy stems and leaves. The white flowers are very slim. It is found along dry, partially shaded roadsides.

P. smallii—Mountain beardtongue has hairy stems, and the leaves directly below the flower cluster are bigger than the leaves at the middle of the stem. The flowers are usually violet and pink. It is found in calcareous soil in shady areas with good drainage.

BLUE PHLOX
Phlox divaricata
Polemoniaceae (Phlox Family)

Many country folk call blue phlox sweet William. Traveling to market with a load of potted phlox is a heady experience. In the closed car, the light floral fragrance concentrates and seems to intensify. Other fragrant annual garden phlox are also called sweet William, so I prefer to use the common name blue phlox.

Phlox is the Greek word for flame. Many species of phlox have panicles of vivid pink, purple, or crimson flowers. *Divaricata* means spreading, referring to the habit of the basal shoots to spread spoke-like from the center of the plant.

FLOWER: Loose cymes of blue to lavender flowers with 5 petals dance atop 12″ stems. A flat-faced pinwheel of petals unfurls from a thin corolla tube. Each flower is perfect and regular with 5 petals, sepals, and stamens. The eye of the flower may be deep blue, magenta, or white. Chance color variations occur among seedlings, resulting in many color forms in the commercial trade, including pure white.

BLOOMS: 3–4 weeks between March and May

LEAVES: The dark green, elliptical to lanceolate leaves are simple, entire, and opposite. Both the leaves and stems are hairy. Except for plants in mountainous areas, the leaves look moth-eaten during the heat and humidity of high summer. In winter or early spring, depending on the climate of the location, new leaves emerge and the plant photosynthesizes during late winter before the spring floral show.

UNDERGROUND STRUCTURES: Blue phlox has stolons with feeder roots. Some nonflowering stems lie on the ground and root at any leaf node that touches a spot of earth.

SEEDS: The tan, ellipsoid capsules have 3 compartments. A capsule splits at 3 sutures to release 3 seeds that germinate the following spring in moist, humus-rich sites.

HEIGHT: 8–18″

HABITAT: Rich, moist, deciduous woodlands; also streamside

CULTURAL TIPS (see page 62)**:** Interplant with other woodland plants to hide the ratty summer foliage. Blue phlox tolerates average or moist conditions if it does not have too much competition from tree roots. If it is planted under shallow-rooted trees like maple or dogwood, it will require irrigation. Open deciduous woods provide strong light in winter and spring which is necessary for good flower bud formation in the woodland phlox species. Once the trees leaf out, filtered light sustains the plant through its less active period.

MOISTURE: Moist, well-draining soil

pH: 5–7.5

EXPOSURE: Full morning sun to filtered shade.

PROPAGATION (see page 66)**:** Stem cuttings are easiest.

SEED STORAGE: Hard to collect; few capsules develop, and they hide in the leaf litter when the stems and leaves decline in late summer. Store temporarily in moist spaghnum at 40°.

SEED TREATMENT: Sow fresh in an outdoor seedbed

CUTTINGS (stem)**:** September through October; no hormone treatment; roots form in 3–4 weeks.

DIVISION: Spring or fall

FAUNA: The eye, or central color dot in the center of the flower, is a guide for insects to the location of the nectar. In this phlox, the stamens are shorter than the corolla tube and some part of an insect or hummingbird must get inside the tube to brush against the pollen-bearing anthers. The flower improves pollination by providing fragrance and a "bull's eye" in a color they can see well to attract nectar-seekers.

OTHER SE SPECIES (moist woodland)**:**
    Phlox stolonifera (creeping phlox)—Creeping phlox blooms at about the same time as *Phlox divaricata* but it has distinguishing characteristics. It has an orange "eye" (stamen). The leaves are obovate to spatulate, and rosettes form on stolons. The flower stalk is shorter and does not leave a messy bunch of straw after the blooms are spent. The flowers are not fragrant like those of wild blue phlox, but the semi-evergreen, ground-covering, and self-cleaning features are good trade-offs. It does need the good moisture it would receive in its natural habitat in deciduous forests and on wooded stream banks.

SUMMER PHLOX,
GARDEN PHLOX
Phlox paniculata
Polemoniaceae (Phlox Family)

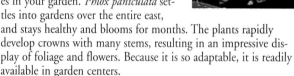

Several perennial species of summer-blooming phlox grace roadsides and cultivated gardens. They are all erect and have large colorful flower clusters in shades of pink to white. Many are fragrant and provide nectar to flights of butterflies. The taxonomic differences have to do with hairs on the leaves and veination. The significant difference for gardeners is whether the plant flourishes in your garden. *Phlox paniculata* settles into gardens over the entire east, and stays healthy and blooms for months. The plants rapidly develop crowns with many stems, resulting in an impressive display of foliage and flowers. Because it is so adaptable, it is readily available in garden centers.

FLOWERS: In this species and all of the species mentioned below, the corolla lobes are not notched, and the style is much longer than the stigma, extending well beyond the lowest anther. This taxonomic division separates these summer-blooming, erect phloxes from many of the shorter, often decumbent, spring-blooming phlox.

The large, smooth, fragrant flower cluster is a compact group of cymes. Individual flowers are regular, perfect, and salverform, with all parts in fives. The pink, purple, or white corolla is pubescent inside. The inflorescence has short, stiff hairs.

BLOOMS: 3 months between June and October

LEAVES: Each upright stem can have 14–25 pairs of 2-6″ long, opposite leaves. The entire, oblong, pointed, sessile leaves have fine hairs along their edges, especially when young. The leaf hairs and the leaf vein pattern differentiate this species from the ones mentioned below. *Phlox paniculata* has obvious lateral leaf veins that curve forward and fuse into a continuous vein near the leaf edge.

UNDERGROUND STRUCTURES: The crown has an extensive network of white rhizomes and attached roots.

SEEDS: The tan, oval capsule splits at 3 seams. Each capsule can contain 3 seeds but usually has only 1. Few capsules seem to mature on phlox plants. Seeds ripen while the plant is still in bloom and for 6–8 weeks after bloom, usually August through October.

HEIGHT: 3–5′

HABITAT: Stream banks and rich, moist places in the open or in thin woods

CULTURAL TIPS (see page 62)**:** Improve the soil with rich humus when planting and dividing. Mildew can be a problem on the foliage of garden phlox. Adequate food, water, light, and air flow are preventive measures. Apply a balanced fertilizer in spring and divide the clump every 3–4 years. If the plants are taller than you like, tip prune the stems until mid-June or early July.

MOISTURE: Average to moist; irrigate during drought

PH: 5–6

EXPOSURE: Full to partial sun, at least a half-day

PROPAGATION (see page 66)**:** If you can catch seeds, this is a good way to produce genetically diverse, healthy plants.

SEED STORAGE: Store dry seeds in an airtight container between 40° and 70°.

SEED TREATMENT: Stratify for 2 months at 40°; sow at 70°. Germinate in 2 weeks.

CUTTINGS: Stem cuttings in May or June; rhizome cuttings in winter—do not pot until the second pair of leaves forms.

DIVISION: Early spring or fall

FAUNA: Many insects visit phlox, but butterflies are the most obvious.

OTHER SE SPECIES: (The following differ from *Phlox paniculata,* in that they have no distinct lateral leaf veining and no cilia on the edges of leaves. Garden phlox are notoriously difficult to differentiate by species.)
  Phlox carolina (thick-leaf phlox)—This 3′ phlox has ovate to lanceolate leaves that taper to a point. The flower cluster is roughly cylindrical. The corolla tube is smooth, and the calyx is bell-shaped. It blooms for 2–3 months between May and August in woodlands and clearings (either wet or dry).
  P. glaberrima (smooth phlox)—The flower clusters of this 3–5′ phlox are broad corymbs. The corolla tube is smooth. It blooms for 2 months between May and July on stream banks and in woods with average to generous moisture.
  P. maculata (meadow phlox)—This 3–5′ phlox has 2.5-6″ leaves that are fairly closely spaced on the stem. The flower cluster is sub-cylindrical. The smooth stem may or may not have red or purple flecks. It blooms for 2 months between May and July on stream banks and in moist, open woods.

PRAIRIE PHLOX,
DOWNY PHLOX
Phlox pilosa
Polemoneaceae (Phlox Family)

Once trees leaf out in the spring, the early floral show bows out. In sites where light still reaches the ground, fragrant masses of prairie phlox take center stage. It inhabits many more sites than just prairies. It can be found in dry sites with sun or light shade from Florida to Texas, north to North Dakota, and east to New York and Connecticut. In the mid-South, in average garden soil, the foliage forms an evergreen ground cover.

Native Americans made a wash of the leaves to treat eczema. They drank leaf tea to purify the blood, and ate (or tricked some-one else into eating) a compound made from the root, which served as a love medicine.

FLOWER: Just when blue phlox begins to look ratty, downy phlox opens in clouds of bloom. Each inflorescence is an open cluster of pink, purple, or white flowers. The regular, perfect flowers are salverform and about 1″ long and wide. Each flower has a short pedicel. The 5 lobes of the corolla are narrow at the base. They broaden and then end abruptly with a sharp tip. The inside of the corolla tube is usually hairy and the 5 stamens do not project from the throat of the tube.

BLOOMS: 6 weeks between April and June; may re-bloom lightly in fall

LEAVES: The stems of downy phlox are loosely upright. The simple, narrow, linear to lanceolate, dark green leaves are opposite. The leaf stems and the calyx are covered with soft hairs.

UNDERGROUND STRUCTURES: The thin, white rhizomes run like crazy about 1/2″ below the ground.

SEEDS: The papery, oval capsule contains copious amounts of small, dry, round seeds.

HEIGHT: 8–20″

HABITAT: Prairies; meadows; glades; rocky or dry, open woods; or the sandy alluvial soil of valleys.

CULTURAL TIPS (see page 62)**:** Prairie phlox spreads rapidly by runners as well as seeds. Do not plant it too close to treasured plants, or prepare to weed out extras. When it looks ratty and goes dormant in summer, mow the entire patch to 2″. New growth emerges with lower temperatures in the fall and persists through winter.

MOISTURE: Dry to average

pH: 5–6.5

EXPOSURE: Full to half-day sun to good filtered light

PROPAGATION (see page 66)**:** Division is easiest.

SEED STORAGE: Seeds dry and can be collected 4–6 weeks after bloom, but why bother?

SEED TREATMENT: Stratify for 3 months at 40°; sow at 70°

CUTTINGS (stem)**:** After new growth becomes firm in the spring, or new growth in fall

DIVISION: Any time

FAUNA: The fragrant flowers attract clear-winged hawkmoths (*Hemaris* species), which resemble bumblebees but have a long proboscis that can reach nectar at the base of the long floral tube of the phlox. These moths feed during the day.

OTHER SE SPECIES (spring-blooming species that like sun)**:**
    Phlox amoena (hairy phlox)—Most people know hairy phlox as the intense pink-flowered phlox found on roadsides in early spring (March to May). It has a 6–18″ mound of densely hairy leaves. The flowers are sessile in a fat cluster. They are usually dark magenta but may be pink or white. Look for this plant on dry road cuts and cut-over oak-hickory-pine woodlands
    P. nivalis—*Phlox nivalis* is similar to *P. subulata* in that it is prostrate and evergreen, but it has woody stems and the stamens are shorter than the corolla tube. It is found in dry, deciduous woodlands.
    P. subulata (thrift, moss pink)—Moss pink also blooms in very early spring (March to May) and it is low (6–12″), but its needle-like leaves are smooth and it has sterile prostrate shoots that root at the nodes and form mats. The flowers can be rose, pink, blue, or white. It inhabits rocky, dry sites.

OBEDIENT PLANT,
FALSE DRAGONHEAD
Physostegia virginiana
Lamiaceae (Mint Family)

The name obedient plant refers to the ability of individual flowers
in a cluster to stay in whatever position they are pushed side to
side. But calling *Physostegia virginiana* obedient plant is a joke.
In cultivation, this species aggressively covers all the space in the
garden with its extending rhizomes. Try to remove it and every
little piece of rhizome sprouts a new shoot. This plant will be
there, along with the ants and cockroaches, at the end of time.
The difference is that it is a beautiful, showy, late-blooming
flower we love to hate. It is unrivaled for longevity in a cut
bouquet. Hang freshly cut flowers upside down in a well-
ventilated area and the dried flowers hold their original color.

The genus name *Physostegia* comes from the Greek root words,
physa, meaning bladder, and *steg,* meaning a cover or roof, in reference to the inflated calyx, which covers the seed. *Virginiana* means
simply of Virginia.

FLOWER: The flower clusters are spikes or racemes. The flowers open
from the bottom up. Individual, 1″ flowers range from white to

pink to lavender, spotted with purple. The calyx has 5 lobes. Each perfect flower is a typical bilabiate mint shape and has 4 stamens.

BLOOMS: 5 weeks between August and November

LEAVES: The smooth stems are upright and 4-sided. They often branch in the flowering section. The simple, toothed, elliptical to lanceolate, 4–5″ leaves are opposite and sessile. The leaf tapers at both ends, to a point at the apex. All the foliage is pale green.

UNDERGROUND STRUCTURES: Rhizomes and their feeder roots form a solid mass.

SEEDS: The fruit has the potential to bear 4 tan, triangular nutlets, but I rarely find more than 2.

HEIGHT: 3–4.5′

HABITAT: River banks; lake shores; prairies; moist, open woodlands; and ditches.

CULTURAL TIPS (see page 62)**:** Cultivars of *Physostegia virginiana* such as 'Vivid' and 'Summer Snow' are shorter and controllable in cultivation. But I refuse to be responsible for anyone who dares to plant the species. If you have lots of space, go for it. Pinch the top third out of each stem by July 4 to create a bushier, self-supporting plant.

MOISTURE: Average to wet

pH: 5–6.5

EXPOSURE: Full sun to half-day sun

PROPAGATION (see page 66)**:** Since seed formation is limited, I recommend propagation by division of rhizomes or stem cuttings.

SEED STORAGE: Store dry seed in an airtight container between 40° and 70°.

SEED TREATMENT: Stratify for 3 months at 40°; sow at 70°. Germinate in 2–3 weeks. Bloom the second year.

CUTTINGS (stem)**:** When new shoots firm in spring

DIVISION: Rhizomes from the edge of a colony can be removed and replanted any time you can work the soil.

FAUNA: Bees are fond of bilabiate flowers and visit obedient plant.

OTHER SE SPECIES:

Physostegia angustifolia (narrowleaf false dragonhead)—This prairie plant has pink to white flowers on erect stems. The leaves are dark green, serrate, linear lanceolate, and clasp the stem. Only a few 1–4′ stems occurs in any one spot because the plant is not rhizomatous. It often grows in heavy, moist, clay soils.

P. purpurea (eastern false dragonhead)—This 3-4′ tall, pink to purple flowering false dragonhead has rounded teeth on the leaves and is more clump forming (i.e., less rhizomatous), than *Physostegia virginiana*. It is found in wet pine savannas and flatwoods, ditches, edges of cypress swamps, and prairies of the Coastal Plain.

SILK GRASS,
GOLDEN ASTER
Pityopsis graminifolia (Chrysopsis graminifolia, Heterotheca graminifolia)
Asteraceae (Aster Family)

Drive down many county roads in the winter and you will soon pass a mass of silvery gray leaves. The angle of the sun is low in winter and highlights the beauty of the leaves of this golden aster. Rub your fingers along a leaf blade, and you can collect a pinch of "silk." The blooms are a lovely feature as well but they must compete with the general riot of yellow fall blooms. The leaves will probably attract you to this plant first.

Choctaws used the plant ash as a treatment for mouth sores.

FLOWER: Many ¹/₂–1″ radiate blooms form a loose corymb. The yellow disc flowers are perfect. The numerous, yellow ray flowers are female.

BLOOMS: 4–5 weeks between July and November

LEAVES: The alternate, entire, linear leaves are mainly basal. These grass-like leaves are .25″ wide, 4-12″ long, and have 3–5 parallel veins. Silky hairs make the evergreen leaves shimmer even in winter. Leaves on the flowering stalk are sparse and much smaller.

UNDERGROUND STRUCTURES: Fibrous roots support a clumping crown.

SEEDS: Both disc and ray flowers produce seeds, but only the inner disc seeds have a long, bristly tail or pappus. The brown achenes (seed plus hull) are ripe and ready to collect when you can pinch the pappus and easily pluck a clump of seeds from the receptacle.

HEIGHT: 1–3′ upright flower stalks

HABITAT: Dry, open pinelands and roadsides

CULTURAL TIPS (see page 62): If the plant looks weather worn in the fall, cut it back to 3–4″, and it will quickly produce fresh new foliage for the winter.

MOISTURE: Silk grass grows better in a dry site but will tolerate moisture if it is on a slope or in well-draining soil.

pH: 4.5–6.5

EXPOSURE: Full to partial sun

PROPAGATION (see page 66): Seeds produce plants quickly and easily.

SEED STORAGE: Store dry seeds in an airtight between 40° and 70°.

SEED TREATMENT: Add grit to seed-starting medium. Apply a light cover of grit. At 70°, germinate in 1 week.

CUTTINGS (stem): When firm; in spring to early summer

DIVISION: Late fall or early spring

FAUNA: Butterflies visit for nectar.

OTHER SIMILAR PLANTS (significant revisions have occurred recently among the genera *Pityopsis, Chrysopsis,* and *Heterotheca*):
   Chrysopsis mariana (Maryland golden aster)—This short-lived perennial has blooms similar to those of silkgrass, but is shorter and has a rosette of furry, dark green leaves. *C. mariana* also likes good drainage.

YELLOW-FRINGED ORCHID
Platanthera ciliaris (Habenaria ciliaris)
Orchidaceae (Orchid Family)

The yellow-fringed orchid is a bright light of summer. A good-sized cluster of apricot-orange, fringy orchids gather on a 1–2′ stem. A single inflorescence may surprise you at a turn in a mountain road, or groups of blooms may shine from among the black tree trunks of a pine woodland that burned not so long ago. They always seem to be in moist drainage areas. I like the old name *Habenaria,* because it makes me think of a Spanish dancer in a fringed shawl, which pretty well describes this flower.

    Orchis is Greek for testicle, referring to the shape of the root of some orchids. For at least four centuries, the roots of orchids have been considered to have aphrodisiac properties. *Platanthera* is Greek for broad or flat anther. *Cilia* is Latin for eyelash or small hair.

FLOWER: Many-fringed, irregular, orange flowers comprise the 3–6″ solitary, compact raceme of this terrestrial orchid. There are 3 sepals and petals. The dorsal sepal forms a hood arching over the reproductive parts. The 2 side sepals are roundish. The lower petal is larger than the others and is called the "lip." It extends at the base into a 1.5″ long spur or nectary. In this species, the lip is oblong and fringed. The 2 side petals are smaller, linear-oblong, and toothed. The stamens, style, and stigma unite in a short column that has sticky pollen. The pollen is not contained in a pouch (pollinia) in this genus.

BLOOMS: 4 weeks between June and September

LEAVES: The alternate, lanceolate leaves are entire and smooth. The longest leaves may be 12″ long and 1.25″ wide. The leaves get markedly smaller near the top of the stem, grading into bracts.

UNDERGROUND STRUCTURES: The roots are a fleshy tuberoid (a thick underground storage organ).

SEEDS: The narrowly cylindrical capsule contains dust-like seeds.

HEIGHT: 1–2.5′

HABITAT: Occasional in many different habitats: bogs, savannas, pinewoods, mixed woods, edges of cypress swamps, marshes, pocosins, and even roadsides.

CULTURAL TIPS (see page 62)**:** This plant and its relatives cannot be propagated and are not for sale in the legitimate plant trade.

MOISTURE: Moist to wet

pH: 5–6

EXPOSURE: Sun to light shade

PROPAGATION (see page 66)**:** This is still a mystery. The plant and the seeds are dependent on a variety of mycorrhizal fungi.

FAUNA: Orchids are a minority species in any given plant population and have developed many different techniques to attract specific insect pollinators. Mosquitoes, small flies, bees, beetles, wasps, moths, and butterflies all help pollinate various orchids. Butterflies pollinate *Platanthera ciliaris.*

OTHER SE SPECIES:

Platanthera blephariglottis—This species is very similar to *P. ciliaris,* but the flowers are white. It may or may not have fringe. The spur measures up to 2″ in length. It is occasional in moist, open areas of the Coastal Plain.

P. clavellata (green rein orchid)—This 18″ tall orchid has greenish or yellowish white flowers and a winged stem. The lip is oblong and blunt. The spur is club-shaped and looks distorted.

P. cristata (crested fringed orchid)—The flowers are orange, but several features differentiate this species from *P. ciliaris.* The ovate lip has less fringe. The spur is shorter, and the raceme is smaller. It can be found in moist open areas, bogs, meadows, savannas, flatwoods, prairies, and along streams and the borders of cypress swamps.

P. flava (southern rein orchid)—This 6″-2′ fragrant orchid has small, fringeless, yellow-green flowers in a loose raceme. The ovate lip is $1/4$″ long. The spur is slender and club-shaped. The stem bears 2 leaves near the middle. It inhabits acidic soils of tidal freshwater swamps and marshes and bald cypress-tupelo gum forests.

P. integra (frog arrow)—This species is almost identical to *P. cristata* but is more yellow than orange and has no fringe. It occurs in swamps, dense woods, and pine barrens. It can disappear for a year or two and then return.

P. lacera (green fringed orchid, ragged orchid)—This 8–24″ fragrant orchid has flowers that are pale yellow or whitish-green. The lip is 3 parted and fringed. It is found in bogs, marshes, and wet meadows.

P. nivea (snowy orchid)—This 1–2′ orchid has white flowers. The fringeless lip is uppermost. It has a long, slender, horizontal spur; 2–3 stiff, keeled, lanceolate leaves sheath the stem near the base. It requires a constant supply of acidic water and can be found in Longleaf Pine Savannas.

MAY APPLE,
RACCOONBERRY
Podophyllum peltatum
Berberidaceae (Barberry Family)

In early spring, pale green umbrellas unfurl in moist woodlands. Closer inspection reveals some plants have a double umbrella. Peer beneath the leaves to see a lovely white-petaled flower with a creamy yellow center. At this stage, all of the plant is poisonous. Later, the flower turns into a small green "apple" which is edible when it turns yellow. Afficionados make chutney of the fruit. Flowers, green fruit, leaves, roots, and seeds should not be eaten!

Podo is a Greek root word for foot and *phylla* refers to the leaf. The original name for the plant was *Anapodophyllum,* Greek for "duck foot leaf." In 1737, Linnaeus shortened the name. *Peltatum* means shield-shaped.

A drug, podophyllin, comes from the rhizome of May apple. This bitter resin is used to treat soft cancers. Another extract, etoposide, is approved for use against certain other cancers. Currently, research continues on the anti-cancer action of the drug. Native Americans used it to treat many different disorders. If they survived the purging, they probably felt cured.

FLOWER: The solitary, 1–2″ flower has 6 sepals and 6–9 white, waxy petals. The stamens are in multiples of 3, usually 12–18. The saucer-shaped, perfect bloom hangs shyly in the fork of the leaf stalks. Photographing this flower is a challenge. Use a reflecting device to cast light under the leaves.

BLOOMS: 2 weeks between March and May

LEAVES: The smooth leaves emerge from the ground enclosed in a whitish sheath. Mature flower-bearing shoots emerge later than barren shoots and have what appears to be a little cap at the end of the thumb-sized protuberance. The cap is the flower bud. (Perhaps nature protects the flower from late frosts. The rhizomes of all the plants in the colony are buried at the same level, so why would flowering plants emerge a week later?) Once the leaves swirl open, they may be as big as 12″ across. Each leaf is loosely, palmately divided into 5–9 segments.

UNDERGROUND STRUCTURES: Thick feeder roots support long, branching, horizontal rhizomes. Members of a colony may all originate from one plant. In cultivation, the rate of spread of a patch of May apple earns it the title of "thug," but in nature, the edges of colonies only increase about half a foot a year. Colonies persist for many generations.

SEEDS: Elliptical, 1/4″, light brown seeds mature in 1-celled, 2″ oval fruits. Seeds are ripe when the fruit turns yellow, probably in June.

HEIGHT: 12–24″

HABITAT: Rich, moist, open deciduous woods

CULTURAL TIPS (see page 62)**:** May apple is a better candidate for the wild garden than the formal garden. It forms solid mats, and its springtime charm fades midsummer as the leaves tatter and melt. Plant it on the high side of a path to display the reticent bloom. Wear gloves when handling May apple or wash soon after handling it. Some people develop dermatitis from the juice of the rhizome.

MOISTURE: Plenty of moisture encourages a healthy colony and keeps the leaves inflated and green longer into the gardening season.

pH: 4.5–6.5

EXPOSURE: Strong light in early spring, before the trees leaf out; filtered to heavy shade in summer

PROPAGATION (see page 66)**:** Division is most successful. Do not try to divide or move after the umbrella has opened in the spring. If you do, the leaves will sulk all of that season, and the rhizomes may decrease in size.

SEED STORAGE: Can store temporarily in moist spaghnum at 40°.

SEED TREATMENT: Clean the seeds and sow in flats to be left outside or in an outside seed bed. Germination is poor in cultivation. Scientists believe passage through the digestive system of a mammal helps germination. From seed, development of a rhizome takes 5 years. The time from seed to flowering plant can be 12 years.

CUTTINGS: No

DIVISION: Divide in fall or very early spring, leaving a bud on each piece of rhizome. The pieces will be 4-5″ long.

FAUNA: Bumblebees pollinate May apple. Eastern box turtles relish the fruit. The common name raccoonberry suggests that raccoons also eat the fruit.

SOLOMON'S SEAL
Polygonatum biflorum
(P. canaliculatum, P. commutatum)
Liliaceae (Lily Family)

The blue-green arching stems of true Solomon's seal form great colonies in rich, moist woodlands. The flowers are inconspicuous, but the blue, almost black, berries add to the architectural interest of the foliage well into the fall. In the South, true Solomon's seal is a more reliable ornamental plant than false Solomon's seal, which looks moth-eaten by late summer.

The genus name *Polygonatum* comes from the Greek root words *polys* and *gony,* meaning "many knees," referring to the rhizome that has knee-like swellings at the previous years' leaf scars. The "seal" of Solomon may refer to the round leaf scar on the rhizome or to the star shape seen on a cross section of the rhizome.

The taxonomy of *Polygonatum* spp. is confusing, because they vary in chromosome numbers and in appearance under varying environmental conditions. Most authorities recognize another species, *Polygonatum pubescens,* with downy undersides to the leaves.

Solomon's seal has a wide range and many different Native American tribes used the plant for a wide variety of ailments, from head to toe. They made a tea or poultice from the root. The rhizomes and stems, minus the bitter leaves, are edible fresh or cooked, but wild collection is verboten. If your culinary interests are adventuresome, purchase plants from a reputable mail-order source (see page 293), and within a few years you will have a crop to sample.

FLOWER: Greenish-white, bell-like flowers dangle from a branched peduncle (flower stalk) at each leaf axil, beginning 4 leaves from the bottom of the stem. The flowers can number 1–9 per cluster but are usually in pairs. The regular, perfect flowers are $1/2$-1″ long. The 6 rounded petals are joined and flared at the lip of the bell. They are less showy than the berries that follow.

LEAVES: The alternate, entire, lanceolate-oval leaves are lime green on top and whitish-green underneath. The leaves are parallel-veined with 3 prominent veins. The stem is shiny smooth, erect, arching, and unbranched. Maroon scales look like gaiters at the base of the stem.

UNDERGROUND STRUCTURES: White, branched rhizomes with knobby swellings, like knees, run horizontally just under the surface of the ground. Feeder roots anchor the rhizomes.

SEEDS: Dark blue, round, 1/4″ fleshy berries persist well into the fall. Each berry contains 3–6 elliptical seeds.

HEIGHT: 1–4′

HABITAT: Woodlands

CULTURAL TIPS (see page 62)**:** Tolerates almost any condition, but will become lush in rich organic soil

MOISTURE: Moist, well-draining soil; highly drought-tolerant

pH: 4.5–6.5

EXPOSURE: Filtered shade of deciduous woods or morning sun/ afternoon shade

PROPAGATION (see page 66)**:** Division is the easiest method.

SEED STORAGE: Store seeds in moist spaghnum at 40°.

SEED TREATMENT: Collect seeds when the blue fruit is soft. Remove pulp. Best sown fresh in an outdoor seedbed. Germinate during 50° temperatures the following spring. Alternatively, stratify in the dark for 2 months at 40°. Sow at 70°. Cover seeds well (dark requirement). May require a second cold period. Bloom in 3–4 years.

CUTTINGS (rhizome)**:** Late summer; pieces may lie dormant for a year.

DIVISION: Early spring or fall

FAUNA: The pendulous, bell-shaped flowers are visited by bumblebees. No plant is deer-proof, but Solomon's seal must be way down at the bottom of their list of preferred plants. I have never seen browse damage.

MOUNTAIN MINT
Pycnanthemum incanum
Lamiaceae (Mint Family)

Mountain mint is a tall, stiff, summer-blooming plant common throughout the Southeast. The mountain reference probably refers to the appearance of the leaves. From early summer onward, the leaves, particularly the middle and upper ones, look like they are frosted with a light dusting of snow.

Pycno is a Greek root word meaning thick or dense, and *anthemon* means flower. *Incan* is the Latin root for hoary or gray, referring to the frosty look on the leaves.

Steep fresh or dried leaves of mountain mint to make a pungent tea. Native Americans used the tea to treat colds, fever, diarrhea, upset stomach, and heart trouble. They used a poultice of the leaves and sometimes the roots to treat headaches.

FLOWER: Mountain mints have clusters of tightly packed flower heads on terminal branches. The 2-lipped bilaterally symmetrical flowers help place the plant in the mint family (as do the square stem and opposite leaves). Some flower heads arise on peduncles from the upper leaf axils. Individual 1/4″ long flowers are white to lavender, spotted with purple. A few flowers in each head bloom at a time, providing a long period of bloom.

BLOOMS: 4–6 weeks from June to August. The white hairs on the bracts and leaves near the bloom heads make the plant look like it is in bloom for a much longer period.

LEAVES: The simple, opposite leaves are ovate to lanceolate, petiolate, lightly toothed, and hairy underneath. The main stem leaves are more than 1/2″ wide. The 3–6′ erect, square stems branch at the leaf axils, but the plant retains an airy look, because the leaf nodes are 3″ apart. At the time of flowering, no basal leaves exist. The leaves frequently drop from the bottom quarter of the stem, especially in times of drought. The bottom two-thirds of the stem is dark purple, and the top one-third is frosty. A pelt of short, closely spaced, curly hairs creates the frosty look on the leaves, stems, and bracts beneath the inflorescence.

UNDERGROUND STRUCTURES: *Pycnanthemum* species have slender rhizomes and can form colonies. Fibrous roots extend from the rhizomes.

SEEDS: Brown, hairy, oblong seeds ripen between September and November. The dried calyx holds the seeds for a long time. The seeds have high fertility rates.

HEIGHT: 3–6′

HABITAT: Dry to wet places in thin woods

CULTURAL TIPS (see page 62)**:** Cut tips back in early spring or after bloom to force basal foliage. Pamper it too much, and it can get invasive, as mints do.

MOISTURE: Dry to moist, with drainage

pH: 5–6

EXPOSURE: Half-day or filtered light

PROPAGATION (see page 66)**:** Seed is easy.

SEED STORAGE: Store dry seeds in an airtight container at 70°.

SEED TREATMENT: Vernalize 6 months. Stratify (optional but increases germination percentages) for 2 months at 40°. Sow at 70°. Cover very lightly (light requirement). Germinate in 1–2 weeks.

CUTTINGS (stem)**:** Terminal shoots in late spring

DIVISION: Late fall or early spring

FAUNA: *Pycnanthemum* species attract bees (lilliputs), wasps (shiny black with white belly bands), flies (medium-sized, not house or horse), beetles, and butterflies, including the sleepy orange.

OTHER SE SPECIES:

Pycnanthemum albescens—This species is similar to *P. incana* but has no bristles on the tips of the calyx teeth and bracts. It is found in dry sites.

P. tenuifolium (slender mountain mint)—*Tenui* is the Latin root for thin. *Folia* means leaf. This 1–3′ plant has terminal, flat-topped clusters of very small heads of tightly packed white to pinkish, 2-lipped flowers. The stem is smooth. The aromatic, linear, sessile leaves are 1/16″ wide and less than 2″ long. This common plant is found in bogs, meadows, low open pastures, and along gravel roads at woods edge.

P. virginianum—This species is similar to *P. tenuifolium,* but the stem is slightly hairy at the angles. The leaves can be needle thin or up to 1/2″ wide. It is an uncommon woodland species.

MEADOW BEAUTY,
HANDSOME HARRY,
ROBINHOOD, DEER GRASS
Rhexia mariana var. *mariana*
Melastomataceae (Melastome Family)

The meadow beauties are easy to identify when in flower or in fruit. All but one species have varieties of pink petals, and all have an urn-shaped calyx and seed capsule. They have rhizomes and/or tubers, and form colonies that are covered with bloom in mid-summer in moist open areas. In fall the leaves turn red, burnishing the meadow for weeks. These decorative, underused jewels bloom even when mowed, and are drought-tolerant.

Most of the 215 genera of Melastomaceae are tropical plants. One of them is a shrub that has black berries that stain one's mouth black when eaten.

Melas is the Greek word for black and *stoma* means mouth. *Rhexia* is Greek for a break or rupture. Evidently, Pliny the Elder originally assigned the name to a different plant, and the reason for the genus name is unclear.

Young leaves of meadow beauty can be eaten fresh in salads or boiled. They have a palate-cleansing lemony flavor. Some species have tubers, which can be a nutty addition to salads.

FLOWER: Because of the branching of the stems, the plant is festooned with many loose cymes of flowers. Each radiate, perfect, 1″ diameter flower has 4 asymmetrical, rose-colored petals, which terminate in an off-center point. The petals, examined during the bud stage, have no hairs; 8 long, bent, sulfur yellow stamens contrast dramatically with the rose-pink petals. The curved anthers release pollen through a pore in the end.

BLOOMS: 4-6 weeks between May and October. Each bloom lasts only 1 day, but the plants have so many flowers that the floral show lasts for several weeks.

LEAVES: *Rhexia mariana* is an erect branching plant with stems that feel 4-angled when rolled between the fingers. Using a hand lens, one can see that 2 opposite sides are rounded or convex and the other 2 are flat or even slightly concave. The flat sides are a lighter green. All the herbage is sparsely hairy. The leaves are opposite with an interesting arrangement on the stem. Each succeeding pair is at right angles to the ones above and below. The leaves are simple, toothed, linear, or lanceolate, and may have a very short stalk or none. Each leaf has 3 prominent veins, a feature of all Melastomataceae. Closer examination shows spots of red pigment, even during the summer. In fall the red coloration dominates. Each tooth on the margin of the leaves has a red hair projecting from it.

UNDERGROUND STRUCTURES: Dark brown, thin but leathery rhizomes run just under the surface of the soil. They create great networks of roots and colonies of plants that may all be clones.

SEEDS: Both the urn-shaped capsules and the snail-shaped seeds are highly distinctive. The plants produce large numbers of seeds, which are held for a considerable length of time in the hard, tan, upright capsules. The surface of the seeds is marked with concentric ridges. In this variety the capsule is less than $1/2''$ long.

HEIGHT: 8–32″

HABITAT: Common throughout the Southeast on moist to wet, disturbed ground; in pine savannas, flatwoods, and bogs; and on the edges of bays, ponds, and swamps.

CULTURAL TIPS (see page 62)**:** No special care is necessary.

MOISTURE: Moist, but tolerant of wet or dry

pH: 4–6

EXPOSURE: Full to partial sun

PROPAGATION (see page 66)**:** Division of rhizomes is easiest.

SEED STORAGE: Store dry seed in an airtight container at 70°.

SEED TREATMENT: Vernalize at least 6 months. Stratify for 2 months at 40°. Sow at 70°. Cover lightly (light requirement). Germinate in 2–3 weeks. The seed has no endosperm and has miniscule seedlings that develop slowly and are subject to rot in pot cultivation. Sow the seeds heavily in plug trays and do not attempt to separate the clumps when moving the plugs to larger pots. Feed every week with a half-strength, balanced, liquid fertilizer. For the first step up, move to a small pot (such as a 3–4″ pint). Bloom the second year.

CUTTINGS (stem or rhizome)**:** In early spring

DIVISION: Any time, but spring or fall probably least stressful for both you and the plant

FAUNA: A patch of meadow beauty is usually alive with busy bumble-bees, stuffing their leg pouches with orange pollen. Deer are reputed to eat meadow beauty, but I have never observed nipped stems and I have certainly had my share of deer and rabbits in the garden.

OTHER SE SPECIES:

Rhexia alifanus (savanna meadow beauty)—The 3′ wand-like stem is smooth. The anthers are curved. This is the only meadow beauty that does not have seeds shaped like snails. It is roughly wedge-shaped. It can be found in moist pinelands of the Coastal Plain.

R. lutea (yellow rhexia)—This 2′ rhexia has yellow flowers. It inhabits wet areas in the Coastal Plain.

R. mariana* var. *interior—The petals are bright lavender-rose. The stem surfaces are equal and flat, and the petals have glandular hairs. The neck of the floral tube is longer than the body. This species is found in wet areas in southeastern states bordering the Midwest.

R. mariana* var. *ventricosa (Maryland meadow beauty)—This variety is nearly identical to *R. mariana* var. *interior.* It differs from var. *interior* by irregular ridges on the seeds and by geographic location. This variety is found in only two southeastern states: North Carolina and South Carolina.

R. nashii *(R. mariana* var. *purpurea)*—This species has a stem similar to *R. mariana* var. *mariana,* since its 2 sides are flat and the other 2 sides are darker green and convex. The difference is that this species has glandular hairs on the back sides of the petals. Look at the flowers in bud to observe this feature most easily. It is found in acidic, wet soils of the Coastal Plain.

R. virginica (handsome Harry)—This species has pink flowers. The stems are either simple or lightly branched. At the midstem, all 4 faces of the stem are equal and winged. The anthers are curved. The rhizomes are thick and spongy and may have tubers. It occurs in wet areas.

BLACK-EYED SUSAN,
BROWN-EYED SUSAN
Rudbeckia fulgida
Asteraceae (Aster or Sunflower Family)

Black-eyed Susans belong in the same category as mom, the flag, and apple pie. Almost everyone recognizes these golden-rayed, dark-centered blooms as black- or brown-eyed Susans.

The genus name *Rudbeckia* honors two professors with the same name: Professor Olaf Rudbeck, (1630-1702) and his son (1660–1740) of Uppsala, Sweden. *Fulg* is a Latin word root for flash or shining, referring to the yellow ray flowers.

Native Americans used the ooze of the root for earaches. They bathed snakebites, worm-swollen bellies, and sores with a concoction of black-eyed Susan. They also used it to treat venereal diseases and dropsy.

FLOWER: The 3″, radiate heads have nonfertile, orange ray flowers and perfect, fertile, dark brown disc flowers. Each disc flower has a bract beside it that becomes the chaff on the dried seed head. In this species, the bracts have rounded upper ends. The receptacle for the flowers is cone-shaped and becomes more so as the seeds develop.

BLOOMS: 6–8 weeks between July and October

LEAVES: The rough, lanceolate to ovate, entire, toothed leaves are alternate. In some varieties, the upper part of the erect stem and the petioles may be winged. Basal and lower stem leaves have very long petioles. Upper stem leaves become sessile, especially where the nodes bear flowering stalks.

UNDERGROUND STRUCTURES: This species is rhizomatous, and colonies or clones tend to spread if given space. Off-white feeder roots extend from the crown and rhizomes.

SEEDS: The seeds are 1/16″ long, sooty black nutlets. The tan to bronze chaff is longer than the seeds. Infertile seeds are flat and tan. Seeds are ripe when they turn grayish-black, sometime in October or November.

HEIGHT: 2–3′

HABITAT: Moist soil of thin woods, meadows

CULTURAL TIPS (see page 62)**:** *Rudbeckia fulgida* spreads by rhizomes and by seeds. It is robust but not dangerously aggressive. *Rudbeckia fulgida* and *R. laciniata* (see page 240) need more water than *R. hirta* and *R. triloba.*

MOISTURE: Average to moist, with drainage

pH: 5.5–6

EXPOSURE: Sun to partial shade

PROPAGATION (see page 66)**:** Although perennial black-eyed Susan self-seeds readily, it can be finicky to germinate. Division of offsets is the easiest method of increase.

SEED STORAGE: Store dry seeds in an airtight container between 40° and 70°.

SEED TREATMENT: Let seed heads ripen fully before collection, so the seeds will fall easily from the head. Stratify for 2-3 weeks at 70°; switch to 40° for 1 month, then sow at 70°-80°. Cover the seed well. Some people recommend sowing at 90° without stratification.

CUTTINGS (rhizome): Late winter

DIVISION: Spring or fall

FAUNA: Butterflies and other flying insects visit black-eyed Susans for nectar.

OTHER SE SPECIES:

Rudbeckia hirta—This annual, biennial, or short-lived perennial begins blooming in May or June before the other black-eyed Susans, and blooms for 2–3 months. All of the 2–3′ plant is roughly hairy. The flower heads are terminal, 1 per stalk. The small bracts next to each disc flower are sharply pointed but not spiny. The lanceolate leaves are simple. The seeds have no pappus. It is common in old fields, prairies, along roadsides, and in thin woods over the entire eastern United States. *R. hirta* is originally from the Midwest. Seeds probably hitchhiked east among other batches of seeds.

R. triloba—This is a highly variable, self-seeding annual or short-lived, multistemmed perennial that has large numbers of small blossoms on a bush-like plant. On any one plant, the leaves may be lobed or unlobed, toothed or smooth-edged. Lobed leaves are usually the lower leaves. The bracts next to each disc flower have a thin, sharp point. It can be found in woodlands and meadows, usually in the mountains or the Piedmont in basic soils. Seeds germinate in 1 week at 70° with no cold stratification.

GREEN-HEADED CONEFLOWER,
CUT-LEAF CONEFLOWER, GOLDEN GLOW
Rudbeckia laciniata
Asteraceae (Aster or Sunflower Family)

This is not your everyday coneflower or black-eyed Susan. This coneflower can reach 6–8′, and the center of the flower head is greenish-yellow, not brown. The leaves are deeply cut and dark glossy green. I have seen it growing in a cypress swamp and at the edge of woods. It adapts to almost any site, moist to average, sun to shade.

Native Americans combined green-headed coneflower with other plants' leaves and flowers to treat indigestion and to apply to burns. In spring, after a long winter without vitamins, they ate cooked young shoots of this coneflower as a spring tonic.

FLOWER: The 2.5-3″ wide, radiate flower heads have a greenish-yellow center and drooping pale yellow "petals," really ray flowers, which are infertile. The tubular green disc flowers are perfect and fertile. The receptacle for the flowers is cylindrical, becoming more pronounced as the seeds develop. The receptacle bracts, or chaff, are densely hairy.

BLOOMS: 6 weeks between July and September

LEAVES: The branched stem is smooth and may look bluish-green. The alternate, petiolate leaves feel like sandpaper. The lower leaves are deeply cut into 3–5 lobes. Upper leaves may be less dissected. The leaves are usually toothed.

UNDERGROUND STRUCTURES: Rhizomes produce new plants at a steady pace. Older plants have a woody crown.

SEEDS: The $3/16''$ long, 4-ribbed seeds are usually fertile and well filled out. They are dark black and easily distinguished from the tan chaff that has a similar length.

HEIGHT: 4–6′

HABITAT: Moist woodlands and edges, and creek banks. At least one of the several varieties occurs in every physiographic province.

CULTURAL TIPS (see page 62): This species is adaptable to sun or shade, wet or dry. It may need irrigation during severe drought if planted in rocky or sandy soil.

MOISTURE: Moist to average

pH: 5–6

EXPOSURE: Sun to light shade

PROPAGATION (see page 66): Seed is easy and highly reliable.

SEED STORAGE: Store dry seeds in an airtight container between 40° and 70°.

SEED TREATMENT: Stratify for 2 months at 40°; sow at 70°. Germinate in 1 week.

CUTTINGS (stem): Firm terminal shoots in spring

DIVISION: Early spring or late fall; slice and dig a portion of the plant with a sharp spade to avoid digging the whole huge plant.

FAUNA: *Rudbeckia laciniata* is host to the silvery crescentspot. Goldfinches feast on the seeds of all *Rudbeckia* spp.

WILD PETUNIA,
PRAIRIE PETUNIA
Ruellia humilis
Acanthaceae (Acanthus Family)

The branching stems of *Ruellia humilis* form a mat studded with lavender tubular flowers. The flowers look like a small version of annual bedding petunias, but the plants are unrelated. Although each flower lasts only a day, the overall bloom period is 4–6 weeks, providing continuous floral display in dry, inhospitable areas.

The genus name *Ruellia* honors Jean Ruel (1474–1537), a French herbalist. *Humil* is Latin for low, referring to the compact habit of this species of petunia.

FLOWER: The lavender, tubular flowers unfurl in the leaf axils. Clusters of buds emerge from one point, but usually only 1–2 of the flowers at that leaf axil are in bloom at the same time. In this species, 4–10 nodes produce flowers. The tube has 5 flaring lobes forming a 1.5″ diameter face. Each 2-3″ long flower has 4 stamens. White anthers contrast with dark purple markings in the throat of the tube.

BLOOMS: 6-8 weeks between June and September

LEAVES: The entire, opposite, medium-green leaves are oval and taper to a blunt point. They vary from 1–3″ in length. They abut directly to the 4-angled, purplish stem. Slim side branches emerge from the leaf axils. The leaves are spaced closely on the stem. Sessile leaves, stem branching, and short internodes give the plant a compactness lacking in *R. caroliniensis,* another common species.

UNDERGROUND STRUCTURES: Seedlings quickly develop fleshy roots, which become thick and knotty with age. A compact root-stock develops slowy.

SEEDS: After a long maturation period, the smooth, woody, ellipsoid capsule splits explosively, flinging seeds several feet from the mother plant. A dry seed looks like a flat, tan lentil. Most capsules contain 2–8 fertile seeds. Seeds are ripe in September and October.

HEIGHT: 1–2′

HABITAT: Dry, open areas throughout the Southeast

CULTURAL TIPS (see page 62)**:** This is a long-lived plant that does not require division.

MOISTURE: Dry to average

pH: 5–6.5

EXPOSURE: Full sun to half-day or strong filtered light

PROPAGATION (see page 66)**:** Seed is easy.

SEED STORAGE: Store dry seeds in an airtight container between 40° and 70°.

SEED TREATMENT: Collect seed capsules when they are tan but before they split. Capsules exploding in the paper collection bag sound like jumping beans. Stratify for 14 weeks at 40°; sow at 70°. Germinate in 10–20 days. Some bloom the first year.

CUTTINGS (stem)**:** April through June; root in 4–5 weeks

DIVISION: Spring or fall

FAUNA: Wild petunias are host plants for the buckeye butterfly.

OTHER SE SPECIES:
  Ruellia brittoniana—This 2–3′ species has smooth, lanceolate leaves. It is uncommon but occurs in the Southeast naturally and is a popular cultivated perennial.
  R. caroliniensis—This 2–2.5′ species has petiolate (stalked) leaves. It appears lankier than *R. humilis* because it does not branch and the internodes are longer. It has flowers in only 1–4 nodes.
  R. ciliosa—This 7″ species has petiolate, spatulate leaves that form a rosette.
  R. strepens—This 1–4′ species has lance-shaped calyx lobes. The stem is mostly smooth. It prefers calcareous soil.

ROSE GENTIAN,
ROSE PINK, BITTER BLOOM, EYEBRIGHT
Sabatia angularis
Gentianaceae (Gentian Family)

This biennial rose gentian is a much showier plant than most of the perennial *Sabatia* spp. In July, it is a mass of clear pink, single, 1–1.5″ blooms. Because the flower color is so pure, it is highly visible along roadsides, even at 70 mph. In order to perpetuate the species, it must set seed before the mowers arrive to tidy the right of way. Luckily, a few plants seem to escape the scythe in out-of-the-way places and can repopulate a whole area.

The genus name, *Sabatia,* honors Liberato Sabbati, the eighteenth-century curator of the Rome botanic garden. The specific epithet *angularis* simply means with angles, referring to the stem of this species.

The Cherokee drank a tea of this species for pain relief. This bitter herb is reputed to have greatly aided in reducing fever during an outbreak of yellow fever in Philadelphia in 1793.

FLOWER: *Sabatia angularis* is a branching biennial. Each branch bears a terminal cymose cluster of flowers. The perfect, tubular flower has 5 rotate, pink or, rarely, white petals or corolla lobes. The base of each lobe has a red line and a triangular, chartreuse blotch that create a 5-pointed star in the center of the flower face. Five backward-curling, yellow anthers arise from the indentations between the points of the star. Five lanceolate sepals caress the backs of the petals.

BLOOMS: 6 weeks between July and August

LEAVES: The smooth-winged stems have 4 sides. The flowering branches are opposite. The simple, entire, opposite, sessile leaves are ovate, softly pointed, and clasp the stem. The length and width of the leaves are about equal, with the length occasionally a bit longer.

UNDERGROUND STRUCTURES: The simple white feeder roots are non-rhizomatous.

SEEDS: The ovoid capsule contains many brown, pitted seeds. A papery membrane, the remains of the corolla tube, is like a stocking around the capsule. Seeds are mature in September or October. Both the number and fertility of the seeds are high. Seedlings germinate the following spring and spend their first year in a basal rosette.

HEIGHT: 1–3′

HABITAT: Old fields, pastures, open upland woods, and prairies

CULTURAL TIPS (see page 62)**:** Allow the seeds to ripen and fall before mowing or removing the declining plant.

EXPOSURE: Full to partial sun

pH: 5–6

MOISTURE: Average; tolerates drying or extra moisture

PROPAGATION (see page 66)**:** The most successful method for biennial species is to sow the seeds to grow in situ.

SEED STORAGE: Store dry seed in an airtight container between 40° and 70°.

SEED TREATMENT: Can be collected green and dried in a paper bag. For pot production and bloom the following summer, start in May or June. Sow heavily at 70°. Germinate erratically over 4–8 weeks.

CUTTINGS: Not on this biennial. Cuttings on perennial species: (stem) May-June or (root) February through March

DIVISION: Not on this biennial. Division on perennial species: early spring or fall

FAUNA: Await observation

OTHER SE SPECIES: (There are many more species. These descriptions can be found in Godfrey and Wooten, *Aquatic and Wetland Plants of SEUS, 1981*).

LYRE-LEAVED SAGE,
CANCER WEED
Salvia lyrata
Lamiaceae (Mint Family)

Lyre-leaved sage is ubiquitous in the entire eastern United States and has naturalized all the way to California. One would think it was propagated and planted at every golden arch across the country to achieve such commonality. It survives so well because it adapts to so many sites. Only the deep sand of coastal areas discourages this survivor.

Salvia comes from the Latin, *salvus,* meaning healthy or safe. Salvias in general were used in tonics to promote overall health. Colonists used a tea of the whole plant of *Salvia lyrata* for colds, coughs, nervous conditions, asthma, constipation, and fever. A salve made from the root is a folk cure for warts and cancer.

FLOWER: The inflorescence is a raceme of 6-flowered whorls. Individual flower corollas are violet and about 0.5-1″ long. The upper lip is shorter than the lower lip. It has 2 pollen-bearing stamens.

BLOOMS: 3 weeks between March and June; may bloom again lightly in the fall

LEAVES: The irregularly lobed, wavy-edged basal leaves are 3-8″ long and resemble the lyre (the musical instrument) in shape. These dark green basal leaves have petioles, while the 2–6 smaller leaves ascending the flowering stalk may or may not have petioles. The stem is square, and the entire plant is hairy. Crushed leaves have a minty fragrance. Leaves take on a bronze appearance in winter.

UNDERGROUND STRUCTURES: Each plant has a clump of fibrous roots. Plants spread by seeds, not rhizomes.

SEEDS: As the flowers fade, the calyx turns brown and gives the plant a decidedly rusty cast in addition to its prominent dark green aspect. Within the dried calyx is a papery container full of dry, tan seeds. Plant self-sows prodigiously.

HEIGHT: 1–2′ flower spike

HABITAT: Rich or rocky, open woods; sandy and gravelly soils along waterways; pastures; thickets; moist, open ground; and roadsides

CULTURAL TIPS (see page 62): Lyre-leaved sage is a good evergreen groundcover that can be kept in bounds by removing dead flower heads before the seeds fall. A lawn mower set at its highest setting would remove the bloom stalks without harming the basal rosette of leaves. If some of the leaves are cut accidentally, the plant will produce fresh new leaves.

MOISTURE: As evidenced by the wide range of *Salvia lyrata,* it tolerates both wet and dry conditions.

pH: 4.5–7

EXPOSURE: Filtered light to full sun

PROPAGATION (see page 66): The easiest way to introduce this sage would be to spread seeds (spring or fall) where you want the plants to naturalize.

SEED STORAGE: Store dry seed in an airtight container between 40° and 70°.

SEED TREATMENT: Sow at 70°. Germinate in 7–14 days

CUTTINGS: Stem cuttings in May

DIVISION: Separate clumps in spring or fall.

FAUNA: Hummingbirds, bumblebees, and some long-tongued butterflies visit blooms frequently, gathering nectar and spreading pollen.

BLOODROOT,
RED PUCCOON, RED INDIAN PAINT,
TURMERIC, SNAKEBITE, PAUSON
Sanguinaria canadensis
Papaveraceae (Poppy Family)

One of the earliest-blooming spring wildflowers, bloodroot, risked decimation by collectors for the medicinal plant trade. Bloodroot contains a compound, sanguinarine, that inhibits plaque formation on teeth. The sanguinarine for toothpaste and mouthwash is now produced from plume poppy, *Macleya cordata,* a large, fast-growing, easily propagated plant.

The myriad uses of the plant, particularly the root, gave rise to many common names. Red puccoon comes from the Indian word *pak,* and refers to the use of the juice of the root to dye skin, clothing, baskets, and mats. Red Indian paint refers to ceremonial skin decoration with the juice. Turmeric refers to the acrid powder of the dried root, which was used for numerous internal and external ailments. Snakebite suggests that ingestion of the root helped stimulate the body and helped cure snakebite. Pauson sounds like poison, and in moderate to large doses, bloodroot is definitely toxic.

FLOWER: Each stalked flower has 8–12 white petals (sometimes more), 2 sepals, and numerous gold-yellow stamens. The emerging bud is sheathed in a leaf as it emerges. The blooms eventually stand 6″ tall. The leaves develop slowly and allow the blooms their limited days in the sun.

BLOOMS: 7–10 days between March and April

LEAVES: The blue-green leaves are palmately lobed, with 5–9 lobes. The petiole is 4-6″ long. The number of lobes and leaf shapes is highly variable.

UNDERGROUND STRUCTURES: The 1/2-1″ thick, branching rhizome is covered with fine roots. The rootstock and roots exude red-orange juice when broken.

SEEDS: The single-chambered, 1″ long capsule is oblong, smooth, and pale green. It contains large numbers of arillate brown seeds, which explode from the capsule when it is ripe and splits. Sometime in May, the color of the capsule will change from bright green to whitish-yellow. Gently squeeze a capsule to check for ripeness. If the seeds are ripe, the seams of the capsule will split and 50–100 slippery brown seeds with a white aril will spill into your hand.

HEIGHT: 6–12″

HABITAT: Rich, wooded slopes

CULTURAL TIPS (see page 62)**:** Bloodroot can withstand competition of shade-loving woodland plants but not grass invasion or too much sun. It needs adequate moisture and good drainage in spring, but withstands moderate drought in summer and fall. Excessive dryness results in early dormancy and, if prolonged, leads to death.

MOISTURE: Moist, well-draining

pH: 4.5–7

EXPOSURE: Shade of a deciduous woodland (bright in spring, shady after the leaves on the trees unfurl)

PROPAGATION (see page 66)**:** Division is easiest.

SEED STORAGE: Store temporarily in moist spaghnum at 40°.

SEED TREATMENT: In cultivation, germination of bloodroot seeds is poor, perhaps 5 percent. They probably need one or more gib-berellins (products of soil fungi), which are unavailable commercially. For now, let ants sow the seeds for you or scatter seeds in an outdoor seedbed.

CUTTINGS: No stem cuttings; the stem is in the form of an underground rhizome.

DIVISION: In early March or in the fall, cut the rootstock, leaving buds or leaves and flowers on each section.

FAUNA: Pollinators include hive bees, bumblebees, mining bees, and bee-like flies. Ants detect the pheromone mimic in the aril and carry the seed to their nests as soon as the seeds fall. They eat the aril and discard the seeds outside their runs. They disperse the seeds widely and large displays of bloodroot can develop.

SALLY KURTZ

LIZARD'S TAIL,
BREASTWEED
Saururus cernuus
Saururaceae (Lizard's Tail Family)

Lizard's tail is a common plant all over the eastern United States. When you see it, you see lots of it. If it has moisture, it spreads rapidly. In spite of its invasive tendencies, it is useful in cultivation as a containerized plant because it will bloom in the shade as well as in the sun. It exudes a delicious fragrance, which smells to me like honey and almond. Others detect a citrus aroma.

It should be used in construction projects instead of the ugly rock called riprap. It stabilizes land more efficiently than the rock and adds beauty and fragrance.

Lizard's tail has a second, rarely used common name, breastweed. Native Americans used a poultice of the root on painful, impacted breasts and on wounds. A dried leaf tea also soothed pain in the chest and back.

FLOWER: Many small, white, perfect flowers comprise a 7–10″ raceme. There are no true petals. The white we see are the stalks of the stamens. With age, the flowers turn into gray-green wrinkled fruits that are tightly massed on the flexible stem, producing

an almost reptilian appearance. The flower stalk is directly opposite the leaf stalk. Each aerial stem has only 1–2 flower spikes but,
en masse, the show is impressive.

BLOOMS: 4 weeks between May and July

LEAVES: The broad, pale green, heart-shaped leaves are entire and
alternate. Plants are full with leaves of many sizes from 2–8″. This
plant has upright stems and underground stems in the form of
rhizomes.

UNDERGROUND STRUCTURES: Fleshy rhizomes run just under
the surface of the soil. A thick network of feeder roots dives down
from the rhizome. They grow rapidly, anchoring the plant and
providing the water and nutrients for the explosive top growth.

SEEDS: Each of the 3–4 parts of the seed capsule contains 1 black dot
of a seed.

HEIGHT: 2–3′ depending on the growing conditions

HABITAT: Swamps, marshes, low woodlands, roadside ditches, and
shallow water along streams and lake edges

CULTURAL TIPS (see page 62)**:** Give lizard's tail plenty of room or
keep it in a container. It is particularly useful in manmade ponds
that are too shady to produce blooms on other water plants.

MOISTURE: Wet to average

pH: The extensive range suggests a wide pH tolerance, perhaps 4–7.

EXPOSURE: Full sun (if lots of moisture) to light shade

PROPAGATION (see page 66)**:** Division is easy.

SEED STORAGE: Can store temporarily in moist spaghnum at 40°.

SEED TREATMENT: Sow fresh seed on saturated soil.

CUTTINGS: Stem cuttings in spring or early summer; rhizome
cuttings can be taken at any time—keep at about 70°.

DIVISION: Early spring or fall

FAUNA: Await observation

NARROW-LEAVED SKULLCAP,
HELMET FLOWER
Scutellaria integrifolia
Lamiaceae (Mint Family)

When it comes to color, visitors to my nursery may say "no thanks" to gold-yellow or orange or red, but everyone loves true blue. Most of the skullcaps have blue flowers. Occasionally, one may be pink or white, but not often. Blue is a retiring color, more so in the shade than in sun. Skullcaps will not catch your eye from a distance, but when you get close to them they take your breath away.

Scutella is Latin for dish, perhaps referring to the plate-like lower petal. The seeds sit on a platform and are covered by a lid, which looks like a helmet.

FLOWER: The 3/4″ blue-violet flowers form showy racemes at the terminal ends of the 1–2′ erect, square stems. The stem is lightly branched with smaller racemes of flowers at the tips of the branches. The perfect, irregular flowers look like snapdragon flowers. Pinch the tube of the corolla and the mouth opens. The petals form 2 lips; the upper lip is a tight hood or helmet, while the lower lip is plate-like. It is violet along the outer edge and white and bearded in the throat, with violet nectary guides. The 4 stamens have purple anthers.

BLOOMS: 3–4 weeks between May and July

LEAVES: Each stem has 3–8 pairs of finely pubescent leaves. The 1-1.5″ long, lower leaves are ovate, roundly toothed, and petioled. The 1″ long, upper leaves are lanceolate, entire, and sessile. Reduced leaves or bracts subtend the flowers of the raceme. Unlike other members of the mint family, the leaves of skullcaps have no minty fragrance and they have a bitter taste.

UNDERGROUND STRUCTURES: The roots are tough, white to purplish rhizomes. The crown becomes somewhat woody with age.

SEEDS: The seed capsule of the skullcaps is unique. The calyx is enlarged and has a helmet-like protuberance on the upper side, which flips off when the seeds are ripe. There are 4 round seeds inside this clever case. They ripen 4–6 weeks after flowering. Flowers and ripe seeds can be on the plant at the same time.

HEIGHT: 1–2′ depending on the amount of available moisture

HABITAT: Moist, open areas; roadsides; and woods throughout the Southeast

CULTURAL TIPS (see page 62)**:** Thrives in any soil, but especially in moist soil. This plant self-seeds aggressively. Site it accordingly.

MOISTURE: Moist to average

pH: 5–6.5

EXPOSURE: Sun to light shade

PROPAGATION (see page 66)**:** Seed is easiest.

SEED STORAGE: Store dry seed in an airtight container between 40° and 70°.

SEED TREATMENT: Using seeds that have been dried 6 months, sow at 70°. Germinate in 20-30 days. If started in a heated greenhouse in the winter, they will bloom the first year. (Other SE Species may benefit from rinsing in a strainer or coffee filter to help remove germination inhibitors.)

CUTTINGS (stem)**:** May; root in 3 weeks

DIVISION: Spring or fall

FAUNA: Bumblebees are one of the pollinators.

OTHER SE SPECIES:

Scutellaria elliptica (hairy skullcap)—This 1–2′ species has blue, violet, or white flowers. The hairy, rounded leaves taper. It inhabits dry upland woods and fields.

S. incana (downy skullcap)—This 3–3.5′ species has blue flowers. It is similar to *S. elliptica,* but several racemes terminate the branches. It inhabits dry woodlands, and offers summer bloom for woodland gardens. It is available commercially and tolerates sun or shade. The Cherokee used a compound of the roots of *S. elliptic* and *S. incana* to ensure monthly menses and to treat diarrhea and neuralgia.

S. lateriflora (mad dog skullcap)—This 1–5′ species has blue, violet, or white to pinkish flowers, which tend to hang from 1 side of the peduncle. Its smooth foliage branches freely, and it has creeping stems. It is common throughout the Southeast in alluvial and nonalluvial swamps, in hardwood bottoms, and in freshwater marshes. It was used as a folk remedy for rabies.

S. ovata (heart-leaf skullcap)—This 3–4′ species has blue flowers. The stems are hairy, and the petiolate leaves are cordate. It inhabits dry to wet woods and marshes.

S. serrata (showy skullcap)—This 18″ tidy clumping plant has dark blue flowers. The leaves are rounded, and the upper leaves are broad. In the summer and fall, a margin of dark magenta coloration outlines the leaves. It is highly desirable for cultivation because it does not get leggy and does not seed prodigiously. Unfortunately, propagation of this species is difficult. A seed stratification involving temperature extremes (70°-32°-70°) shows promise. Stem cuttings form callus, but rarely develop roots. Division is successful in the spring or fall.

BUTTERWEED,
SQUAW WEED
Senecio glabellus
Asteraceae (Aster or Sunflower Family)

Whether annual or perennial, *Senecio* species brighten many habitats from late winter through spring. *Senecio glabellus* is called butterweed, because the flowers are the smooth, shiny texture and color of butter. In moist areas, whether roadside ditches or woodland, it shines like a yellow slicker on a rainy day.

Senex is Latin for old man, referring to the fluffy white pappus of the seed head of *Senecio* spp. *Glaber* is Latin for smooth. The genus name was chosen by Linnaeus in 1737 for a large genus of 1,200 plants, 25 of which are poisonous. *S. glabellus* may be poisonous to cattle.

FLOWER: This single-stemmed annual has a terminal corymb of radiate flower heads. Both disc and ray flowers are yellow. The disc flowers are perfect, and the ray flowers are female.

BLOOMS: 3 months between February and June

LEAVES: The simple, alternate leaves are pinnately divided into rounded lobes having large teeth. The terminal lobe is usually the largest. Lower leaves have a petiole; upper leaves are sessile. The upright stem is hollow.

UNDERGROUND STRUCTURES: These annuals have an octopus-shaped network of roots that readily releases its grip on the earth when pulled. Perennial species have rhizomes as well as roots, and resist a tug from above.

SEEDS: Each seed is a smooth but ribbed achene.

HEIGHT: Variable; 6–36″

HABITAT: Roadside ditches, wet pastures, swamps, cypress ponds, and lakes

CULTURAL TIPS (see page 62)**:** Butterweed makes a good winter ground cover. Mow before or after seed set depending on how many plants you want the following year.

MOISTURE: Average to wet

pH : 5–6.5

EXPOSURE: Sun or light shade

PROPAGATION (see page 66)**:** Seed for annuals, division for perennials

SEED STORAGE: Store dry seeds in an airtight container between 40° and 70°.

SEED TREATMENT: For annuals, collect when the fluff pulls easily from the receptacle. Sow in the area that you want the plants. For perennial species, stratify 45 days at 40°. Sow at 70°-80°.

CUTTINGS: Not on annuals; spring to early summer for perennials

DIVISION: Spring

FAUNA: Bees visit butterweed.

OTHER SE SPECIES:

Senecio aureus (golden ragwort)—This rhizomatous perennial has a cluster of stems and cordate basal leaves. The leaves are dark green above and purple below. It is found naturally in more northern areas of the Southeast. It is companionable in the South but highly invasive by seed and runner in the mid-Atlantic area. The solid mass of roots causes a monoculture to develop in spite of summer dormancy.

S. obovatus—This species has thick, shiny, obovate basal leaves. It is found in limestone areas.

S. anonymous (*S. smallii*)—This species is a perennial of drier sites. The leaves are mostly basal, and it is common in the Blue Ridge Province.

S. tomentosa —This perennial has a furry, white stem and basal off-shoots. It is found in moist to wet sands and sandy clays of pinelands, along roadsides, in openings in moist woodlands, and in the seasonally wet soil of Piedmont granite rock outcrops.

FIRE PINK,
CATCH FLY
Silene virginica
Caryophyllaceae (Pink Family)

The flowers of fire pink are a startling pure red among the pastels of spring. The simple pinwheels of red on weakly erect, branching stems insert the spot of unexpected color so often used by Impressionist painters and by observant landscape designers. The plant is a short-lived perennial but replaces itself by seed when properly sited.

Silenus was the foster father of Bacchus and leader of the satyrs. Satyrs were hairy, light-footed, cavorting woodland gods or demons; they were half beast, half human. *Silene* spp. are frequently viscid-pubescent (i.e., sticky hairy). Each petal has a hairy claw at its base that resembles a satyr's hoof.

The "pink" part of the common name refers to the resemblance of the pinked petal tips to those of dianthus or pinks.

FLOWER: The 1–2″, red, perfect, regular flowers have 5 notched petals and 5 sepals. Inspect the petal carefully and you will find the claw toward the orifice of the tube. The sparse terminal cluster of stalked flowers forms a cyme. All parts of the flower are sticky, giving many of the *Silene* species the common name, catchfly.

BLOOMS: 4–6 weeks between April and July

LEAVES: All the leaves are simple, entire, and hairy. Basal leaves are 3-5″ long, spatulate, and opposite. There are usually 2–4 pairs of lanceolate stem leaves. The lax, watery stem angles ever so slightly at each leaf node. Basal offshoots hug the ground.

UNDERGROUND STRUCTURES: The roots, like the stems, are watery and easily broken.

SEEDS: Dry, brown, kidney-shaped seeds fill ellipsoid capsules, which open at the end. The sticky green calyx persists around the tan capsules. When the capsules split, they tip down to spill the seeds. Plants bear flowers and ripe seeds simultaneously.

HEIGHT: 1–1.5′

HABITAT: Rich, moist, or dry woods

CULTURAL TIPS (see page 62)**:** Transplant when dormant. All but the basal rosette disappears in summer. Rocky soil is preferable to highly organic soil.

MOISTURE: Average to moist, with excellent drainage

pH: 5–6

EXPOSURE: Filtered light or full sun part of the day (in the morning or midday)

PROPAGATION (see page 66)**:** Seed collection piecemeal over 4 weeks

SEED STORAGE: Store seeds temporarily in moist spaghnum at 40°.

SEED TREATMENT: Sow as fresh as possible outside in a seed frame or in a flat containing soil amended with grit. Stratify for 3 months at 70°. Switch to a temperature between 40° and 60°. About 10 days after exposing to lower temperatures, check for germination and prick out those plants that have germinated when they have 2–3 sets of true leaves. Over-winter the ungerminated seeds outside. Bloom in 1–2 years.

CUTTINGS: Stem cuttings after bloom (late May, early June); root in 4–6 weeks

DIVISION: Late fall or early spring; separate basal rosettes

FAUNA: The long corolla tube limits pollinators to those with long tongues, like hummingbirds. Bees often chew holes in flowers and rob the nectar. The leathery calyx on *Silene* spp. offers some protection against such assaults.

OTHER SE SPECIES:

Silene caroliniana (wild pink)—This species is a low-growing mound with white to pink, barely notched flowers and gray-green leaves. It has a thin taproot. It needs 4–6 hours of sun each day and excellent drainage. It inhabits sandy, open woodlands. Seeds germinate readily at 70°.
Silene stellata (starry campion)—This tall, airy species has white terminal flowers with fringed petals. The leaves are whorled. It is found in rich, moist woodlands.

STARRY ROSINWEED
Silphium astericus (S. dentatum)
Asteraceae
(Aster or Sunflower
Family)

The rosinweeds are more
of those tall, summer- and
fall-blooming plants with
yellow blooms. The easiest
way to distinguish them
from a sunflower is to tear
apart a bloom. The rosinweed forms seeds in a crown or ring
around the disc. The middle of the disc has sterile flowers. The
sunflower has seeds covering the entire disc except for the very
outside ring. The rosinweeds tend to have more lemon-colored
flowers, but color can be a tricky feature of identification, since
odd seedlings can appear with different colors or a different shade
of the same color.

The genus name *Silphium* comes from the Greek root word
silphi, meaning "a plant with medicinal properties." Various
species were used to stop bleeding, relieve lung ailments, stop and
induce vomiting, and expel worms from horses. For head colds
and general pains, its smoke was inhaled from burning roots. For
rheumatism, the smoke was directed to the crippled joint.

FLOWER: The inflorescence is a branching cluster of 2″ diameter
flower heads. Several rows of large recurved bracts beneath the
disc of flowers form a cup-like shape, which is evident in any
stage of the flower: bud, bloom, or seed. Ray and disc flowers are
yellow. (Disc flowers may be brown in other species.) In this
species, each head has 8–13 ray flowers with each ray ¹/2″ long
or just under. The ray flowers are fertile and make seeds (the ring
or crown mentioned above). The disc flowers are sterile.

BLOOMS: 8 weeks between June and September

LEAVES: The thick, erect stem is purple and hairy. The alternate (or
opposite), simple, entire, elliptic leaves are coarsely hairy. They are
5″ long near the bottom of the stem and decrease to 2″ just under
the flower cluster. The lower leaves have a petiole; the upper leaves
are sessile. The red pigment of the stem runs out into the midrib
of the leaves and recurs in the bristly hairs along the leaf edges.

UNDERGROUND STRUCTURES: The stout rhizomes create a
central mass in a mature plant group. Roots extend from the
rhizomes.

SEEDS: The flat, dark gray seeds are broadly winged and have two
horns at the top. The overall shape reminds me of a Halloween

devil's mask. The seeds in this species are ¹/₄″ long but can be smaller or much larger in other species.

HEIGHT: 3–4′

HABITAT: Thin woods and clearings

CULTURAL TIPS (see page 62)**:** Rosinweeds are no-care plants: no pruning, no staking, no division, no fertilizer. It can't hurt, but it just isn't necessary.

MOISTURE: Average to dry

pH: 5–6

EXPOSURE: Partial sun or filtered light

PROPAGATION (see page 66)**:** Seed is easiest.

SEED STORAGE: Store dry seeds in an airtight container between 40° and 70°.

SEED TREATMENT: Stratify for 2 months at 40°; sow at 70°. Or sow in a flat and place it outdoors from November through January. Germinate in 2.5 months. Bloom in 2–3 years.

CUTTINGS (stem)**:** Early spring; terminal shoots

DIVISION (on species without taproots)**:** Early spring or late fall

FAUNA: Bumblebees are frequent visitors to rosinweeds.

OTHER SE SPECIES:

Silphium compositum—This species has a large, loose inflorescence of numerous small flower heads (¹/₂″ diameter disc) on a 4–8′ almost leafless stem. The large (12″ long) basal leaves look like leaves of rhubarb, with wavy edges or lobes. The petioles and midribs may be green or red. It can be found in dry, sandy, or rocky soils in thin woods and at woods edge.

S. integrifolium—This species has many large flowers with 16–35 rays. The leaves are broad and smooth edged but rough; they frequently clasp the velvety stem. The plants can be found in prairies and along roadsides.

S. laciniatum (compass plant, gum plant)—This species has deeply lobed (nearly to the midrib) leaves and a taproot. The basal leaves orient their edges so they point north and south, exposing the blade surface to the sun. It is found on prairies, glades, and roadsides. Grazing animals such as white-tailed deer eat the young leaves. Native Americans chewed the gummy resin.

S. perfoliatum (cup plant)—This taprooted species has a square stem that pierces the joined opposite leaves, forming a cup that can hold rainwater. It inhabits moist woods, meadows, and the edges of streams and ponds.

S. terebinthinaceum (prairie dock, rosin plant)—This taprooted species is similar to *S. compositum,* but the flower disc is larger (³/₄″ diameter). It has huge toothed, basal leaves. The 2–10′ stem is nearly leafless. It inhabits prairies, glades, and limestone outcrops. *Terebinthinaceum* means "like turpentine."

S. trifoliatum (whorled rosinweed)—This fibrous-rooted species has many small heads in an open inflorescence. The lanceolate or lance-ovate leaves are found mainly on the smooth, round, bluish stem. They can be whorled or opposite. It inhabits open woods and fields.

BLUE-EYED GRASS,
SATIN FLOWER,
IRISETTES
Sisyrinchium angustifolium
Iridaceae (Iris Family)

Blue-eyed grass is one of the first wildflowers that beginners meet. It is everywhere, in sun and shade; in moist and dry sites. Until it is kissed by the sun each day, the pale, steely blue flowers are furled like a closed umbrella. Once light touches them, they unfurl into a flattish face with a yellow eye. In masses, these small flowers are quite showy.

Blue-eyed grass is not a grass, nor is it blue-eyed. It is a member of the iris family and has a yellow eye. Here we have one more example of the confusion caused by common names.

Sisyrinchium is a Greek word meaning swine snout. The entire genus is encumbered with a name for a Greek plant whose roots were savored by pigs. *Angustifolium* means narrow-leaved.

The Cherokee used an infusion made from the roots to treat diarrhea in children. They also ate the greens to keep their bowels regular.

FLOWER: Each winged scape (flower stalk) ends in clusters of 2–15 stalked flowers. The scape may branch once or twice at the end and have more than one cluster of flowers. The flower clusters emerge from a spathe (modified leaf) that looks like a small, flat, green crab's claw. Each perfect, regular flower has 6 petals that may be blue (aging to violet) or white. Each petal culminates in a sharp tip. At the base of each petal is a sulfur-yellow patch. These blotches and the yellow pollen of the anther create the "eye" of the flower. The 3 stamens are united.

BLOOMS: 4 to 5 weeks between March and June (each bloom lasts only 1 day)

LEAVES: The smooth, bluish-green, linear, entire leaves are alternate and basal.

UNDERGROUND STRUCTURES: This clumping monocot has bright-yellow, fibrous roots.

SEEDS: The globular capsule has 3 compartments containing round black seeds. Seeds ripen about 1 month after a flower fades. Ripe seeds and flowers can be on the plant at the same time.

HEIGHT: 12–18″; plants in full sun are shorter and more upright.

HABITAT: Meadows and moist, open woods

CULTURAL TIPS (see page 62)**:** In the sun, blue-eyed grass makes an excellent border plant. Plant in any soil, but avoid heavy mulch. It tolerates mowing or clipping. Lean soil promotes an upright, tight clump.

MOISTURE: Moist to average

pH: 4.5–6.5

EXPOSURE: Full sun to light shade

PROPAGATION (see page 66)**:** Division or collection of self-sown seedlings is easiest.

SEED STORAGE: Store dry seeds in an airtight container at 40°.

SEED TREATMENT: Sow at 50°–80°. Germination is slow and erratic over 6 months.

CUTTINGS: No

DIVISION: Early spring or fall

FAUNA: Bees are frequent visitors to blue-eyed grass.

OTHER SE SPECIES:

Sisyrinchium albidum *(S. capillare)*—This 6–15″ species has blue or white flowers and a mat of old fibers at the base of the plant. It stands out from other species because the stalk has 2 sessile spathes, each with a flower cluster. It inhabits sandy soils in open areas or in dry, open woodlands.

S. arenicola—This 8–18″ species has blue flowers, and the old leaves remain as erect bristles around the base of the plant. It grows in sandy soils in dry fields, woodlands, or seasonally wet savannas.

S. atlanticum—This species is similar to *S. angustifolium,* but the scapes are only $^1/16″$ wide. It inhabits moist areas, including marshes, prairies, shores, roadsides, and savannas.

S. exile *(S. brownei)*—This 4–10″ annual species has yellow or cream flowers with a red-brown eye. It is naturalized from South America and becomes weedy in moist, sunny areas.

WREATH GOLDENROD,

BLUE-STEMMED GOLDENROD,

SYLVAN GOLDENROD

Solidago caesia
var. *caesia*

Asteraceae (Aster or Sunflower Family)

Wreath goldenrod is a non-pushy woodland plant ideal for the shade garden. Just when all colors other than shades of green seem to disappear from the woodland, *Solidago caesia* begins to bloom. The sulfur-yellow flowers contrast nicely with the blue-green foliage. It rarely exceeds 2.5′ in height and develops a lovely violet "bloom" on the stems. Although it slowly spreads by rhizomes, it never engulfs its neighbors.

Solidago spp. are in the aster family because they have both disc and ray flowers. They differ from the genus *Aster* and the genus *Erigeron* by having yellow rays (except for one species, *Solidago bicolor,* which has white ray flowers). Other genera with yellow rays that bloom in late summer and fall at the same time as the goldenrods include: *Rudbeckia* (black-eyed Susans), *Helianthus* (sunflowers), *Bidens* (tickseeds), *Silphium* (rosinweeds), and *Helenium* (sneezeweed). In general, these differ from goldenrods in that they have opposite leaves, especially the lower ones, and the receptacle has chaff between the disc flowers (and thus between the seeds). But, of course, any general statement like this is dangerous. Sometimes a species within these genera will have alternate leaves. If you are interested in taxonomy, consider using some of the books listed in the Bibliography on page 288.

The genus name *Solidago* comes from the Latin *solido,* meaning "to make whole or strengthen," referring to the healing properties of goldenrods. *Caesi* is a Latin word root meaning "blue-gray," referring to the stem color.

FLOWER: Clusters of blooms, racemes, emerge from leaf axils along the top half of the stem. The flower heads contain both female ray flowers and perfect, yellow, disc flowers. The rays are bright yellow, not orange at all.

BLOOMS: 3–4 weeks between July and October

LEAVES: The leaves are alternate, simple, toothed, sessile, and lanceolate to lance-elliptical, tapering to a point. Young plants have a basal clump of foliage, but blooming plants have leaves only on the stem. The leaves are more than 3 times as long as wide, and vary from 1–3″ in length. The 2–2.5′ erect, slightly arching stem is blue-gray, smooth, and round in cross section. It may or may not have a bit of a zigzag effect between leaf nodes near the top of the stem. It has a hazy warm color on the stem like the bloom on a freshly picked grape or plum (but does not always have this trait).

UNDERGROUND STRUCTURES: The plant can have both short, stout rhizomes and long, creeping rhizomes. Feeder roots extend from the rhizomes.

SEEDS: The hairy seeds have a single row of white pappus bristles. The seeds are mature when the pappus dries and fluffs out, giving the plant a blousy look. The seeds can fly a short distance on the wind. Frequently, a large number of seeds are infertile.

HEIGHT: 1-3′

HABITAT: Woodlands, moist and rich or dry; widespread in eastern United States

CULTURAL TIPS (see page 62): This is a no-care plant but it will develop richer foliage colors if it is in rich, moist soil.

MOISTURE: Average to moist, with drainage

pH: 5–6

EXPOSURE: Filtered light

PROPAGATION (see page 66): Propagation from seed is quick and easy.

SEED STORAGE: Store dry seeds in an airtight container between 40° and 70°.

SEED TREATMENT: Sow heavily at 70°-80°. Cover very lightly or surface sow. Keep humidity high using plastic film over the flat until germination occurs in about 2 weeks.

CUTTINGS (stem): Tip cuttings in early spring, as soon as the stem gets a bit firm

DIVISION: Divide basal rosettes in late winter.

FAUNA: Goldenrods are pollinated by bees and butterflies. Their pollen is not loose on the wind to tickle allergic noses. The pollen that causes hay fever comes from the *Ambrosia* spp. (ragweeds).

OTHER SE SPECIES (or varieties with flower clusters in the leaf axils): ***Solidago caesia* var. *curtisii***—In this variety, the branched flower clusters are usually shorter than the subtending leaf. It has a more restricted range than *S. caesia* and is found most often at moderately high elevations. *S. flexicaulis*—This species has a broad leaf (less than 2.5 times as long as wide). It has a terminal flower cluster as well as axillary clusters, and the leaves are greatly reduced in the upper part of the stem, so the overall appearance is of a terminal inflorescence. Its range is more northern and midwestern, but it occurs in mountainous provinces of the Southeast in basic soils.

JESSIE HARRIS

SWEET GOLDENROD,

ANISE-SCENTED
GOLDENROD
Solidago odora
Asteraceae
(Aster or Sunflower
Family)

Books say that rainfall is abundant in the Southeast, but I fight a period of drought every summer. This is the time of year when I realize I have planted way too many plants out of their usual habitats. Any plant that can thrive in drought conditions in sandy or rocky pine woodlands is welcome in my garden. *Solidago odora* is one such plant. It has several appealing features: triangular clusters of bright yellow blooms in late summer and fall, aromatic foliage, and none of the coarseness or aggressiveness associated with goldenrods.

Native Americans introduced settlers to the culinary and medicinal values of sweet goldenrod. The Cherokee, in particular, drank sweet goldenrod tea to treat fever, colds, coughs, nerves, and measles. They also used it as a tonic, a stimulant, a carminative (to relieve gas pains), and a diaphoretic (to induce sweating).

The leaves can be prepared like regular tea. After the Boston Tea Party, colonists resorted to drinking herbal teas, among them Liberty Tea made from *S. odora.*

FLOWER: The terminal inflorescence is a panicle of small flower heads aligned on 1 side of the flowering branch. The heads are less than 1/2″ wide and have no chaff. The slender involucral bracts overlap in more than 1 row. Both disc and ray flowers are yellow. The disc flowers are perfect and fertile.

BLOOMS: 6–8 weeks between July and October

LEAVES: The dark, upright, leafy stems zigzag slightly, and there are no basal leaves at the time of bloom. The smooth, entire, alternate, sessile, linear-lanceolate, pointed leaves are glandular punctate (unusual for a goldenrod). Hold a leaf up to a window and look at it with a hand lens. Translucent dots are scattered regularly all over the leaf. These gland-like structures are the source of the aromatic oil. Sometimes a plant lacks the fragrance—don't buy that one, the tea from it won't be worth drinking.

UNDERGROUND STRUCTURES: Sweet goldenrod has fibrous roots and a thick central root. It is not rhizomatous.

SEEDS: The dry seeds have a single row of bristles that are as long as the seeds.

HEIGHT: 2–5′

HABITAT: Dry, open woods

CULTURAL TIPS (see page 62)**:** This is a noninvasive species, but other species with long creeping rhizomes may be too invasive for small gardens. Selected cultivars are often exceptions to this rule. Goldenrods are tough plants that will grow in poor soils.

MOISTURE: Average to dry

pH: 4.5–6

EXPOSURE: Light shade to a half-day of sun

PROPAGATION (see page 66)**:** All methods are easy.

SEED STORAGE: Store dry seeds in an airtight container between 40° and 70°.

SEED TREATMENT: Dry storage for 6 months may aid germination. Sow heavily at 70°. Cover lightly. Germinate in 2 weeks.

CUTTINGS (stem)**:** Spring to early summer

DIVISION: Spring or fall

FAUNA: Goldenrods are favorites of bees and butterflies.

OTHER SE SPECIES: (In all of these species, yellow flowers are aligned on 1 side of the arching flower branches of terminal panicles.)

SPECIES WITH MAINLY SMOOTH LEAVES:

Solidago arguta (cut-leaf goldenrod)—This 2–5′ clumping species has mainly basal, petiolate leaves that are elliptical and toothed. It forms a dark evergreen rosette. It blooms from late summer to fall in woodlands and meadows and on road banks.

S. gigantea (late goldenrod)—This bushy, rhizomatous, 2–7′ species has a long inflorescence. The bell-shaped flower heads have numerous rays. The smooth stem is waxy white beneath the flower cluster. It has numerous, thin, narrowly elliptical, pointed, toothed, cauline (on the stem), nonclasping leaves, with 3 or more prominent veins. It blooms between July and October in moist, open places.

SPECIES WITH HAIRY STEMS:

S. canadensis var. scabra (*S. altissima*) (tall goldenrod)—This leggy, rhizomatous, 3–7′ species has 12″ long, dense flower clusters with an ashy pubescence. The thick, rough cauline leaves are lanceolate, short toothed, pointed, and prominently 3-veined. It blooms in the fall in dry or moist soils in old fields and meadows. Tea from this species was said to unite (solido) wounds both inside and out.

S. nemoralis (dyersweed goldenrod, dwarf goldenrod, or gray goldenrod)—This clumping 1–4′ species has pale yellow flowers. The stem and leaves have a fine, gray pubescence. Elliptical cauline and basal leaves are both present at the time of bloom. The leaves are much smaller at the top of the stem. They are rough, 3-veined, and petiolate (at least the lower ones). It blooms from summer into fall in open, baked, poor soils of old fields, roadsides, and pastures.

S. rugosa (rough or wrinkle-leaf goldenrod)—This rhizomatous, 2–5′ species has cauline leaves. They are thin, lance-oval, toothed, subsessile, and net-veined. They bloom in the fall in old fields and meadows.

INDIAN PINK,
PINK ROOT
Spigelia marilandica
Loganiaceae (Logania Family)

In the native woodland garden, knock-your-socks-off bright colors are rare. The primary red and yellow of the upright flowers of Indian pink is an exotic visual surprise. A mound of rich green leaves adds to the feeling of lushness.

The common name, Indian pink, is a confusing appellation. Pink refers not to color but to the sharply cut lobes of the flower face. Indian refers to Native American use of the plant medicinally. The word root in pink root refers to the plant part used medicinally.

The genus name honors Adriaan van den Spieghel (1578–1625), a Flemish botanist and anatomist. Spieghel changed his name to Spigelius.

Native Americans taught the colonists to use pink root to treat intestinal worms. Up until the early 1900's pharmacies regularly dispensed Pink and Senna, a combination vermifuge and laxative. The poisonous side effects of pink root saved the plant from being over-collected by the pharmaceutical trade.

FLOWER: Indian pink has perfect, regular, 1.5″ long flowers with all their parts in fives. Each scarlet, tubular corolla opens to reveal a yellow interior. The 5-pointed lobes look like a star. The inflorescence is an arched, 1-sided spike of ranked blooms at the end of leafy stems.

BLOOMS: 6-8 weeks between May and June

LEAVES: The true green leaves are simple, entire, opposite, and oval, stretching to a point. Each 4-angled stem has 4–7 pairs of leaves.

UNDERGROUND STRUCTURES: Mature plants have a crown with thick feeder roots and thinner rootlets.

SEEDS: The green 2-lobed capsule is broader than it is tall. It holds a few dark-brown, angled seeds. The seeds ripen about 1 month after the blooms fade. They catapult before the capsule appears to be ripe.

HEIGHT: 1–2′

HABITAT: Rich, moist woodlands

CULTURAL TIPS (see page 62)**:** Indian pink grows best on basic or sweet soil that retains a bit of moisture. If the leaves look chlorotic (yellow-streaked), sprinkle granular or powdered lime around the plant. Keep the lime off the leaves.

MOISTURE: Moist to average

pH: 5.5–7

EXPOSURE: Filtered light with 2–4 hours strong light daily

PROPAGATION (see page 66)**:** No method is quick or easy.

SEED STORAGE: Store dry in a closed container between 40° and 70°. Length of viability unknown.

SEED TREATMENT: Cover green seed capsules with mob caps of pieces of old stocking. Secure with a twist tie. Sow the seeds in a flat to leave outside over the winter. Cover the seeds to their depth with medium. Alternatively, stratify for 6 weeks in the dark at 70°; switch to 32° for 6 weeks; switch to 70° with light.

CUTTINGS (stem)**:** New but firm growth in early spring or after bloom

DIVISION: Early spring or fall

FAUNA: Protect newly planted, rooted cuttings from deer.

RUE ANEMONE,
WINDFLOWER
*Thalictrum thalictroides (Anemonella thalictroides)**
Ranunculaceae (Crowfoot Family)

Rue anemone appears delicate but is, in fact, a tough plant. It
blooms happily through hard frosts in March and pops up after
the dog treads on it. Of all the spring-blooming wildflowers, it
has the longest period of bloom, a good 3 months. It is a tiny
plant with every part in proportion. This windflower shivers with
the touch of the slightest breeze. Surely it was created to charm us
with its daintiness.

   The leaves look like those of the plants known as rues to which
it is allied. This visual similarity explains part of the common
name "rue anemone." The blooms must have reminded some
taxonomist of anemones and, for years, we called the plant
Anemonella, meaning "looks like an anemone."

FLOWER: Umbels of 1–5 white flowers dance on wiry stems. What
   look like petals are really sepals, anywhere from 5–10 in number.
   They are white to pinkish in the bud stage. The flowers are
   perfect and regular with showy yellow stamens.

BLOOMS: 3 months between March and June

LEAVES: The smooth, ovate-to-round green leaves have 3 gentle lobes
   at the outer edges. The leaves are stalked and compound in threes.
   When the plant is first emerging from the earth, it has a rosy
   brown color, which gradually changes to green. The flexible stems
   are thin and dark.

UNDERGROUND STRUCTURES: The tuberous roots look like
   miniature sweet potatoes clutched together at one end. Leaves and

flowers develop from the top. Feeder roots grow from the bottom.

SEEDS: A cluster of pale green, oval, pointed seeds sits loosely atop a platform. When they are ripe they are still green, and tumble from their perch with the slightest nudge. Each flower produces 5–10 seeds, each within its own nonsplitting capsule. Seeds ripen quickly; seeds and flowers can be present at the same time.

HEIGHT: 3–9″

HABITAT: Rich woods and stream banks

CULTURAL TIPS (see page 62)**:** Rue anemone increases by seed quickly if the soil is moist, friable humus. They persist in challenging soil but will not reproduce enthusiastically.

MOISTURE: Moist, but well drained

pH: 4.5–6

EXPOSURE: Filtered shade to heavy deciduous shade or morning sun

PROPAGATION (see page 66)**:** Division is easiest.

SEED STORAGE: Store temporarily in moist spaghnum at 40°.

SEED TREATMENT: Sow fresh or keep moist until sown. Stratify for 3 months at 40°. Sow at 60°-70°. Best grown in an outdoor seedbed since the seedlings are tiny and take 3 years to bloom.

CUTTINGS: No

DIVISION: In early spring or in fall, separate the tubers. Each little piece can survive on its own. Try to keep the leaf end up, or place the tuber horizontally in the soil.

FAUNA: Flies so small they are almost unnoticeable visit the flowers, and presumably they carry pollen from one flower to another.

OTHER SE SPECIES (all of which are dioecious)**:**
　　Thalictrum dasycarpum (purple meadow rue)—This 4–6′ meadow rue often has purple stems. It has the typical ternately compound petio-late leaves. The leaf right below the lowest flower cluster is petiolate. The loose, domed flower mass is creamy white. It is found in wet meadows and prairies.
　　T. dioicum (early meadow rue)—This early-blooming, 1–2′ plant has gray-green petiolate leaves. Male flowers have yellow dangling stamens and no petals. Female flowers are nondescript. They can be found in moist, deciduous woods north of the Coastal Plain.
　　T. pubescens (T. polygamum) (tall meadow rue)—Tall meadow rue can be 6′ tall, but the blue-green, rue-like leaves do not obstruct the view. Upper leaves are sessile. The large, white inflorescence consists of masses of petal-less flowers in domed clusters. Male flowers are showier than female flowers. Plants may have single sex or bisexual flowers. It is found in moist meadows and woods but is highly drought-tolerant in cultivation
　　T. revolutum (waxy meadow rue)—The leaves on this 4–6′ meadow rue may have glandular hairs on the underside. It is found in dry or rich woods.

　　* Rue anemone is listed in the USDA Plant Database for all the south-eastern states except Louisiana. Featherman recorded it in Louisiana in 1870, and Caroline Dorman writes about it in her books. Perhaps some sharp-eyed plant enthusiast will rediscover it.

SPIDERWORT
Tradescantia virginiana
Commelinaceae
(Spiderwort Family)

The rich blues and purples of the small iris-like flowers of spiderwort attract insects and people alike. The plant is showy in spite of the small flower size because it rapidly forms clumps, and many flowers in a clump are open at one time. *T. virginiana* is found in all the Southeastern states, but other species of *Tradescantia* might be more common in some states.

To the American ear, the word "wort" sounds like "wart," imbuing the name spiderwort with a negative connotation. In fact, "wort" comes from the Old English word, "wyrt" (and several other languages with various spellings) and simply means plant, often a plant used for food or medicine.

The genus name honors John Tradescant (d. 1637), gardener to King Charles I. The common name spiderwort may come from the appearance of a clump of leaves. The long, strappy leaves bend midway and touch the ground. If you have a good imagination, you might picture a long-legged spider.

The young leaves and stems of spiderwort can be eaten fresh or boiled. Native Americans drank a root tea for stomach, kidney, and "female" disorders. But be warned: the tea is a laxative. They also used a mash of the leaves on insect bites and root mash on tumors.

FLOWER: Each perfect, regular, 1-1.5″ diameter flower has 3 ovate, blue to purple (occasionally white) petals; 6 yellow, bearded stamens sparkle against the purple petals. A group of stemmed flowers form a loose umbel-like cyme. Only 1–2 flowers in each group is open on any given day. The green sepals behind the petal and the flower stems are furry. A pair of green, leaf-like bracts clutch the inflorescence into a nosegay. The flower faces close when touched by intense midday sun. Individual flowers come and go in a day.

BLOOMS: 6–10 weeks between April and July

LEAVES: Alternate, linear, parallel-veined, 6–18″ leaves clasp the erect, round stem. The foliage is a bright, medium green and is usually smooth. The sheath where the leaf clasps the stem is hairy. The leaves fold lengthwise along the midrib.

UNDERGROUND STRUCTURES: Fleshy, white underground organs spread from the base of the stem. They produce offsets next to or several inches from the parent plant.

SEEDS: The 3-celled, oval capsule turns brown and splits in 3 places, dispersing 4–12 flat, gray, pitted seeds. Seedlings of spiderwort show great variability in flower color. Seeds are ripe in July and August.

HEIGHT: 18–24″

HABITAT: Meadows and open woodlands. In the Midwest, one species is called railroad iris, because it is frequently found alongside railroad tracks.

CULTURAL TIPS (see page 62): Rapid removal of the spent bloom stalks results in a second flush of bloom. When the leaves look ratty in the summer, chop them to the ground. In September, fresh, new leaves will replace the spent ones. Spiderwort is not a good cut flower. Plant it where you can enjoy it in the garden.

MOISTURE: Moist to dry; robust and aggressive in rich, boggy sites

pH: 5–7

EXPOSURE: Morning sun or light shade

PROPAGATION (see page 66): Division or transplanting self-sown seedlings is easiest.

SEED STORAGE: Store dry seeds in an airtight container at 40°.

SEED TREATMENT: Capture seeds in a cap of cheesecloth or nylon stocking. Sow fresh or store. Stratify for 3 months at 40°. Sow at 70°. Germinate in 2–3 weeks.

CUTTINGS (stem): May through July; root in 3 weeks

DIVISION: Early spring or fall

FAUNA: Cross-pollination is essential, because *Tradescantia* species are self-incompatible. An individual plant rejects its own pollen as soon as the pollen tube starts to grow at the stigma surface. Ground-dwelling bees and small bumblebees are two of its pollinators. Visiting butterflies may or may not be pollinators.

OTHER SE SPECIES:

Tradescantia hirsuticaulis—This early-blooming spiderwort is covered with glandular hairs. The blooms are violet, and the leaves have a purplish cast.

T. ohiensis—This species has smooth flower stems and sepals, except for the very tips. The leaves are bluish.

T. rosea—This 1′ species has thin leaves and rose-colored flowers. It can be found in dry, sandy soils.

T. subaspera—This species is technically differentiated from the others by leaf width. When the whole leaf is flattened, it is wider at the tip end than at the sheath end. By gestalt, the plant is taller and rangier and the stem has a zigzag aspect. The flowers are a pale, blue-lavender. It does better in limy soils.

WAKE ROBIN, TRILLIUM
Trillium **spp.**
Liliaceae (Lily Family)

The genus *Trillium* is well represented in every state in the Southeast, but no one species is found in all the states. All have 3 leaves, 3 sepals, and 3 petals. The flowers are usually white, maroon, or less commonly, yellow or chartreuse. As development reduces natural habitat and deer populations grow, the number of trillium falls. In addition, trillium are slow to reach flowering age—7 years from seed. Never dig trillium unless you have written permission to collect it. Buy plants from a reputable nursery.

Native Americans used a rhizome tea to help induce childbirth and to treat menstrual complaints and symptoms related to menopause. They also made a poultice of the entire plant to treat tumors and skin problems. Doctors once prescribed the rhizome tea for coughs, bowel troubles, hemorrhage, and lung problems.

FLOWER: The flowers are terminal and may or may not have a stalk. There are 3 green to reddish-purple sepals, and 3 white to maroon, occasionally yellow or chartreuse, petals. The petals may be erect or opened loosely or curved backwards or twisted. There are 6 stamens and 3 stigmas. Occasionally the sepal, petal, stamen, and carpel number can be 4, 5, 6, or 7.

BLOOMS: 3–4 weeks between February and June

LEAVES: The whorl of 3 ovate to lanceolate leaves top a thick "stem" that is usually upright but may be decumbent. This stem is really a peduncle or flowering branch. The net-veined "leaves" may or may not have a stalk. These leaves are actually bracts since they occur on a flowering stalk, but most people just call them leaves (Case, 1997). They may be pure green or mottled.

UNDERGROUND STRUCTURES: Underground dwells a stocky, ringed rhizome that is full of starch. These food storage devices are about the size of a man's thumb in older plants. Their size is relative to the flower size of the particular species. For example, *T. pusillum* is a petite, white-flowered species with a small rhizome. The terminal bud is at one end of the rhizome. It is softly pointed and whiter in color than the rest of the structure, and the rear end is flat. Old growth decays from that end each year. Feeder roots descend from the newer portion of the rhizome. The appearance of rhizomes and roots is slightly different for each species.

SEEDS: As many as 60–120 reddish brown, BB-sized seeds pack a 1″ diameter, pulpy, 3-ridged capsule. The fruit varies in color from off-white to red, depending on the species. Red berries have a fruity smell. White berries are small, dry, and lack fragrance. The brown seeds have a white, fleshy, oily aril that is nearly as large as the seed. Seeds take 2–3 months to ripen after the bloom withers. The capsule softens at the base first and falls from the leaf platform. The seams may or may not split. Seeds may just fall out the bottom.

HEIGHT: 6–18″

HABITAT: Moist, open, deciduous woodlands

CULTURAL TIPS (see page 62)**:** Trillium need plenty of humus. In the fall, remove heavy layers of leaves, chop the leaves, and mulch the plants with the now friable material. Irrigate during periods of drought. In late winter, while the plant is still dormant, the application of a balanced, dry fertilizer is acceptable but not absolutely necessary.

MOISTURE: Moist, well-draining

pH: 5–7 (But varies with species.—The common *T. cuneatum* will grow in almost any southeastern soil. The presence of *T. lancifolium* indicates a slightly sweeter substrate.)

EXPOSURE: Light shade

PROPAGATION (see page 66)**:** Seed is easiest but slow.

SEED STORAGE: Store in moist sphagnum in a closed container in the refrigerator or a cooler until the seeds can be processed.

SEED TREATMENT: Stratify for 6 weeks at 70°; switch to 40° for 3 months; switch to 70° for 3 months; switch to 40° for 3 months; and finally sow at 60°. The first leaf above ground is a simple, single leaf. The main growth will occur below ground for several years. The characteristic 3-leaved whorl does not appear until the fourth year after sowing the seed. 7 years will pass before the rhizome contains enough food to support a blooming, fruiting stalk. Some species may require giberrelin #3 to germinate. Sowing in an outdoor seedbed is one way to meet this requirement.

CUTTINGS: No stem cuttings! A mature rhizome can be decapitated to induce bud formation. In July or August, lift a mature rhizome from the ground and rinse it with water. Cut across the rhizome about 3/4–1″ behind the terminal growing point. Dust the cut ends with fungicide and replant them about 2″ deep in good woodland humus. The lateral buds take about 2 years to form, and a blooming plant takes about 4 years. No process is quick with trillium. Another way to induce lateral bud formation without disturbing the parent plant is to pull aside the soil and cut a groove along the top of the rhizome. Dust the rhizome with fungicide, replace the soil, and hope for bulbils in a year.

DIVISION: Divide clumps of trillium after leaf senescence, when the weather is cooling in the fall.

FAUNA: Trillium may have a delicious floral or lemon fragrance or the smell of carrion. Bees pollinate the pleasant-smelling species, and beetle and carrion flies pollinate the offensive-smelling species. One must get down to "beetle level" to detect the nasty smell. I haven't smelled a truly repugnant trillium, but have not met the West Coast species that is said to have a ghastly aroma. Ants harvest trillium seed for the aril which contains a pheromone.

MERRYBELLS,
BELLWORT
Uvularia perfoliata
Liliaceae (Lily Family)

Nature has a knack with color and form. The combination of the pale lemon-yellow of the flowers and the blue-green, smooth foliage of merrybells refreshes and calms. When color and line of foliage are strong, the bloom can be charming and retiring and doesn't lessen the overall appeal of the plant.

The uvula is the piece of tissue hanging in the back of your throat. The flowers of the *Uvularia* spp. hang in a similar manner. *Perfoliata* refers to the piercing of the leaf by the stem.

The Iroquois used the roots of *U. perfoliata* as a cough medicine, as a wash for sore eyes, and to treat broken bones.

This species is edible, prepared like asparagus, but to eat a dwindling wildling would be sacrilege.

FLOWER: A pale yellow, 6-petaled, loosely bell-shaped flower hangs shyly on a stalk. The flower is terminal, perfect, and regular. It has 6 stamens about equal in length to the styles. The flower is 1-1.5″ long.

BLOOMS: 3 weeks between March and May

LEAVES: The base of the erect stem is white and scaly just under the leaf litter. As it ascends it becomes smooth and blue-green. A mature plant stem is exceedingly stiff, and when broken, reveals snapped fibers. The stem pierces the base of the 2–5″, oval, pointed leaves. The leaves are smooth, blue-green, entire, and alternate.

UNDERGROUND STRUCTURES: The individual root structure of a plant of bellwort resembles the radial design of an octopus. The roots are pristine white and have the thickness of spaghetti. Slightly thinner rhizomes which appear to have vestigial leaf bases extend out from the center about 6″ and surface to form new plants.

SEEDS: The green, 3-cornered capsule is about 1/3″ long. The seeds are a flattened round shape, with up to 3 seeds in each of 3 chambers.

HEIGHT: 6–20″

HABITAT: Slopes of rich, moist, deciduous woodlands

CULTURAL TIPS (see page 62): This is one tough plant! The rhizomes will grow into blacktop, and the plant withstands winter road salt. It even tolerates transplanting when in bloom, if watered.

MOISTURE: Moist, well-draining, but drought-tolerant.

pH: 4.5–6.5

EXPOSURE: Filtered light of a deciduous woodland

PROPAGATION (see page 66): Division of offsets is easiest.

SEED STORAGE: Store temporarily in moist spaghnum at 40°.

SEED TREATMENT: Sow outdoors as soon as they are ripe.

CUTTINGS: No

DIVISION: Early spring or fall

FAUNA: Await observation

OTHER SE SPECIES:

Uvularia grandiflora—The flowers of this 1–2′ species are larger and brighter yellow. The undersides of the leaves are hairy. It thrives in a sweet soil, with a pH of 6–8.

U. sessifolia—This 6–10″ species does not have perfoliate leaves, and the leaves are a medium green with no blue cast. It forms colonies rapidly.

ROSE VERBENA,
EASTERN VERBENA
Verbena canadensis
Verbenaceae (Vervain Family)

When you see an expanse of intense pink, low-growing flowers or a 4′ haze of purple along the roadside in midsummer, chances are good that you are seeing verbena. It may be a native or a naturalized plant, but whatever its country of origin, it has several admirable qualities: showy, long-lasting blooms, a tendency to form colonies, and drought-tolerance.

Verbena is a Latin name for sacred plants used in religious ceremonies. The French name for verbena is *verveine*, hence the common name vervain, often used instead of verbena. American verbenas were used medicinally. Native Americans and settlers drank a tea made from the leaves or roots of blue vervain to treat consumption and stomach and bowel problems. A weak tea was used as a "female tonic." A strong tea causes vomiting.

FLOWER: The flat-topped inflorescence is similar to a garden phlox, but the individual flowers of verbena are slightly irregular. The fragrant flowers are about 1/2″ in diameter. The corolla is usually a shade of pink, magenta, or violet, but may be red or white. Each tubular flower has 5 lobes and 4 stamens, 2 of them being longer than the others. The calyx has gland-tipped hairs.

BLOOMS: 4–6 weeks between March and June

LEAVES: The 3″ dark green, petiolate leaves are opposite, toothed, and variably lobed. The hairy, above-ground stems are angled and sprawling. Wherever the branches of this perennial touch the ground, roots form.

UNDERGROUND STRUCTURES: Rhizomes with feeder roots run shallowly, forming colonies.

SEEDS: The fruit has 4 sections, each one containing a brown nutlet.

HEIGHT: 12″ (stem 12–24″ but lax)

HABITAT: Rocky glades (especially limestone), open and rocky or sandy wooded slopes, sandhills, ledges of bluffs, fields, pastures, prairies, gravel bars along streams, and along roadsides and railroads.

CULTURAL TIPS (see page 62)**:** Good drainage is imperative, but go easy on the fertilizer. Mow patches to the 2″ level (no lower) when they become leggy. Provide a loose soil to encourage rooting along the decumbent stems.

MOISTURE: Moderate to dry

pH: 5–6.5

EXPOSURE: Full sun to partial shade

PROPAGATION (see page 66)**:** Stem cuttings are easiest

SEED STORAGE: Store dry seeds in an airtight container between 40° and 70°.

SEED TREATMENT: Stratify for 3-4 weeks at 40°. Sow at 60-70°. Germination is erratic over 3–5 weeks.

CUTTINGS (leaf node cuttings): Spring through summer, you can take cuttings all along the stem.

DIVISION: Spring or fall

FAUNA: All verbenas are good nectar plants for hummingbirds and butterflies. The genus is one of several host plants for the buckeye butterfly. The seeds are a favorite food of wild turkey.

OTHER SE SPECIES:

Verbena bonariensis—This species is a naturalized plant with tiny violet flowers in a dense, 1″ spike. It is 6-8′ tall and has a rough, square stem. The leaves are elliptic or lanceolate, sessile, clasping, and downy underneath.

V. brasiliensis (Brazilian verbena)—This naturalized species is similar to *V. bonariensis,* but the non-clasping leaves and the stem are smooth.

V. hastata (blue vervain)—This 2-4′ tall species has a candelabra of thin spikes of blue-violet flowers, which open from the bottom up. The toothed, petiolate leaves are lanceolate-halberd shaped, and the hairy stem is square. It prefers moist sites. Thoreau's grandfather made a tea of blue vervain for his cough. Roasted, ground seeds make a bitter but life-sustaining flour.

V. x hybrida (garden verbena)—This plant is a hybrid of 4 South American species of verbena grown as garden annuals in all the colors of the rainbow.

V. rigida (stiff verbena)—This invasive species has naturalized across the Southeast. It has bright magenta clusters of flowers on 6-12″ tall erect stems. The leaves are roughly hairy, clasping, lanceolate, and toothed. It is common on roadsides.

V. stricta (hoary vervain, fever weed)—This 3.5′ tall species has blue-violet, terminal spikes of flowers on erect stems. The sessile leaves are hairy, oval, and coarsely toothed.

V. tenuisecta (moss verbena)—This naturalized, prostrate species has showy flower heads of pink (in every hue) to purple or white. The branching stems tolerate mowing. The opposite leaves are deeply cut.

TALL IRONWEED
Vernonia gigantea (V. altissima)
Asteraceae
(Aster or Sunflower Family)

Ironweeds rival the goldenrods for attention in the fall. The flower color in this species is magenta-purple. In the New York ironweed, the color is almost black-purple. Cattle must find ironweed unpalatable because it remains untouched in pasturelands. The white *Eupatorium* species repel ruminants as well, and the combination of purple ironweed, white thorough-wort, and Black Angus cattle is a sight to behold.

Native Americans used infusions of various species of ironweed to regulate menses, relieve post-partum pain, and to treat stomach ulcers and bleeding.

The genus name, *Vernonia,* honors William Vernon, (1680s–1710s), an English botanist who collected plants in Maryland.

FLOWERS: The potentially 3′ x 3′ flower cluster is loose, terminal, and flat-topped. These clusters contain large numbers of heads. Each head is composed of 9–30, purple-magenta, perfect disc flowers. There are no ray flowers; 2 rows of overlapping involucral bracts clutch the bases of the flowers. The outer row is purplish and pubescent. Ironweeds have no chaff-like material between the flowers.

BLOOMS: 4 weeks between August and October

LEAVES: The stout, unbranched, upright stems are smooth or slightly hairy and very leafy. The 4″ to 12″ long leaves are simple, alternate, lanceolate-ovate, petiolate, pointed, and toothed. The leaves are generally smooth above and lightly furry below.

UNDERGROUND STRUCTURES: Ironweeds have a heavy crown with fibrous roots. Some of these "roots" are larger than the others, and new stems emerge from these large roots 4–12″ from the mother plant.

SEEDS: The dark gray nutlets are ribbed and hairy on the ribs. The purplish-tan pappus is twice as long as the seed and is in 2 rows, an inner, long ring and an outer, short ring. The seeds begin ripening while the plant is still flowering and continue to ripen for 6 weeks.

HEIGHT: 5–10′

HABITAT: Moist to wet woods

CULTURAL TIPS (see page 62)**:** Fall-blooming ironweeds can be cut back up until July 4 to produce a shorter but still blooming plant.

MOISTURE: Average to wet

pH: 5–6

EXPOSURE: Partial shade to sun

PROPAGATION TIPS (see page 66)**:** Seeds of the wet species have high germination rates, and the young plants develop a large root system rapidly.

SEED STORAGE: Store dry seeds in an airtight container between 40° and 70°.

SEED TREATMENT: Stratify for 3 months at 40°; sow at 70°. Germinate in 1–2 weeks.

CUTTINGS (stem)**:** Late spring to early summer; roots form in 4–5 weeks

DIVISION: Spring or winter

FAUNA: Many insects and butterflies seek nectar from ironweeds. One butterfly in particular may be sighted perching on the flowers. The tiger swallowtail will feed on an assortment of flowers, but prefers flowers more than 5′ tall such as ironweed, Joe Pye weed, thistles, and buttonbush. Other butterflies you will find on ironweed include: diana, great spangle fritillary, painted lady, monarch, fiery skipper, peck's or yellowpatch skipper, cross line skipper, sachem, southern golden skipper, and the carolina roadside skipper. Later, goldfinches eat the seeds.

OTHER SE SPECIES:

Vernonia angustifolia (narrowleaf ironweed)—This 2-3′ tall species has magenta blooms. There are 8–30 disc flowers per head, and the pappus is a tawny purplish color. Many linear leaves crowd on each fuzzy stem. It blooms in summer in piney woods and on dunes.

V. noveboracensis (New York ironweed)—The common and scientific names of this 4-7′ tall species are misleading, since it is common in the Southeast. It has 30–65 disc flowers per head, making individual heads (not the overall inflorescence) larger than those of *V. gigantea*. It has long, pointed, involucral bracts. At the time of flowering, the long, pointed, dark-green leaves are mainly on the stem. The pappus is brown to purple. It can be found in low woods and wet fields, blooming from August to October.

Culver's Root,
Beaumont's Root, Bowman's Root, Brinton's Root, Cubeun's Root
Veronicastrum virginicum
Scrophulariaceae (Figwort or Snapdragon Family)

Culver's root is a handsome 3–5′ plant found in roadside ditches and open moist areas all over the East Coast. It has dark green whorled leaves and white flowers in 6–9″ spikes. The leaves are spaced 4″ apart on the unbranched, erect stems, so the foliage does not seem coarse or obstructive. The white bloom spikes shine from the darkness of a woodland edge.

The genus name, *Veronicastrum,* refers to the similarity of the bloom spike to the flowering spikes of *Veronica* spp.

The large number of common names based on surnames indicates the frequent usage of Culver's root among colonists as the basis of folk medicine. They learned about the drug from the Native Americans who drank a tea made from the dried root as a laxative, a diuretic, an emetic, and a diaphoretic. The fresh root can be toxic.

FLOWERS: Each thin bloom spike has numerous small, white (sometimes blue or pink), 2-lipped flowers. When the flower bud is just beginning to open, the rose-colored style and 2 stamens peak from the opening bud. Viewed with a hand lens, it looks like a tiny white whale sticking out his tongue. The corolla of white petals has an upper lip with 2 lobes and a lower lip with 3 lobes. They fuse in a tube which is lined with white hairs. The stamens and style extend way beyond the open flower, giving the inflorescence a pinkish cast. Mature plants have a terminal flower spike (raceme) and several subtending spikes in the leaf axils of the 2 top whorls of leaves.

BLOOMS: 4–6 weeks between June and August

LEAVES: Each dark green, smooth leaf is simple, lanceolate, serrate, and sessile. Groups of 3–7 leaves form whorls at 4″ intervals on the round, erect, unbranched stem. The undersides of the leaves and the stem may be lightly pubescent.

UNDERGROUND STRUCTURES: The expanding crown of easily separable plants has fibrous roots supporting each rosette.

SEEDS: The dark brown seeds are like dust within the oval, dark brown capsule. They are ripe when the capsule begins to split at its 4 seams, usually in September or October.

HEIGHT: 3–4′ (or, less commonly, 6′)

HABITAT: Prairies, wet meadows, roadsides, bogs, stream edges, and moist open woodlands

CULTURAL TIPS (see page 62): Add humus to the planting site. The clump does not die out in the middle, so division is only necessary if one wishes to increase the number of plants.

MOISTURE: Moist (with less moisture, decrease the amount of light)

pH: 4.5–7

EXPOSURE: Full sun to half-day or strong filtered light

PROPAGATION (see page 66): All methods are successful.

SEED STORAGE: Store dry seed in an airtight container between 40° and 70°.

SEED TREATMENT: Stratify for 1 month at 40°. Sow at 70°. Cover very lightly (light requirement). Germinate in 2–4 weeks. Keep at 60 degrees for 2–4 weeks if possible. Newly emerged seedlings are miniscule, and develop strength most readily at a cool temperature. Blooms the second year. Some people germinate Culver's root at 70° with good light, but they say it takes 4–6 weeks. I find a period of cold stratification hastens germination, thus reducing the time when seedlings are most vulnerable to dessication, rot, or disease.

CUTTINGS (stem): Terminal in April or May when the stem is firm, but as long as possible before bloom buds develop; (root): February through March

DIVISION: Early spring or fall

FAUNA: Await observation

BIRD'S FOOT VIOLET
Viola pedata
Violaceae (Violet Family)

Before the advent of herbicides, country roads were festooned with violet pansy faces in early spring. *Viola pedata,* literally, "foot-like violet," disdains rich garden soil and thrives in lean, gravelly, open areas. The deeply dissected leaves look like the feet of birds. This delicate-looking violet can survive in habitats that would be inhospitable to many other plants. The entire plant is edible.

FLOWER: The 5 beardless petals of the perfect, solitary flowers are usually violet, but the upper 2 petals may be velvety purple and the lower 3 violet. The bottom petal of the lower 3 is larger and spurred. The stamens project from the flower tube and accent the center of the bloom with a complementary orange dot.

BLOOMS: 3–6 weeks between March (even January in mild years) and May

LEAVES: The simple, stalked leaves are deeply, palmately cut. Most of the leaves are basal. The stem is underground in the form of a rhizome.

UNDERGROUND STRUCTURES: The fleshy rhizome is carrot-like in young plants, but has 3–4 branches with feeder roots in older plants.

SEEDS: As the capsule ripens, it turns from green to tan and splits open explosively, casting seeds in a broad area around the plant. The tan to brown seeds are quite small but not dust-like, and can be collected when the capsule turns translucent yellow.

HEIGHT: 6–8″

HABITAT: Roadside banks and thin, rocky woods

CULTURAL TIPS (see page 62)**:** Because bird's foot violet requires lean soil and good drainage, it never becomes a pest. Other common violets are unwelcome in monoculture lawns because they spread so aggressively. Violets can be divided into 2 classes: "leafy stemmed" (flower stalk arises from a leaf axil of the stem), and "stemless" (flower stalk rises directly from the rhizome). With the exception of bird's foot violet, the stemless species are the most aggressive ones. The common blue violet is a stemless violet.

MOISTURE: *Viola pedata* is highly drought-tolerant. It can live in areas of high rainfall as long as it has excellent drainage.

pH: 5–6

EXPOSURE: Full to partial sun

PROPAGATION (see page 66)**:** Challenging

SEED STORAGE: Can store temporarily in moist spaghnum at 40°

SEED TREATMENT: Sow fresh on a medium amended with sand or grit. Protect the container from heavy rains. Seeds need a cold, moist period.

CUTTINGS (leaf cuttings)**:** After bloom, remove leaves with a piece of the crown attached. Stick the cuttings in a tray of sand, place in the shade, and mist 3–4 times per day, or create a high humidity chamber. Roots should emerge in 6 weeks.
(root)**:** In February in a warm greenhouse

DIVISION: Late winter or early spring; cut completely through the crown, leaving at least 1 leaf on each division.

FAUNA: Fine directional lines etch the lower petal of the flower face. These are nectary guides to direct pollinators (small bees and butterflies) to the nectar and pollen. The sleepy orange butterfly is one visitor. Many species of fritillary butterflies use violets as host plants.

Yucca,
Adam's Needle
Yucca filamentosa
(Y. flaccida, Y. smalliana,
Y. concava)
Agavaceae
(Century Plant Family)

Yuccas have a bushel basket–size basal rosette of pointed dark green leaves with shredding threads curling along the edges. The bloom stalk of large white flowers stands 6-8′ tall. This noble plant suggests desert, but it is a plant of the Southeast.

Fili is a Latin word root for thread. *Tosa* is a Greek word root for very. The specific epithet *filamentosa* describes the threads that peel from the sides of the leaves.

Yucca has economic importance in the form of food, fiber, and soap. The flowers can be eaten fresh, cooked with meat, or dipped in batter and deep fried. Native Americans produced rope and fabric from the fiber. The strong strap-like leaves were also used to hang meat for smoking. Saponins in the roots of yuccas can be used in soap and shampoo, but are toxic to lower forms of life, such as fish. Because of its usefulness, settlers carried the plants west, and yucca has naturalized all the way to California. Native Americans may have spread the plant throughout the East.

FLOWER: The fragrant, perfect flowers are waxy, white, and bell-shaped. Masses of flowers nod in the branched panicle. The inflorescence itself can be 2′ in height. The flowers are pollinated by the night-flying yucca moth *(Tegeticula yuccasella)* and are said to turn to face upward in the evening.

BLOOMS: 4 weeks between April and August

LEAVES: The linear leaves are leathery and evergreen. They clasp the base of the plant and taper to a sharp point at the outer end, thus the name Adam's needle. Strong fibers fray from the leaf margins. The tall erect stem is a flowering stalk with leaves reduced to the point that it looks almost bare.

UNDERGROUND STRUCTURES: Each rosette has 1 main white-pithed rhizome with fibrous feeder roots.

SEEDS: The tan, oblong, erect capsule has 3 chambers. Within each chamber, 2 vertical rows of seeds stack neatly. The seeds are black, triangular, and flat.

HEIGHT: 5–8′

HABITAT: Rich, dry, or draining soil in open woods, roadsides, thickets, and railroad embankments

CULTURAL TIPS (see page 62)**:** Plant in rocky loam or any soil with good drainage. Unless planted in pure sand, yucca needs no supplemental moisture once established. It is not a succulent, so it does not store a large reservoir of water in its leaves.

MOISTURE: Average to dry

pH: 4.5–6.5

EXPOSURE: Filtered light to full sun

PROPAGATION (see page 66)**:** Slow

SEED STORAGE: Store dry seed in an airtight container between 40° and 70°.

SEED TREATMENT: Collect in September or October; vernalize 6 months; stratify 3 months at 40°; sow at 70°. If sowing directly in the ground outside, allow seeds to mature on the plants until late fall.

CUTTINGS: No stem

DIVISION: Spring or fall

FAUNA: *Yucca filamentosa* has a cooperative arrangement with the yucca moth. The female moth collects pollen from a yucca. She then pierces a hole in the pistil, lays 1 egg, and packs the hole with pollen. She pollinates the plant in exchange for a few seeds for her baby. Some seeds always escape the hungry larvae.

OTHER SE SPECIES:

Yucca aloifolia (Spanish bayonet)—This species is more like a shrub or small tree. It differs from *Y. filamentosa* in several ways. Several sets of leaves stack into a sizeable mass as the plant ages. The leaves lack shredding filaments, leaf points are much sharper, and the fruit dangles instead of standing erect.

GOLDEN ALEXANDER,
ZIZEA
Zizea aurea
Apiaceae (Parsley Family)

In late March or early April, nature mounts a display that rivals the work of any floral artist. In moist to wet woodlands, pure white atamasco lilies, pink spring beauties, blue phlox, purple spiderwort, and mustard-yellow zizea mingle in masses. The light, at this debut of the year, pierces to the woodland floor, unfiltered by leaves, infusing the blooms with an inner glow.

The genus name *Zizea* honors I.B. Ziz, a Rhenish botanist. *Aurea* is Latin for golden.

Native Americans and colonists used zizea medicinally, but all plants in the parsley family are toxic. If you eat a root, expect violent vomiting to follow.

FLOWER: The 1–2″ compound umbels of bright gold flowers have inflorescence stalks 1.5″ long. These peduncles emerge from leaf axils along the top one-third of the stem. Each 5-petaled flower is perfect and regular. The central flower in each umbellet is sessile (has no stalk or a very stubby one).

BLOOMS: 2 months between March and June

LEAVES: A wedge of 3 or more leafy flowering stalks rises from the thick rootstalk. The alternate, smooth, toothed, compound, medium-green leaves have petioles of varying lengths, long at the base and very short at the top of the plant. Each leaflet is 1-1.5″ long and 0.25-5″ wide; 3–5 leaflets comprise a leaf. The first true leaf on a seedling is a toothed half-circle.

UNDERGROUND STRUCTURES: Golden Alexander has the thick rootstock typical of a plant in the parsley family.

SEEDS: The dark brown, dry seeds are oblong and ribbed. They look like dill seeds. They are ripe between June and August.

HEIGHT: 1–3′

HABITAT: Moist meadows and moist to wet woodlands

CULTURAL TIPS (see page 62)**:** Zizea thrives in any woodland, wet or dry. It seeds actively but can be controlled because it has fibrous roots, not underground rhizomes.

MOISTURE: Moist or dry

pH: 5–6.5

EXPOSURE: Light shade

PROPAGATION (see page 66)**:** Seed is easiest. Collect the seeds when you can rub them off the receptacle. It may be greenish or brown.

SEED STORAGE: Store dry seeds in an airtight container between 40° and 70°.

SEED TREATMENT: Stratify 4 months at 40°; sow at 70°. Blooms the second year.

CUTTINGS (stem)**:** May through June

DIVISION: Early spring or fall

FAUNA: Zizea prevents self-pollination by having all the flowers of one head male and all the flowers of another head female. A solitary bee seeking nectar transfers pollen from male flowers to female flowers as he makes his rounds. As a member of the parsley family, zizea can serve as a host plant for the black swallowtail caterpillar.

OTHER SE SPECIES:
   Zizea aptera—This species has similar flowers, but the simple, basal leaves are ovate. It is found in the mountains and Piedmont.

BIBLIOGRAPHY

Ajilvsgi, Geyata. *Wild Flowers of the Big Thicket.* College Station, Texas: Texas A & M University Press, 1979.

Armitage, Allan M. *Herbaceous Perennial Plants.* Athens, Georgia: Varsity Press, Inc., 1989.

Art, Henry W. *A Garden of Wildflowers.* Pownal, Vermont: Storey Communications, Inc., 1986.

Art, Henry W. *The Wildflower Gardener's Guide.* Pownal, Vermont: Storey Communications, Inc., 1987. (2nd printing 1989).

Batson, Wade. *Wild Flowers in the Carolinas.* Columbia, South Carolina: University of South Carolina Press, 1987.

Borror, Donald J. *Dictionary of Word Roots and Combining Forms.* Mountain View, California: Mayfield Publishing Co., 1960.

Bradley, Jeff. *Tennessee Handbook.* Chico, California: Moon Publications, 1997.

Brandt, Robert S. *Tennessee Hiking Guide.* Sierra Club, Tennessee Chapter. Knoxville, Tennessee: The University of Tennessee Press, 1988.

Braun, E. Lucy. *Deciduous Forests of Eastern North America.* Philadelphia, Pennsylvania: The Blakiston Company, 1950.

Brown, Lauren. *Grasses, An Identification Guide.* Boston, Massachusetts: Houghton Mifflin, 1979.

Burrell, C. Colston. *A Gardener's Encyclopedia of Wildflowers.* Emmaus, Pennsylvania: Rodale Press, Inc., 1997.

Campbell, Carlos C., William F. Hutson, and Aaron J. Sharp. *Great Smoky Mountains Wildflowers,* 4th ed. Knoxville, Tennessee: The University of Tennessee Press, 1988.

Carlton, Mike. *Tennessee Wonders, A Pictorial Guide to the Parks.* Nashville, Tennessee: Rutledge Hill Press, 1994.

Case, Frederick W. Jr., and Roberta B. Case. *Trilliums.* Portland, Oregon: Timber Press, 1997.

Clay, James W., Paul D. Escott, Douglas M. Orr, Jr., Alfred W. Stuart. *Land of the South.* Birmingham, Alabama: Oxmoor House, 1989.

Coffey, Timothy. *The History and Folklore of North American Wildflowers.* New York: Facts on File, New York, 1993.

Coombes, Allen J. *Dictionary of Plant Names,* 7th ed. Portland, Oregon: Timber Press, 1985.

Cronquist, Arthur. *Vascular Flora of the Southeastern United States,* Vol. I, Asteraceae. Chapel Hill, North Carolina: The University of North Carolina Press, 1980.

Darke, Rick and Mark Griffiths, Mark. *Manual of Grasses.* Portland, Oregon: Timber Press, 1994.

Dean, Blanche E., Amy Mason, and Joab L. Thomas. *Wildflowers of Alabama.* University, Alabama: University: The University of Alabama Press, 1973.

DeHart, Allen. *Hiking South Carolina Trails,* 3rd ed. Old Saybrook, Connecticut: The Globe Pequot Press, 1994.

Denison, Edgar. *Missouri Wildflowers,* 4th ed. Jefferson City, Missouri: Missouri Department of Conservation, 1989.

Deno, Norman C. *Seed Germination, Theory and Practice,* 2nd ed. State College, Pennsylvania: self-published, 139 Lenor Drive, State College, PA 16801, 1993. 1st Supplement, 1996. 2nd Supplement, 1998.

Dormon, Caroline. *Wild Flowers of Louisiana.* Garden City, New York: Doubleday, Doran & Co, Inc., 1934.

Duncan, Wilbur H. and Leanard E. Foote. *Wildflowers of the Southeastern United States.* Athens, Georgia: The University of Georgia Press, 1975.

Erichsen-Brown, Charlotte. *Medicinal and Other Uses of North American Plants.* New York: Dover Publications, Inc., 1979.

Fenneman, Nevin M. *Physiography of Eastern United States.* New York: McGraw-Hill Book Company, Inc, 1938.

Foster, Steven and James A. Duke. *Medicinal Plants, A Peterson Field Guide.* Boston, Massachusetts: Houghton Mifflin Co., 1990.

Godfrey, Robert K. and Jean W. Wooten. *Aquatic and Wetland Plants of Southeastern United States, Dicotyledons.* Athens, Georgia: The University of Georgia Press, 1981.

Godfrey, Robert K. and Jean W. Wooten. *Aquatic and Wetland Plants of Southeastern United States, Monocotyledons.* Athens, Georgia: The University of Georgia Press, 1979.

Greer, Jennifer. *Alabama's Natural Wonders.* Alabama Outdoors, Montgomery, Alabama: Summer 1997.

Grossman, D. H. et al. *International Classification of Ecological Communities: Terrestrial Vegetation of the United States,* Vol. 1. Arlington, Virginia: The Nature Conservancy, 1998.

Harper, Roland M. *Economic Botany of Alabama,* Monograph 9, Part 2. University, Tuscaloosa, Alabama: Geological Survey of Alabama, 1928.

Harper, Roland M. *Forests of Alabama,* Monograph 10. University, Alabama: Geological Survey of Alabama, 1943.

Haywood, Paulette. *Creating Butterfly Habitats with Native Plants,* talk given at the Landscaping With Native Plants Conference, Cullowhee, North Carolina: July 1998.

Headstrom, Richard. *Nature in Miniature.* New York: Alfred A. Knopf, Inc., 1968.

Hemmerly, Thomas E. *Wildflowers of the Central South,* Nashville, Tennessee: Vanderbilt University Press, 1990.

Hunter, Carl G. *Wildflowers of Arkansas,* 3rd ed. 1992, Ozark Society Foundation, Arkansas Game and Fish Commission, 1992.

Jacobs, Don L. and Rob L. Jacobs, *American Treasures, Trilliums in Woodland and Garden.* Decatur, Georgia: Eco-Gardens, 1997.

Jones, Samuel B., Jr., and Leanard E. Foote. *Gardening with Native Wild Flowers.* Portland, Oregon: Timber Press, 1990.

Kniffen, Fred B., and Sam Bowers Hilliard. *Louisiana, Its Land and People,* revised ed. Baton Rouge, Louisiana: Louisiana State University Press, 1988.

Kuchler, A. W. *Potential Natural Vegetation of the United States,* (Map and Illustrated Manual). Special Publication No. 36. New York: American Geographical Society, 1964.

Leidolf, Andreas and Sidney McDaniel. *A Floristic Study of Black Prairie Plant Communities at Sixteen Section Prairie.* Vol 63, No. 1., Oktibbeha County, Mississippi: 1998.

Leopold, Aldo. *A Sand County Almanac.* New York: Oxford University Press, 1949.

Lindsey, Anne. *The Intricate and Intimate Relationship of Flowers and Their Pollinators,* a talk given at the Landscaping With Native Plants Conference., Cullowhee, North Carolina:. July 1998.

Lineback, Neal G., *Atlas of Alabama*, University, Alabama: The University of Alabama Press, University, AL., 1973.

Lipscomb, B.L. and E.B.Smith. *Morphological Intergradation of Varieties of Bidens aristosa (Compositae) in Northern Arkansas,* 79:203-213. Rhodora, 1977.

Lowe, E. N. *Plants of Mississippi.* Mississippi State Geological Survey, Bulletin # 17, Feb. 1921.

Martin, Alexander C., Herber S. Zim, and Arnold L. Nelson. *American Wildlife & Plants, A Guide to Wildlife Food Habits.* New York: Dover Publication, Inc.,1951.

Martin, William H., Stephen G. Boyce, and Arthur C. Echterancht. *Biodiversity of the Southeastern United States, Lowland Terrestrial Communities.* New York: John Wiley & Sons, Inc., 1993.

Martin, William H., Stephen G. Boyce, and Arthur C. Echterancht. *Biodiversity of the Southeastern United States, Upland Terrestrial Communities.* New York: John Wiley & Sons, Inc., 1993.

Martin, Laura C. *Southern Wildflowers.* Atlanta, Georgia: Longstreat Press, 1989.

Mathew, Brian. *A Taxonomic and Horticultural Review of Erythronium L. (Liliaceae). Botanical Journal of the Linnean Society* (1992), 109: 453-471, 1992.

McNeal, Pat. *The Grass Menagerie,* Chicago, Illinois: American Nurseryman, July 15, 1998.

Mills, Robert H. and Sam B. Jones, Jr. *The Compositiona of a Mesic Southern Mixed Hardwood Forest in South Mississippi.* Castanea,1969, 34:62-66, 1969.

Moerman, Daniel E. *Medicinal Plants of Native America.* Technical Reports, # 19. Ann Arbor, Michigan: The University of Michigan Museum of Anthropology, 1986.

Mohr, Charles. *Plant Life of Alabama,* Contributions from the U. S. National Herbarium, Vol. VI, U.S. Government Printing Office, 1901.

Mount, Robert H. *The Reptiles & Amphibians of Alabama,* Auburn, Alabama: Auburn Printing Co., 1975.

Native Plants for Georgia Gardens. Bulletin 987. Athens, Georgia: Cooperative Extension Service, The University of Georgia, 1992.

North Carolina Wildflower Preservation Society, Inc. Chapel Hill, North Carolina: Propagation Handbook, 1977.

Oosting, Henry J. *The Study of Plant Communities,* 2nd ed. San Francisco, California: W.H. Freeman and Company, 1956.

Opler, Paul A., and George O.Krizek. *Butterflies East of the Great Plains.* Baltimore, Maryland: The Johns Hopkins University Press, 1984.

Ottesen, Carole. *The Native Plant Primer.* New York: Harmony Books, 1995.

Parks, Clifford and James W. Hardin. *Yellow Erythroniums of the Eastern United States.* Brittonia 15: 245-259, July 1963.

Peterson, Lee Allen. *Edible Wild Plants, A Peterson Field Guide.* Boston, Massachusetts: Houghton Mifflin Co., 1977.

Phillips, Harry R. *Growing and Propagating Wild Flowers.* Chapel Hill, North Carolina: The University of North Carolina Press, 1985.

Porcher, Richard D. *Wild Flowers of the Carolina Lowcountry and Lower Pee Dee.* Columbia, South Carolina: The University of South Carolina Press, 1995.

Proctor, Michael, Peter Yeo, and Andrew Lack. *The Natural History of Pollination.* Portland, Oregon: Timber Press, 1996.

Quarterman, Elsie. *A Fresh Look at Climax Forests of the Coastal Plain.* Association of Southern Botanists Bulletin, Vol. 28, No. 4, October 1981.

Quarterman, Elsie and Catherine Keever. *Southern Mixed Hardwood Forest: Climax in the Southeastern Coastal Plain, U.S.A.* Ecological Monographs, Ecological Society of America, 32: 167-185, 1962.

Radford, Albert, E., Harry E. Ahles, and Ritchie C. Bell. *Manual of the Vascular Flora of the Carolinas,* 9th ed. Chapel Hill, North Carolina: The University of North Carolina Press, 1968-1987.

Schafale, Michael P. and Alan S. Weakley. *Classification of the Natural Communities of North Carolina,* 3rd Approximation. Raleigh, North Carolina: North Carolina Natural Heritage Program, Division of Parks and Recreation, 1990.

Steyermark, Julian A. *Flora of Missouri,* (7th printing). Ames, Iowa: The Iowa State University Press, 1996.

Stokes, Donald. *The Natural History of Wild Shrubs and Vines.* New York: Harper & Row, 1981.

Taylor, Kathryn S. and Stephen Hamblin. *Handbook of Wild Flower Cultivation.* New York: The McMillan Co., 1963.

Thompson, Peter. *Creative Propagation, A Grower's Guide.* Portland, Oregon: Timber Press, 1995.

Wasowski, Sally, with Andy Wasowski. *Gardening with Native Plants of the South.* Dallas, Texas: Taylor Publishing Co, 1994.

Wharton, Charles H. *The Natural Environments of Georgia.* Bulletin 114. Atlanta, Georgia: Georgia Geologic Survey, 1989.

Wharton, Mary E. and Roger W. Barbour. *Wildflowers & Ferns of Kentucky.* Lexington, Kentucky: The University Press of Kentucky, 1979.

Whitley, James R., Barbara Bassett, Joe G. Dillard, and Rebecca A. Haefner. *Water Plants for Missouri Ponds.* Jefferson City, Missouri: Missouri Department of Conservation, 1990.

Wilson, Craig. *"May Apple."* Missouri Conservationist. Jefferson City, Missouri: Missouri Department of Conservation, pp. 30-31, April 1993.

APPENDIX

NATIVE PLANT RESOURCES

Atlanta Botanical Garden
Piedmont Park at the Prado
P.O. Box 77246
Atlanta, GA 30357
404/876-5859

Atlanta History Center
130 West Paces Ferry Rd., NW
Atlanta, GA 30305
404/814-4000

Birmingham Botanical Garden
2612 Lane Park Rd.
Birmingham, AL 35223
205/879-1227

Brookgreen Gardens
US 17
Murrells Inlet, SC 29576
803/237-4218

Callaway Gardens
US 27
Pine Mountain, GA 31822
404/663-2281
800/282-8181

Crosby Arboretum
1801 Goodyear Blvd.
P.O. Box 190
Picayune, MS 39466
601/798-6961

DeKalb Botanical Garden
3251 Panthersville Rd.
Decatur, GA 30034
404/244-5077

Hilltop Arboretum
11855 Highland Rd.
P.O. Box 82608
Baton Rouge, LA 70884
504/767-6916

**Huntsville-Madison County
Botanical Garden**
4747 Bob Wallace Ave.
Huntsville, AL 35805
205/830-4447

J. C. Raulston Arboretum
4301 Beryl Rd.
Department of Horticultural
Sciences, Box 7609
Raleigh, NC 27695
919/515-7641

**Lady Bird Johnson
Wildflower Research Center**
4801 La Crosse Ave.
P.O. Box 550
Austin, TX 78739
512/292-4100
email: nwrc@onr.com

Lichterman Nature Center
5992 Quince Rd.
Memphis, TN 38119
901/680-9756

**Magnolia Plantation
and Gardens**
Route 4, Hwy 61
Charleston, SC 29407
803/571-1266

Memphis Botanic Garden
750 Cherry Rd.
Memphis, TN 38117
901/685-1566

Missouri Botanical Garden
4344 Shaw
St. Louis, MO 63110
314/577-9400

Mobile Botanical Gardens
Pat Ryan Dr., Langan Park
P.O. Box 8382
Mobile, AL 36608
334/342-0555

**Mt. Cuba Center for the
Study of Piedmont Flora**
Barley Mill Rd.
P.O. Box 3570
Greenville, DE 19807
302/239-4244

**United States National
Arboretum**
3501 New York Ave., NE
Washington, DC 20002
202/475-4815

New England Wildflower Society
Garden in the Woods
180 Hemenway Rd.
Framingham, MA 01701
508/877-7630
email: newfs@newfs.org

North Carolina Arboretum
100 Frederick Law Olmsted Way
Asheville, NC 28806
828/665-2492

**North Carolina
Botanical Gardens**
CB# 3375, Totten Center, UNC-CH
Chapel Hill, NC 27599-3375
919/962-0522

Sarah P. Duke Gardens
Duke University
Durham, NC 27706
919/684-5579

Shaw Arboretum
P.O. Box 38
Gray Summit, MO 63039
314/577-5138

**State Botanical Garden
of Georgia**
2450 South Milledge Ave.
Athens, GA 30605
706/542-1244

**Southern Appalachian
Botanical Society**
c/o Charles N. Horn
Newberry College, Biology Dept.
2100 College St.
Newberry, SC 29108

**Tennessee Botanical Gardens
and Fine Arts Center
at Cheekwood**
1200 Forest Park Dr.
Nashville, TN 37205
615/356-8000

**University of Alabama
Arboretum**
4400 Arboretum Way
Tuscaloosa, AL 35487
205/553-3278

S T A T E   S O C I E T I E S

Alabama Wildflower Society
11120 Ben Clements Rd.
Northport, AL 35475
alawild@aol.com

Arkansas Native Plant Society
c/o Eric Sundell
School of Mathematical &
Natural Sciences
University of Monticello
Monticello, AR 71656
sundell@uamont.edu

Florida Native Plant Society
P.O. Box 6116
Spring Hill, FL 34611
fnpsbetsy@aol.com

Georgia Botanical Society
2 Idlewood Court NW
Rome, GA 30165

Georgia Native Plant Society
P.O. Box 422085
Atlanta, GA 30342

Kentucky Native Plant Society
Dept. of Biological Sciences
Eastern Kentucky University
Richmond, KY 40475

Louisiana Native Plant Society
216 Caroline Dormon Rd.
Saline, LA 71070

Maryland Native Plant Society
P.O. Box 4877
Silver Spring, MD 20904

Mississippi Native Plant Society
c/o MS Museum of
Natural Science
111 North Jefferson St.
Jackson, MS 39202

Missouri Native Plant Society
Box 20073
St. Louis, MO 63144

**North Carolina Wildflower
Preservation Society**
c/o North Carolina
Botanical Garden
CB# 3375, Totten Center, UNC-CH
Chapel Hill, NC 27599-3375
919/962-0522

**South Carolina Native
Plant Society**
PO Box 759
Pickens, SC 29671

Tennessee Native Plant Society
Dept of Botany
University of Tennessee
Knoxville, TN 37996

Native Plant Society of Texas
P.O. Box 891
Georgetown, TX 78627
dtucker@io.com

Virginia Native Plant Society
Blandy Experimental Farm
Route 2, Box 214
Boyce, VA 22620

**West Virginia Native Plant
Society**
P.O. Box 75403
Charleston, WV 25375

MAIL-ORDER
NURSERIES

Applachian Gardens, Inc.
Box 87
Waynesboro, PA 17268
888/327-5483
email: appgarden@innernet.net

Ben Meadows Company
3589 Broad St.
Atlanta, GA 30341
800/241-6401

Carroll Gardens
444 E. Main St.
P.O. Box 310
Westminster, MD 21157
800/638-6334

Eco-Gardens
P.O. Box 1227
Decatur, GA 30031
404/294-6468

Fairweather Gardens
P.O. Box 330
Greenwich, NJ 08323
609/451-6261

Louisiana Nursery
Route 7, Box 43
Opelousas, LA 70570

Lower Marlboro Nursery
P.O. Box 1013
Dunkirk, MD 20754
301/812-0808

Mail Order Natives
P.O. Box 9366
Lee, FL 32059
850/973-4688
email: monatives@aol.com

Missouri Wildflowers Nursery
9814 Pleasant Hill Rd.
Jefferson City, MO 65109
573/496-3492
email: mowldflrs@sockets.net

Native Gardens
5737 Fisher Lane
Greenback, TN 37742
423/856-0220

Nature's Nook
1578 Marion Russell Rd.
Meridian, MS 39301
888/485-5161

Niche Gardens
1111 Dawson Rd.
Chapel Hill, NC 27516
919/967-0078
email: mail@nichegdn.com

Pine Ridge Gardens
832 Sycamore Rd.
London, AR 72847
501/293-4359

Plant Delight's Nursery
9241 Sauls Rd.
Raleigh, NC 27603
919/772-4794

Prairie Moon Nursery
Route 3, Box 163
Winona, MN 55987
507/452-1362

Prairie Nursery
P.O. Box 306
Westfield, WI 53964
608/296-3679

The Primrose Path
R.D. 2, Box 110
Scottsdale, PA 15683
412/887-6756

Shooting Star Nursery
444 Bates Rd.
Frankfort KY 40601
502/223-1679

Sunlight Gardens, Inc.
174 Golden Lane
Andersonville, TN 37705
423/494-7086, 800/272-7396

Virginia Natives
P.O. Box D
Hume, VA 22639
540/364-1665

Water Ways Nursery
Route 2, Box 247
Lovettsville, VA 22080
703/822-5994
email: wwnursery@aol.com

We-Du Nurseries
Route5, Box 724
Marion, NC 28752
704/738-8300
email: wedu@wnclink.com

Wild Earth
49 Mead Ave.
Freehold, NJ 07728
732/308-9777

Woodlanders
1128 Colleton Ave.
Aiken, SC 29801
803/648-7522
803/648-7522

INDEX TO PLANTS PROFILED